COMPLEX TEXT DECODED

COMPLEX TEXT DECODED

How to Design Lessons and
Use Strategies That Target
Authentic Texts

KATHY T. GLASS

ASCD | Alexandria, VA USA

1703 N. Beauregard St. • Alexandria, VA 22311-1714 USA
Phone: 800-933-2723 or 703-578-9600 • Fax: 703-575-5400
Website: www.ascd.org • E-mail: member@ascd.org
Author guidelines: www.ascd.org/write

Deborah S. Delisle, *Executive Director;* Stefani Roth, *Publisher;* Genny Ostertag, *Director, Content Acquisitions;* Julie Houtz, *Director, Book Editing & Production;* Jamie Greene, *Editor;* Donald Ely, *Senior Graphic Designer;* Mike Kalyan, *Manager, Production Services;* Kyle Steichen, *Senior Production Specialist;* Valerie Younkin, *Production Designer*

PAPERBACK ISBN: 978-1-4166-2037-2   ASCD product #115006   n8/15

PDF E-BOOK ISBN: 978-1-4166-2101-0; see Books in Print for other formats.

Quantity discounts: 10–49, 10%; 50+, 15%; 1,000+, special discounts (e-mail programteam@ascd.org or call 800-933-2723, ext. 5773, or 703-575-5773). For desk copies, go to www.ascd.org/deskcopy.

Library of Congress Cataloging-in-Publication Data
Glass, Kathy Tuchman.
    Complex text decoded : how to design lessons and use strategies that target authentic texts / by Kathy Glass.
        pages cm
    Includes bibliographical references and index.
    ISBN 978-1-4166-2037-2 (pbk. : alk. paper) 1. Reading comprehension. 2. Lesson planning. I. Title.
    LB1573.7.G55 2015
    372.47--dc23
                                                                                                    2015019013

23 22 21 20 19 18 17 16 15   1 2 3 4 5 6 7 8 9 10 11 12

COMPLEX TEXT DECODED

· · · · · · ·

How to Design Lessons and Use Strategies That Target Authentic Texts

List of Figures

Many of the forms and figures found in this book can be downloaded and customized for classroom use. To access these documents, please visit www.ascd.org/ASCD/pdf/books/Glass2015.pdf

Use the password "ASCD115006" (no quotes) to unlock the files.

Acknowledgments

As teachers know, there are few clear boundaries between the professional and personal demands and joys of life. My own journey has been full and rewarding; many people have helped make it so. My husband Mike has enthusiastically supported me as I pursue my passion for education. For this and so much more, I am deeply indebted. My parents, who are my staunch champions and first teachers, continually serve as models for me in boundless ways. My children, Kimmie and Marshall, have taught me innumerable life lessons and have enabled me to see a firsthand window into a differentiated classroom.

Genny Ostertag, my editor, and Julie Scheina encouraged me to envision a fuller and broader scope for this book. Their advice set me on a clear path toward that larger vision. I thank Genny for arduously providing instrumental feedback and keen insights to help me shape this book. I appreciate her invaluable advice and direction along the way. A considerable measure of appreciation goes to Jamie Greene, the magnificently skilled and talented developmental editor. His astute comments gently nudged me to aim higher and were invaluable in eliciting the best I could offer.

Over the years, many esteemed educators have impacted the development of my own work. Grant Wiggins, Jay McTighe, Doug Fisher, Nancy Frey, and Lynn Erickson are the predominant inspiration and influences for this text. I continually marvel at their wealth of knowledge.

I hope my rendition and contribution to this field will support the dedicated educators who serve our children and schools with constancy, commitment, and full hearts.

Complex Text and Disciplinary Literacy

Synonyms for complex include *intricate, involved, complicated,* and *convoluted.* These modifiers can perhaps all apply to some form of complex text. However, what is considered complex varies depending on the reader's characteristics, and it is incumbent upon us as educators to match the right complexity level to our pupils. In order to access such material, readers need to be skilled at close or deep reading. "By deep reading, we mean the array of sophisticated processes that propel comprehension and that include inferential and deductive reasoning, analogical skills, critical analysis, reflection, and insight. The expert reader needs milliseconds to execute these processes; the young brain needs years to develop them" (Wolf & Barzillai, 2009, p. 32).

We all have different reading goals that are based on a multitude of factors. Sometimes we fancy reading something "light." When we read for entertainment or to gather information so we can stay current with newsworthy events, it does not necessarily require close, focused reading. One exposure is likely enough in these instances. Other times, however, we delve into heady text to research a medical condition, augment our understanding of a somewhat unfamiliar topic on a deeper level, or read an op-ed piece from an erudite and well-informed writer. If we were to limit our inventory of reading solely to the latter, more challenging type of text every time we read, it might be a laborious and cumbersome—though enlightening—process.

By the same token, it's important to give students the opportunity to read a wide variety of texts for different purposes and along a spectrum of difficulty and length. To meet the goal of comprehensively grasping complex text, students must have concrete tools to help them become highly skilled readers, which is an intensely active endeavor toward deep understanding.

No matter which standards apply—Common Core State Standards (CCSS), content area, state or province, or district—students are expected to read and comprehend text that is complex. Therefore, they need the guidance and support of trained educators who can usher them through the process of reading this kind of material with a keen eye. In doing so adeptly, students can bolster their abilities and transfer what they learn to different challenging texts across content areas and even outside of school. Ultimately, this training provides them with the skills necessary to be successful in meeting the demands of life beyond a K–12 setting.

It is no easy feat to teach students how to read complex text in a way that contributes to keen introspection and comprehension. After all, as adults, we likely grapple with reading our own versions of challenging content. When we confront such text, we ratchet up strategies that we perform with automaticity to make sense of it. Students, however, need our support to learn developmentally appropriate skills aligned to specific texts so they can glean the most from them.

This book is intended to support you in not only measuring and defining the full spectrum of what is meant by *complex text* across content areas but also conducting robust and rigorous instruction around whatever that means in the subject you teach. What I provide is a full ensemble for teaching complex text, including strategies, activities, and assessments largely suited for students in upper elementary through 10th grade (although much of what is presented can be adapted to other grades). I present discussion topics and real-life examples around vocabulary, annotation options, text structure, text-dependent questions, questioning techniques, reciprocal teaching, Socratic discussions, writing tasks, criteria for scoring, and more.

Additionally, when gaining access to complex text, it's important to understand the tenets of unit and lesson design, since complex text is a rich resource used within an overarching plan. Any strategies or activities used to access it should not be conducted in isolation but rather serve to target specific skills and curricular goals. Therefore, I include the components of backward planning, lesson plan models, and a proposed preparation and sequence for teaching complex text.

As the esteemed historical figure Francis Bacon states in *The Essays*: "Some books are to be tasted, others to be swallowed, and some few to be chewed and digested; that is, some books are to be read only in parts; others to be read, but not curiously; and some few to be read wholly, and with diligence and attention" (2012, p. 157). This book focuses on the latter category of text. I aim to support you with a repository of practical tools and information so you can guide your students to read challenging and complex text ably and comprehensively.

What Is Complex Text?

When reading, sometimes we speed along and acquire information fairly easily. Other times, we slow our pace because the material is difficult and we recognize the need to grasp something that isn't quite within our sphere of comfort. Perhaps we've encountered unfamiliar and demanding text and realize we are not absorbing what the author intended us to. When this occurs, we are faced with what many in educational circles call *complex text*, which consists of good material well worth reading but that demands certain skills to unlock what may seem daunting at first. Text of this sort necessitates analytical reading—an intense endeavor required for challenging material.

> Good books are over your head; they would not be good for you if they were not. And books that are over your head weary you unless you can reach up to them and pull yourself up to their level. It is not the stretching that tires you, but the frustration of stretching unsuccessfully because you lack the skill to stretch effectively. To keep on reading actively, you must have not only the will to do so, but also the skill—the art that enables you to elevate yourself by mastering what at first sight seems to be beyond you. (Adler & Van Doren, 1972, p. 24)

Complex text refers to printed, visual, auditory, digital, and multimedia texts that complement each standards-based unit, align to curricular goals, and represent an appropriate level of challenge for students. The following examples reflect what typically comes to mind when considering the use of complex text:

- Biographies
- Autobiographies
- Memoirs
- Journals
- Letters
- Fictional work in short stories, novels, novellas, or graphic novels
- Plays
- Poetry
- Newspaper and magazine articles
- Radio or television interviews
- Historical documents
- Speeches
- Essays
- Lab reports
- Periodicals
- Technical manuals
- Reports
- Video
- Audio

Across the disciplines, students question, examine, analyze, compare, scrutinize, and probe—which represent some of the mental processes required to engage fully with complex text. However, this does not always pertain to text that students read or speech they hear (as shown in the previous list). Complex text can also suggest a broader definition across content areas. To this point, authenticity is imperative when considering what constitutes complex text in various subject areas that include sources that are not limited to the written or spoken word.

In technical subjects—science, social studies, graphic arts, home economics, industrial arts, and so forth— students will likely experience some variety of traditional texts such as those mentioned earlier. They will also encounter other material as part of a larger repertoire to build their capacities in subject-matter content. In physical education, for example, students might read complicated directions and strategic maneuvers for a particular sport. Alternatively, they may watch a video to critique a particular play or an opponent's performance of this same sport. In art, students could read biographical information about Johannes Vermeer or Paul Klee before they study the actual artwork produced by those masters, which constitutes a significant version of complex text in this subject area. Figure 1.1 shows a sampling of the kinds of complex text students might intently study in various disciplines.

Selected speaking and listening standards might also provide opportunities for using complex text. For example, when students engage in discussions or collaborate with one another, their conversations might qualify as a form of nontraditional text to be examined. In addition, the content presented in person orally or through technology, such as a guest speaker, TED talk, or lecture, can be interpreted as complex text. The point is that the term *complex text* can encompass traditional and broad forms of material, such as the many examples featured and discussed in this section.

True that not all text students read is complex; however, the text you intentionally choose at the center of instruction needs to be complex so students increase their capabilities to work with challenging material. When selecting text, consider targeted standards and curricular goals, and critique the text to ensure it is indeed complex enough. Does the text provide opportunities for students to examine and analyze it thoroughly, make inferences, draw conclusions, uncover new insights, and think critically?

Resource A (at the end of this book) provides a thorough treatment and additional resources for determining the complexity level of texts you plan to use. If your school or district already has a designated list of complex text selections, Resource A might come in handy to verify that titles qualify as complex. If there is no school or district list, consider using the suggested process in Resource B to support you and your colleagues in compiling such a list. Even if you already have a list, you might still have the freedom to augment it, in which case either resource can prove useful. In fact, a provision for supplementing a formally compiled list is prudent so new texts that become available are given careful consideration.

FIGURE 1.1
Diverse Forms of Complex Text

Subject	Examples
Advertising	print and Internet advertisements, billboards, radio and television storyboards and scripts
Architectural Drafting	renderings of building styles, floor plans, landscape plans with contours and topographical profiles, building codes and regulations, schematic drawings
Art	paintings, drawings, sculpture, color palettes, museum exhibits
Auto Mechanics	demonstrations of an engine tune-up, tire rotation, oil change
Carpentry/Construction	blueprints, estimates for building costs, demonstrations of power tool usage and materials installation
Child Development	lesson plans, classroom observations
Cosmetology	video demonstrations of someone administering a facial, haircut and styling, or manicure
Culinary Arts	recipes, final food products, demonstrations of knife sharpening or basic knife cuts for various food items, diagrams of sections of a cow to identify cuts of meat
Fashion Design	textiles, sewing patterns, clothing designs
Foreign Language	audio, video, or live conversations between speakers
Forensic Studies	evidence reports, blood and DNA test results, crime scene diagrams, police reports
Math	data, bar graphs, statistics, scaled drawings, equations
Music	musical scores, ensembles, choral performances, lyrics
Nutrition	nutrition facts labels, balanced diet plans, calorie count data, recipes, food pyramids
Performing Arts	dance performances, drama productions, set designs
Physical Education	live or video demonstrations of techniques (e.g., tossing a football, shooting a basketball, performing sit ups), diagrams of the muscle groups in the human body, PE equipment (e.g., racquets used in various sports; dumbbells, kettle balls, medicine balls; balance beam, parallel bars, vaulting horse)
Science	charts, graphs, diagrams, photographs, specimens, dissected organisms, labs, experiment results
Social Studies	political cartoons, graphs, timelines, artifacts, propaganda posters
Technology	computer graphics, graphic designs and layouts, web pages, clip art, sound

What Standards Address Text Complexity?

It is imperative that within a given school year and across the grades, you conduct lessons around targeted reading skills that require students to grapple with complex text. Doing so propels them to new levels of competencies. In the Common Core State Standards (CCSS), the term *staircase of complexity* is often used and relates to the practice of exposing students to increasingly more challenging literary and informational texts from year to year. Anchor Standard 10 states that students "read and comprehend complex literary and informational texts independently and proficiently" (2010a).

To achieve deep understanding of this increasingly difficult text independently, conduct learning experiences aligned to the other reading standards. Collectively, there are about 20 of them—10 pertaining to literature and another 10 related to informational text. These standards point the way for you to empower students to acquire knowledge, understand various viewpoints, and gain insights so they can become competent readers of all kinds of text with progressively more sophisticated expertise. This quote further elucidates the expectations:

> The Reading standards place equal emphasis on the sophistication of what students read and the skill with which they read. Standard 10 defines a grade-by-grade "staircase" of increasing text complexity that rises from beginning reading to the college and career readiness level. Whatever they are reading, students must also show a steadily growing ability to discern more from and make fuller use of the text, including making an increasing number of connections among ideas and between texts, considering wider range of textual evidence, and becoming more sensitive to inconsistencies, ambiguities, and poor reasoning in text. (CCSSI, 2010a, p. 8)

Although the term *complex text* is used pervasively in this age of the Common Core State Standards, preparing students to adeptly read challenging text is also a priority in states that did not adopt the CCSS. In short, it is simply good teaching to expose students to such text. It opens the door for them to learn and interact with material they might not necessarily encounter on their own. The following comments from standards documents adopted in Ontario (Canada) and Texas are examples illustrative of the pervasive expectation of text complexity across school systems.

- The Ontario Curriculum Grades 1–8 *Language* document includes this introductory remark under the Reading strand: "Within each grade and from one grade to another, students should be assigned texts of increasing complexity as they develop their reading skills, and should also have many opportunities to select their own reading materials" (Ontario Ministry of Education, 2006, p. 11).

- The Texas Essential Knowledge and Skills (TEKS) contain many expectations for reading comprehension. The following excerpt is included for K–12 reading/comprehension skills, which reflect a commitment to text complexity: "Students use a flexible range of metacognitive reading skills in both assigned and independent reading to understand an author's message. Students will continue to apply earlier standards with greater depth in increasingly more complex texts as they become self-directed, critical readers" (Texas Education Agency, 2010, Figure 19 TAC §110.10(b)).

Who Should Teach Complex Text?

Teachers across the content areas are responsible for exposing their students to rigorous text and incorporating literacy into their instruction. This is true not only for language arts teachers but also for teachers of social studies, science, and technical subjects, which the CCSS defines as "a course devoted to a practical study, such as engineering, technology, design, business, or other workforce-related subject; a technical aspect of a wider field of study, such as art or music" (CCSSI, 2010b, p. 43). This collective ownership is an explicit expectation of the CCSS.

> The Standards insist that instruction in reading, writing, speaking, listening, and language be a shared responsibility within the school. The K–5 standards include expectations for reading, writing, speaking, listening, and language applicable to a range of subjects, including but not limited to ELA. The grades 6–12 standards are divided into two sections, one for ELA and the other for history/social studies, science, and technical subjects. This division reflects the unique, time-honored place of ELA teachers in developing students' literacy skills while at the same time recognizing that teachers in other areas must have a role in this development as well. Part of the motivation behind the interdisciplinary approach to literacy promulgated by the Standards is extensive research establishing the need for college and career ready students to be proficient in reading complex informational text independently in a variety of content areas. (CCSSI, 2010a, p. 4)

This may seem daunting, but it doesn't mean that every teacher—regardless of his or her area of expertise—is a reading teacher. Rather, teachers should use their respective content areas as the focus and determine optimal literacy strategies to employ when teaching that content. Science, math, social studies, language arts, and other subjects all incorporate print text that is organized and written in idiosyncratic ways that make it challenging for students. For example, science textbooks are replete with labeled diagrams, realistic drawings or photographs, and captions that carry essential information to augment the main text. Reading observational notes and lab reports are also commonplace in these classes. In social studies, students study timelines and graphs that relay fundamental facts about historical periods. In addition, historical documents and letters that students read sometimes contain archaic language that is far afield from modern prose. Then consider language arts classes in which students read novels that require a completely different set of skills from what's required when reading informational text. Disciplinary literacy requires that students be taught tools and strategies to grant them access to each kind of text they will encounter so they can glean pertinent subject-area content from it.

With this in mind, it is professionally prudent for you to work with colleagues to plan for the best learning experiences for students. Indeed, subject-area teachers can benefit from collaboration with language arts teachers when the need arises. For example, if students are expected to write an argumentative paper in science class, both the language arts and science teachers can discuss how best to serve students so they are able to produce a well-written and content-rich paper. The language arts teacher can focus on cohesion, sentence structure, and mechanics while the science teacher focuses on research techniques, credibility of sources, and identification of sound reasons and supporting evidence. This collaboration puts the needs of the students at the forefront.

Why Is It Important to Engage Students in Complex Text?

The standards across most school systems make it clear that students are expected to read and experience a variety of complex text as they progress from grade to grade. There is irrefutable and well-documented evidence that complex text should matter. According to the ACT (2006), the data reveal the following significant takeaway, which is just one among many of this organization's key findings:

> ACT data suggest that the readiness of the nation's high school students for college-level reading is far too low. But ACT data also show that, while it is important for students to be able to comprehend both explicit and implicit material in texts and understand how various textual elements (such as main ideas, relationships, or generalizations) function in a text, what matters most in reading achievement is the ability to comprehend complex texts. We must find ways to help all students to read at the level of proficiency necessary to ensure that they are ready to succeed in college without remediation. Students must be able to read and comprehend texts that are complex with respect

to "RSVP": Relationships, Richness, Structure, Style, Vocabulary, and Purpose. (pp. 27–28)

Other research studies have determined that the reading demands after high school have remained at the same level of complexity (or higher) while texts used in K–12 classrooms have decreased in rigor. Furthermore, emphasis has not been on teaching students to read on their own and grapple with complex texts; too much support is given, which robs students of struggling to ascertain the core meaning of text independently. These resources and a plethora of other salient findings about what has not served students well and what needs to happen in classrooms to prepare students for the future can be accessed through the following resources:

- Common Core State Standards Appendix A; see sections "Why Text Complexity Matters" on pages 2–4 (http://www.corestandards.org/assets/Appendix_A.pdf)
- "Why Complex Text Matters" by David Liben (http://achievethecore.org/content/upload/Why_Text_Complexity_Matters.pdf)
- "Reading Between the Lines: What the ACT Reveals About College Readiness in Reading" by ACT (http://www.act.org/research/policymakers/pdf/reading_report.pdf)
- "Advancing Our Students' Language and Literacy: The Challenge of Complex Texts" by Marilyn Jager Adams (https://www.aft.org/pdfs/americaneducator/winter1011/Adams.pdf)

What Does Close Reading Mean?

Now that the need for exposing students to complex text has been established, what does *close reading* mean? It might seem intuitive that you enact learning experiences in which students examine complex text—and that is where close reading comes into play. Students will not have adequate access to a complex text unless they are taught to read it carefully and purposefully. Reading a text closely means reading it multiple times; repeated readings allow students to gain new insights and investigate different aspects of the text to satisfy different purposes.

During the first encounter of an argumentation essay, for example, students might get the gist of the reading selection and begin to see an argument unfold. Another reading has them focus on details and determine if the author provides sufficient and sound evidence for his or her major premise. On subsequent readings, students might look more carefully at counterarguments, determine their overall impressions, and make inferences. During these repeated interactions with the text, students will also look at sentence syntax and word choice to support their assertions and analyses. A similar scenario applies for other types of text. When students first read a short story, they might begin to get a picture of the protagonist and his or her motivations. Upon further examination, other factors emerge that were overlooked during the first pass, such as the impact of setting, a character's preconceived beliefs, or innuendos in dialogue that reveal implied intent. Taking the time to reread for different purposes yields new information that enhances the whole text and develops an understanding that is impossible to glean during a first, quick read.

> Close, analytic reading stresses engaging with a text of sufficient complexity directly and examining meaning thoroughly and methodically, encouraging students to read and reread deliberately. Directing student attention on the text itself empowers students to understand the central ideas and key supporting details. It also enables students to reflect on the meanings of individual words and sentences; the order in which sentences unfold; and the development of ideas over the course of the text, which ultimately leads students to arrive at an understanding of the text as a whole. (Partnership for Assessment Readiness for College and Careers, 2011, p. 7)

Closing

Reading complex text to uncover deep meaning is an expectation across standards documents for all grade levels. Doing so equips students with necessary skills that position them well in whatever endeavor they pursue after high school. Various interpretative and critical reading skills are in play when learning to read a variety of complex text intently, so students need practice with a wide assortment of strategies to acquire and apply what they learn to new situations.

Complex text is not relegated to written text; nontraditional text is also a mainstay in particular classrooms. In different content areas, complex text can take on a broader definition. For example, studying an engine in automotive class, critiquing a soufflé in home economics, studying a sports maneuver, or analyzing the results of a lab experiment are just some of the many types of complex texts that students encounter within school. With each experience, students need appropriate tools to comprehend complex text and learn from it.

Essential Elements of Unit Design and Models for Lesson Planning

Choosing complex text, the focus of the previous chapter, is just one aspect of meeting high standards. The instructional plan you devise around such text is another key factor in positioning students to progress yearly in reading competencies. Therefore, in this chapter, I discuss a framework that articulates necessary components of sound unit design and features research-proven lesson models that align to clearly articulated unit goals. If we are to prepare our students for life beyond high school, this combination is critical: the right text that complements curricular goals taught using effective learning experiences. In abiding by this practice, you prime students to advance along a continuum of becoming more proficient readers who can independently tackle difficult text.

Each strategy, activity, or assessment you use within an instructional sequence should naturally be embedded into a particular lesson, but it is important to note that each lesson resides within a greater unit of study predicated on overarching goals. Therefore, you must clearly delineate these unit goals prior to launching into lesson design. When you build or find discrete lessons—which are easily accessible online and in print—I advise you not to teach these lessons in isolation. Instead, the research around backward design shows that once you are clear about the goals of a given unit, you'll be well positioned to launch into formal instructional experiences.

> The concept of planning backward from desired results is not new. In 1949, Ralph Tyler described this approach as an effective process for focusing instruction. . . . Although not a new idea, we have found that the deliberate use of backward design for planning courses, units, and

individual lessons results in more clearly defined goals, more appropriate assessments, and more purposeful teaching. (Tomlinson & McTighe, 2006, p. 27)

Many professional works support this direction and urge all teachers to first identify what students should know, understand, and be able to do—commonly referred to as KUDs—before beginning lesson design. Once KUDs are clearly defined using standards as a guide, along with ways students can demonstrate their understanding and show evidence of what they have learned, lesson design will have a clear focus rooted in intentional teaching and learning.

John Hattie's seminal work *Visible Learning* (2009), which is based on a synthesis of more than 800 meta-analyses, highlights this approach and discusses other effective practices aligned with the backward design pedagogy. He and his team mention the imperative of clear learning intentions and criteria for student success—the former to articulate what we want students to learn, and the latter so outcomes are transparent. These essential elements pave the way for you to devise meaningful and targeted curriculum and aligned instruction.

A Deep Look at KUDs

The following sections provide an explanation and examples of each of the components of KUDs that can be included on a curriculum map and used to drive unit design. When defining these overarching goals up front, you pave the way for targeted, purposeful learning that can lead to growth and achievement. Considerations for complex text can be made at different points in unit design. Sometimes you might know your content standards well, select a text you will use, and then build a unit around that text. For example, depending on what you teach, you might use a textbook, novel, or historical documents aligned to content standards. Other times, you might need to conduct research to determine complex text while in the process of developing a unit map as ideas come forward. If your school or district has a core text list (see Resource B for a process to compile this list), then you should consult this list when building your unit. However, new texts become available and teachable moments occur all the time, so augmenting the school or district list might make sense for parts of the unit. What is imperative is that the text aligns to standards-based curricular goals; therefore, your unit map is a tool for clarity and direction.

What Students Should Know (Foundational Knowledge)

Knowledge represents the factual information that you expect your students to know within a unit or lesson and is based on content standards. At the most basic level, students should have surface knowledge of a topic, which forms the foundation for them to understand deeper concepts. This knowledge encompasses facts, dates, people, places, examples, and vocabulary terms. It can be itemized in a list, written on a graphic organizer, or even shown on a labeled diagram or chart (e.g., Habsburg family tree, circuit board). See Figure 2.1 for an example of what you might identify as important content information students should know for a poetry unit. Figure 2.2 shows a small excerpt of knowledge items for a social studies unit on early hominids and human evolution.

FIGURE 2.1
What Students Should Know: Poetry

Types of Poetry	Sounds of Poetry	Meter	Figurative Language	Poets
• Haiku • Limerick • Concrete Poetry • Ballad • Epic • Lyrical • Free Verse • Blank Verse • Sonnet • Cinquain	• Alliteration • Assonance • Consonance • Onomatopoeia • Repetition • Rhyme • Rhythm	• Foot • Accent (stress) • Iambic • Pentameter	• Imagery • Simile • Metaphor • Personification	• Cummings • Dickinson • Frost • Hughes • Longfellow • Poe • Sandburg • Shakespeare • Shelley • Soto • Walker • Whitman • Yeats

Although standards need to be reflected in your knowledge list, they do not have to be the only source. When considering what students should know for a particular unit, also rely on textbooks, other resources, your previous experiences teaching the unit, or even your colleagues so what you have is comprehensive. Refer to multiple resources so you are clear about the foundational knowledge that is important to teach as the basis for deeper, conceptual understanding.

Likewise, when teaching a particular complex text within a unit, it is important to identify what you want students to know. For example, in addition to key terms, vocabulary, and facts, you may want your students to know other relevant information, such as text structure, text features, the author's background, the main idea, key details, structure and elements of argumentation, the idea of motif versus theme, and so forth. To prepare for the entire unit in general and a specific complex text in particular, a knowledge list will help you begin to focus on overarching curricular goals and will serve as a resource when building text-dependent questions during the lesson design phase.

FIGURE 2.2
What Students Should Know: Hominid Groups

Time Period	Name	Physical Characteristics	Tools	Socialization	Location/ Migration	Diet
between 1.5 and 2 million years bce	*Homo habilis* or "handy man"	• over 4 feet tall • brain twice the size of *Australopithecus africanus* ("southern ape of Africa") • brain about 2/3 the size of modern human • slightly more humanlike than *A. africanus*	simple tools: animal bones as digging sticks; rocks as chopping tools; sharp pieces of stone for cutting	lived in groups	eastern Africa	meat and animal marrow

What Students Should Understand (Essential Understandings and Guiding Questions)

You might have heard the term *enduring* or *essential understandings*. This component of unit planning refers to what we want students to understand at a gut level and really wrap their heads around. It represents the vital, intrinsic ideas of a unit and stands on the shoulders of the foundational knowledge. These essential or enduring understandings are predicated on key concepts and are lofty statements that encompass the essence of what you want students to realize and remember—even after they may have forgotten the facts that are enumerated in the knowledge category. Hattie (2012) states that "conceptual understandings form the 'coat hangers' on which we interpret and assimilate new ideas, and relate and extend them" (p. 115).

On the next page, there are several examples of essential understandings that you can use as a guide for writing your own. Notice that each statement contains key concepts, such as *argument, balance, labor, truth, art,* and *environment*. Related concepts are grouped together with strong verbs that also carry meaning (e.g., *facilitate, promote, contribute, adapt*). There may be five or six essential understandings for a long unit of study that spans four to six weeks, or possibly one or two for a mini-unit lasting a couple of weeks. If you conduct an interdisciplinary unit, you will have essential understandings associated with each content area.

When you craft these understandings, which represent the direction a unit will go, you are better positioned to select targeted complex text that aligns to them. Sometimes you can find essential or enduring understandings from a standards document or textbook; other times, I find that I need to write them myself to clearly articulate what I intend to teach.

1. A well-organized and developed argument facilitates the flow of ideas and promotes understanding.
2. The structural organization of government can contribute to equity, balance, and the division of labor.
3. People create memoirs to share personal experiences that can teach a lesson, relieve themselves of a burden, or explain the truth to the world.
4. Individuals can create artistic works to convey their beliefs or political views, which might cause people to react emotionally.
5. The structures and behaviors of living organisms help them adapt to their environments so they can survive.

To write essential understandings, look to the standards and key concepts implicit in them, which should be included in your knowledge list. A key feature is that they are transferrable across grade clusters and sometimes can apply to similar units of study within a particular grade. To achieve this, statements are written without proper nouns or past-tense verbs, because constructing them in that way could ground them in a particular situation. For example, look at the second essential understanding about government. You can plan instruction and assessment around this understanding in various units of study perhaps within and across tangential grades as students compare and contrast different governmental systems. However, if you were to write it with a different beginning (e.g., The governmental structure of the United States during the 19th century . . .), the statement might no longer be essential or enduring because it is then associated with a particular period in history.

The essential understandings are for you; they help identify the conceptual thinking that drives a unit's instruction including the complex text necessary to teach the content. However, near the end of a unit, it might be helpful to conduct an activity in which students brainstorm a list of concepts they learned and then fashion statements from that list. They can then compare their statements to the essential understandings you devised. This acts as an extremely telling form of assessment.

By contrast, guiding questions emanate from these essential understandings and are written in student-friendly language rather than solely teacher-speak. Stated succinctly, they are provocative and establish a purpose for learning. It's a good idea to post these questions so students are grounded in the work they are expected to complete. Use Figure 2.3 as a guide for writing your own or critiquing (and possibly revising) those you find in textbooks or other resources. Note the difference between essential understandings and guiding questions: the essential understandings answer the related guiding questions and articulate the learning goal—what you want students to grasp.

FIGURE 2.3
Essential Understandings and Guiding Question Examples

Essential Understandings *(Students will understand that . . .)*	Guiding Questions
Geographic tools enable professionals to locate and analyze information about people, places, and environments.	Why and how do professionals use geographic tools?
People can purposely display the same data in different ways to facilitate various interpretations and conclusions.	How and why do people display data differently?
Writing about personal experiences can help authors reconcile their feelings about a detrimental situation and provide insight and guidance to readers.	Why might people write autobiographies?
Innovators can utilize technology to improve and transform daily life; however, sometimes unintended consequences might result that cause more harm than good.	Do all technological innovations benefit society in positive ways?

For example, the answer to the guiding question "Why and how do scientists use geographic tools?" is expressed in the following essential understanding: Geographic tools enable scientists to locate and analyze information about people, places, and environments. The guiding questions are purposefully brief because you should plan and conduct a series of lessons around these questions so students discover for themselves the deeper meaning embedded in the essential understandings. If a question is leading, then you have revealed the answer too easily rather than give students the opportunity to discover answers on their own. The complex text you choose should expressly support your unit goals (articulated in your knowledge items), essential understandings, and guiding questions.

What Students Should Be Able to Do (Skills)

Skills are what we want students to *do*, and all written descriptions of skills begin with observable action verbs. The CCSS and many other standards are essentially a series of expectations expressed as skills. Examples include the following skills:

- Assess how point of view or purpose shapes the content and style of a text.
- Draw evidence from literary or informational texts to support analysis, reflection, and research.
- Develop a model to predict and/or describe phenomena.
- Apply scientific ideas to solve a design problem, taking into account possible unanticipated effects.
- Analyze patterns and relationships.
- Graph points on a coordinate plane to solve real-world and mathematical problems.

Lynn Erickson (2002) defines skills as "the specific competencies required for complex process performance. Skills need to be taught directly and practiced in context. For example, some of the skills required for doing the complex performance of research include 'accessing information,' 'identifying main ideas and details,' 'notetaking,' and 'organizing information'" (p. 166). Skills are transferrable and can be applied to new situations. For example, when someone learns to bake, these skills (and others) are required: read a recipe, define and differentiate between measurement amounts, measure dry and liquid ingredients, select and utilize baking utensils, and operate kitchen appliances. Once these skills are mastered through a set of experiences (e.g., baking chocolate chip cookies), they can be transferred and applied to different scenarios (e.g., baking brownies, lemon bars, and ginger snap cookies). It is important that you devise and conduct formal lessons that target standards-based skills aligned to content and then conduct assessments to ensure students have mastered these skills.

Figure 2.4 features three distinct examples of KUDs—one for an introduction to an argumentative essay, another for theme, and a third for a social studies unit on an aspect of the Holocaust. Each example is an excerpt from a larger unit map; a comprehensive unit entails a grouping of many standards with associated KUDs and guiding questions. When developing a unit map, select a range of appropriate texts that align with overarching goals.

Learning Evidence

Once you identify the KUDs and craft appropriate guiding questions, determine what evidence is acceptable that reflects the level at which students have grasped content knowledge, understandings, and skills. What can you collect or observe and assess to show proficiency? This can include a variety of informal and formal data from formative and summative assessments and even self-assessments. A unit map accounts for the summative assessment and other forms of assessment you will use to plan your instruction.

Formative assessments are assessments *for* learning. They are meant to check for understanding and allow students the opportunity to practice skills and strategies in order to eventually achieve proficiency in them. Use the results of these assessments to determine if you need to reteach, enrich, or redirect. For example, as students participate in various focused discussions and collaborate with their peers, your observations of these dialogues and exchanges provide evidence that can determine to what extent students are meeting pertinent learning goals. If a targeted skill is to write using a consistent point of view, the evidence you collect will be writing samples to assess students' ability to maintain the same point of view and avoid unnecessary shifts. The former example is more informal evidence; the latter is formal since students submit written evidence that you study and review. A combination of observing, collecting, and analyzing formative assessments serve as opportunities to inform your instruction so you can intentionally guide learning toward growth.

FIGURE 2.4
KUD Examples

Standards	What Students Should Know	What Students Should Understand (Essential Understanding)	Guiding Question	What Students Should Be Able to Do
Introduce claim(s) about a topic or issue. (WHST.6-8.1a)*	• Debatable versus nondebatable topics • Thesis statement purpose and structure • Introduction strategies	Effective argumentation introductions can leave an impression on readers by providing a clear context and establishing a well-defined position on a debatable topic.	How can I effectively begin my argument essay?	• Provide context. • Choose a debatable topic. • Introduce a claim through a thesis statement.
Determine central ideas or themes of a text and analyze their development. (CCRA.R.2)*	• Definition of *theme* • Details in text that authors use to develop theme • Plot versus theme • Universal themes • Literary works that share common themes	Thoughtful readers use textual evidence to analyze and support their impression of the theme and verify their reasoning at intervals to enhance meaning.	How and why do readers determine the theme of a text?	• Analyze development of a theme. • Use context clues to determine a text's theme. • Identify universal themes. • Connect themes across literary works.
• Understand the influence of Nazism on European society and Jewish culture. (McREL 41: Level III.3) • Cite specific textual evidence when writing or speaking to support conclusions drawn from the text. (CCRA.R.1)*	• Definition, background, and examples of Righteous Gentiles or Righteous Among the Nations • People: Oskar Schindler, Irena Sendler, Raoul Wallenberg • Context of Holocaust	Morally upstanding and courageous individuals may put their lives at risk to confront unjust tyrannical forces.	How and why might people courageously help others to survive?	• Cite evidence from text. • Compare and contrast human deeds. • Analyze human motivations.

*abbreviated

Students use your feedback—and the results of self-assessments—to improve in targeted areas. Self-assessment is an important form of assessment that is often overlooked but should be a mainstay in classrooms. Students can monitor their own learning by reviewing their work against a checklist or rubric, making entries in learning logs to pose questions and reflections, and responding to prompts that lead them to new understandings. They can share their impressions with you and their classmates to validate or revise their work and keep abreast of their progress. By doing so, they develop a sense of self-agency and advocacy in their own learning so they know when to ask for help, when to proceed, or when to redirect.

By contrast, summative assessments are assessments *of* learning because they measure how well students have demonstrated understanding of targeted learning objectives. Summative assessments provide evidence of what students have mastered at the culmination of a unit of study and can also be used at pivotal points within a unit. Whereas formative assessments may not be graded since they are opportunities for practice and a means for informing your instruction to steer students' learning toward proficiency, a summative assessment is scored using a rubric that includes clearly defined criteria.

> Summative assessment can occur at the end of a unit when all of the learning objectives have been taught, at the end of several lessons that form a subset of meaning in the unit, or even at the end of a single lesson if the lesson objective has been fully met and students have had adequate opportunity to achieve mastery. Using summative assessments at the end of a lesson or set of lessons helps teachers ensure that students have developed the foundation on which subsequent lessons will build. Summative assessment takes its name from its purpose of 'summing up' what students have learned at a logical point in time. (Tomlinson & Moon, 2013, p. 92)

Once your KUDs, guiding questions, and evidence of learning are well defined, you have targeted goals around which instructional experiences can be built. In line with backward planning, you're now ready to tackle lesson design. When conducting lessons and issuing assessments, remember to be transparent with students about what constitutes success. When students are cognizant of the expectations for achievement, they are in a better position to self-monitor and work with you and their peers to move their learning forward. Having a vision of success is a key contributing factor to students' academic growth; it's therefore imperative to share expectations with them so they can self-assess at intervals along the way to mastery and be accountable for their own learning.

Writing solid lessons can be a creative process. However, each one needs to be a well-framed and choreographed instructional plan that is based on clearly delineated goals so it yields dividends of measurable results. In the following sections, I feature two approaches that are closely aligned: the gradual release of responsibility and direct instruction. Both are proven frameworks for lesson planning that positively influence student achievement. Keep them in mind when you read the strategies and activities later in this book and when you consider your own instructional toolkit.

Gradual Release of Responsibility
What Is the Gradual Release of Responsibility?

The gradual release of responsibility model can be used to address skills, strategies, and concepts across the content areas (Pearson & Gallagher, 1983a). The name of this model is apt because it begins with you, the teacher, taking on the bulk of responsibility to teach new content through explicit instruction, such as modeling or demonstrating. You then assume a gradually diminishing role along a continuum of support until students eventually apply what they have learned on their own. In other words, the lesson moves in stages. Initially, you take control but then institute guided practice so students work together with you and one another. Ultimately, you release control entirely so students independently practice and apply the skill.

> When the teacher is taking all or most of the responsibility for task completion, he is "modeling" or demonstrating the desired application of some strategy. When the student is taking all or most of that responsibility, she is "practicing" or "applying" that strategy. What comes in between these two extremes is the gradual release of responsibility from teacher to student. The hope in the model is that every student gets to the point where she is able to accept total responsibility for the task, including the responsibility for determining whether or not she is applying the strategy appropriately (i.e., self-monitoring). But the model assumes that she will need some guidance in reaching that stage of independence and that it is precisely the teacher's role to provide such guidance. (Pearson & Gallagher, 1983b, p. 35)

The stages of this model, which move students from a teacher-run experience to independence, are as follows:

1. *I do it.* The teacher models, demonstrates, and explains the targeted skill or strategy so students see how it is done.
2. *We do it.* The teacher invites students to share some of the responsibility for the task but remains careful to maintain most of the support.
3. *You do it together.* The teacher orchestrates a guided learning experience that allows students to work collaboratively and assume more responsibility. This is the critical step in the process. When moving students toward independent proficiency, it is necessary to provide consistent feedback so students are clear about their expectations, if they are on track, or if they need redirection or support.
4. *You do it alone.* Students independently practice and apply the targeted skill or strategy.

Inspired by this model, Doug Fisher and Nancy Frey (2014) have identified four instructional steps that are necessary when introducing a new concept, skill, or strategy.

1. **Focused Instruction:** First, set the purpose for learning. To do so, you might establish a guiding question(s) so there are clearly stated teaching points. Include situations when you would use and apply this new learning. Then model or demonstrate the new skill or strategy to show students how to actually do what they will eventually complete on their own. Use the Think Aloud strategy to invite students to hear what's going on in your brain while you're explaining how to accomplish the task. Insert appropriate terms you need them to learn and use (e.g., *subordinating conjunction, argumentation*) within the context of the lesson. While modeling, explain instances in which you might question what should be done or explain common errors to illustrate what students should do when they encounter these potential pitfalls. Student participation at this point is fairly minimal, since they're primarily listening and watching what you are doing. Nevertheless, formatively assess to ensure that students are acquiring the information as intended and to collect data, which will help you determine next steps to differentiate instruction. These data might consist of your observations during partner or small-group discussions, students' notes, or students' brief written responses to a prompt. You can also use the following activities to formatively assess students' learning:
   - Respond on mini-whiteboards, with finger symbols, or on handheld electronic devices. (See Chapter 6.)
   - Turn and talk with a neighbor to ask and answer questions, summarize, or restate information.
   - Draw a picture or symbol.
   - Point to, underline, or highlight a portion of the text.

2. **Guided Instruction:** Using the data collected from pre- or formative assessments, arrange students into small groups for guided instruction. In these groups, students will begin to practice applying the new skill or strategy. It remains your responsibility to interact with students to guide, observe, question, prompt, listen to, respond to, and even explain or provide more modeling. In so doing, you facilitate understanding of the task and offer specific feedback that enables and deepens student comprehension. Differentiation is expected during this step since students require varying levels of scaffolding and assistance, depending on their readiness levels. With this in mind, groups should vary in size and might work at different paces. All students—regardless of their proficiency level or starting point—should receive adequate support so they are appropriately challenged. Feel free to regroup students, as needed, based on data from formative assessments.

3. **Collaborative Learning:** In heterogeneous groupings, provide opportunities for students to engage in discussions, interact with one another collaboratively, and apply the new skill or strategy in authentic situations. As students work together, they can validate, problem solve, clarify, confirm, explain, question, experiment, and apply the new learning. This step is a time for students to "figure it out" together, which is a critical component that is often overlooked. Even though this step focuses on collaborative behavior, students should still be held individually accountable. Continue to formatively assess, check for understanding, and implement additional guided instruction scenarios, as needed.

4. **Independent Practice:** After students have been exposed to thoughtful, guided instruction and had opportunities to collaborate with their peers, assign a task that requires them to apply what they learned to a new situation. This is a time for them to demonstrate understanding independently. Even though students are working on their own, it's important to continue to provide them with constructive feedback so they're able to demonstrate their abilities and produce an end product that is truly indicative of their knowledge and skills.

What Is an Example of Gradual Release of Responsibility in Action?

This section outlines an example of how the four steps can be used in the classroom for a lesson on close reading—in this case, teaching students how to identify similes and their effect on readers. Although the specific example centers on this figurative language device for a text suited for 4th or 5th grade—*Tuck Everlasting* by Natalie Babbitt—the strategies and assessments included in this example can be used and adapted for other forms of figurative language and pertinent text in different grade levels. Pay attention to the scaffolded learning experience and consider ways you can parallel instruction for your students. For younger learners, you might still target similes but use a picture book or easier chapter book. For older students, delve into symbolism, metaphor, personification, or a combination related to age-appropriate text.

Step 1: Focused Instruction—"I do it."

The following bullets describe the beginning of what you might say and do to satisfy this step of the gradual release of responsibility process. It involves establishing a clear purpose, modeling, and thinking aloud to make what goes on in your brain about new learning transparent to students.

- Today's lesson goal is to find similes in our class novel, *Tuck Everlasting*, and to consider the effect of similes on us as readers. Let's look at the definition from yesterday that is on the board: *Similes are a form of figurative language that use the words* like, as if, *and* as *to make a comparison between two unlike objects.*

- Our guiding questions for today are: *Where are similes in this text? What does each mean?*
- When I read, I pay attention to forms of figurative language such as similes, metaphors, and personification because writers use these devices to make reading more interesting and to add richness and depth to their writing. When I spot indicators that trigger a simile—*like, as if, as*—I then reread the sentence to make sure there is a comparison between two things that are very different, since we've already learned that is what similes do. Then I try to figure out what the passage means.
- I think of figurative language like a good meal that should be savored. I can eat a burger and fries at any local hamburger joint, or I can savor and derive more pleasure from a gourmet burger with guacamole, cheese, a special sauce, and grilled mushrooms and onions to get a grander experience. When writers add figurative language to their work, I know they intend to create a richness that adds to deeper comprehension. It might be messy to get to the meaning, but that is part of the enjoyment, so I'm going to look deeply at Babbitt's use of similes to determine any hidden meanings and how they add to my understanding of the text.
- I will read a passage from *Tuck Everlasting* and talk aloud about how I discover where the similes are located. I'll be careful to distinguish between a sentence that uses *like* to form a simile and one that merely uses *like* as a verb. Then I'll continue to open up my mind to you by sharing my thoughts about what the similes really mean. To do that, I'll have to read the text surrounding the simile to understand its context. That way, I can fully understand its effect.

Continue this step by reading excerpts from the novel that have similes. Use the Think Aloud strategy to explain how you locate the similes, point out and read the surrounding text for context, reread for deeper meaning, and provide your interpretations of the similes and how they enhance the text. Repeat with more than one excerpt, moving toward more complicated examples. Be sure to show students a variety of similes and how some require more cognitive work to interpret than others such as these examples from *Tuck Everlasting*:

- "I'm about dry as dust."
- "Queen Anne's lace lay dusty on the surface of the meadows like foam on a painted sea."
- "She always pictured a troupe of burly men with long black moustaches who would tumble her into a blanket and bear her off like a sack of potatoes while she pleaded for mercy."
- "The pastures, fields, and scrubby groves they crossed were vigorous with bees, and crickets leapt before them as if each step released a spring and flung them up like pebbles."

After you model and use the Think Aloud strategy to locate and decipher passages with similes, invite students to turn and talk to their neighbors about the meaning and effect other simile excerpts have on readers. During these discussions, circulate around the room and listen carefully for clues that reveal students' levels of understanding. Invite some pairs to share their thinking with the class. In addition, instruct students to complete an exit card about a text excerpt with a simile, and ask for their impressions of the simile's meaning and effect. These two simple forms of formative assessment can help determine if you need to conduct more modeling or continue with the next step: guided instruction.

 ## Think Aloud

The Think Aloud strategy is something you have probably conducted and might not have known you were doing. It's a simple strategy that reflects what the name implies: you are thinking aloud—or making your thinking audible to others—as you complete a task. In this way, students are essentially hearing your brain at work. Thinking aloud can be embedded in the modeling strategy.

When using the Think Aloud strategy for complex text, stop at intervals and allow students to hear you dialogue with yourself as you ask and answer questions or talk about how to respond to a particular task. Since reading can be a solitary and silent activity, mystery can surround what happens inside someone's mind as he or she tries to construct meaning from text. Thinking aloud makes the process visible and allows students to emulate what they hear you do, such as cull evidence, determine clues from a source text to determine whether or not it is credible, or identify the key details that support an author's argument.

State the purpose for conducting a Think Aloud by articulating the guiding questions and posting them on the whiteboard so students are grounded in the day's lesson.

· · · · · ·

 ## Modeling

Fisher and Frey (2014) make a clear distinction between demonstrating and modeling—two strategies that are sometimes used interchangeably but ought not to be used that way. In both, students watch a task being conducted or performed that they will ultimately do themselves. "Think of modeling as an instructional move used when the lesson addresses using a cognitive process, such as reading, writing, mathematics, and such. Demonstrating is what a teacher does when focusing on physical tasks, such as the proper stance for swinging a baseball bat or the procedure for turning on a Bunsen burner" (p. 26). While modeling or demonstrating, interact with students by soliciting their input and responding to their questions or comments. In addition, stop and engage students along the way and even repeat or revise actions based on their responses.

Think Aloud and Modeling/Demonstrating form a powerful duo. You can think aloud as you model or demonstrate strategies, skills, or tasks associated with complex text so students see what they are expected to accomplish on their own. They can also be effectively implemented across content areas. For example, write topic sentences to support a thesis, illustrate an art technique that mirrors a notable artist, conduct a lab experiment, demonstrate proper safety measures, or use context clues to predict a future event.

. . . . . .

Step 2: Guided Instruction—"We do it."

In this step, students practice applying what they learned about similes. Instruct them to read *Tuck Everlasting* and find examples of similes they can annotate (that were not the focus of the last activity but rather new ones they find on their own). Their task is to emulate what you showed them previously: identify a simile, read the surrounding text, then write about the effect the simile has on the passage.

Meet with each group and pose questions around similes, such as "Can you show me where you find a simile? What evidence proves that this is a simile? What does it mean in context? Does it leave an impression on you? How so? Would the passage be more effective without the simile? Explain what you mean." For high achievers, pose more challenging questions, such as "Could the author have used a different form of figurative language, such as a metaphor or personification, to express his or her intent?" For struggling learners, you might narrow down a part of the text where similes are present so students can more easily find them. Allow time for students to reread the text during question-and-answer sessions; perhaps model how to break down difficult passages into parts to better understand it.

Rotate among groups and assess students' levels of proficiency. Based on the information you observe and collect, determine if any student needs further modeling or explanation before moving on to the next step. It might be that you need to regroup students and work with only those who need a little more exposure to a point that is not quite sticking. As you work with those needing extra support, expect other groups to continue annotating their similes. If these students are finished, provide an enrichment opportunity by asking them to identify places in the text where similes could be added—perhaps because the author chose to write more literally. Individuals or pairs could write their own similes and then compare what they wrote with each other. When you finish meeting with the small groups, ask for volunteers to share their newly created similes with the whole class.

Step 3: Collaborative Learning— "You do it together."

Prepare copies of the three graphic organizers presented in Figure 2.5 (pp. 28–29). Arrange students into trios and distribute the organizers so each group member has one with a different quote. If students have already analyzed the quotes featured in these graphic organizers, then find and write a new quote in the center of a blank organizer. The activity goes like this:

 ## 4-Square Collaborative Graphic Organizer

- Each student begins by writing his or her name in the Student #1 quadrant and then reads the text passage featured in the center of the organizer.
- In the #1 quadrant, the student writes the meaning of the simile within the context of the passage plus his or her opinion of its effect. When finished—or when you call time—students rotate their papers so they now have a group member's graphic organizer with a different quote from the text.
- During this second round, students read the new passage along with the entry from Student #1. He or she then uses the #2 quadrant to expand, revise, or provide an alternative impression to the first student's comments about the text passage.
- This process is repeated once more so Student #3 has an opportunity to read the passage and group members' ideas and then offer any new insight or changes. While students are working on this activity, circulate around the room and offer comments, as needed, to redirect students' thinking or provide additional support in an effort to help students master the new learning. In addition, challenge more able students by extending the activity to encourage them to look at other forms of figurative language in the quotes (e.g., imagery, metaphor, personification).
- When all three group members have had a chance to add their thoughts and ideas to each of the graphic organizers, they work together to complete the last quadrant and record their collective impressions.
- To help cement learning, facilitate a whole-class sharing in which students read the collective group comments for each quote while discussing the similarities and differences among groups.

· · · · · ·

Step 4: Independent Practice—"You do it alone."

To truly demonstrate understanding, students must be able to apply what they learned to a new situation. Therefore, give students this opportunity by asking them to interpret and analyze simile passages from sections of *Tuck Everlasting* that they have not yet examined. What follows are two examples of independent writing tasks linked to the goals and content of this lesson:

- How do similes enhance a text? Write an essay in which you interpret the meaning and analyze the effect of similes within a specific passage. Use examples from the text to clarify your analysis.
- Write a description of a setting or a particular character in the novel that the author did not include. In your description, include similes that leave an impression on readers and demonstrate your understanding of not only this form of figurative language but also the content of the text. If you choose, feel free to include other forms of figurative language as well.

Direct Instruction

What Is Direct Instruction?

Direct instruction is another lesson planning model that you can implement across content areas and in diverse contexts to teach a new skill, strategy, or process. Originally outlined by Adams and Engelmann (1996), this method involves specific stages that you employ in a systematic fashion. The original version included seven stages, but it's subsequently undergone many iterations. Hattie (2009, 2012) makes an emphatic point that direct instruction is not didactic teaching in which a teacher stands in front of the room talking at students. Rather, he cites direct instruction as a very successful method that contributes to student achievement.

What follows is a synthesis of many different resources. The first two stages aren't readily found in recent documents; however, they are indeed contributing factors to effective instructional design (and discussed earlier in this chapter). As you read the stages in this model, you will undoubtedly recognize some aspects of the gradual release of responsibility approach, including regular opportunities for formative and self-assessment that help move students forward on a learning path.

- Stage 1: Identify learning intentions.
- Stage 2: Determine the criteria for success.
- Stage 3: Set the stage and articulate the goal.
- Stage 4: Model or demonstrate new material.
- Stage 5: Engage in guided practice.
- Stage 6: Provide closure.
- Stage 7: Apply new learning through independent practice.

FIGURE 2.5
Figurative Language 4-Square

Student #1: _____

Student #2: _____

"He laughed, gesturing in self-depre-cation with long, thin fingers. His tall body moved continuously; a foot tapped, a shoulder twitched. And it moved in angles, rather than jerkily. But at the same time he had a kind of grace, like a well-handled marionette." (p. 18)

Collective impressions:

Student #3: _____

Student #1: _____

Student #2: _____

"Winnie herself was speechless. She clung to the saddle and gave herself up to the astonishing fact that, though her heart was pounding and her backbone felt like a pipe full of cold running water, her head was fiercely calm. Disconnected thoughts presented themselves one by one, as if they had been waiting their turn in line." (p. 32)

Collective impressions:

Student #3: _____

Student #1: _____

Student #2: _____

"And Winnie, laughing at him, lost the last of her alarm. They were friends, her friends. She was running away after all, but she was not alone. Closing the gate on her oldest fears as she had closed the gate of her own fenced yard, she discovered the wings she'd always wished she had. And all at once she was elated. Where were the terrors she'd been told she should expect? She could not recognize them anywhere. The sweet earth opened out its wide four corners to her like the petals of a flower ready to be picked, and it shimmered with light and possibility till she was dizzy with it." (p. 45)

Collective impressions:

Student #3: _____

Student #1: _____

Student #2: _____

Collective impressions:

Student #3: _____

Stage 1: Identify learning intentions.

To prepare for the lesson, identify what students should know, understand, and be able to do as a result of the learning. Earlier in this chapter, I presented KUDs. This stage of direct instruction expressly addresses these kinds of intentions so you are crystal clear about what you plan to teach.

Stage 2: Determine the criteria for success.

Before beginning a lesson, be aware of what constitutes success. What is expected of students? What will they be held accountable for in an activity or lesson? At what point in the activity or lesson will they be held accountable? Furthermore, students need to be aware of the standards for performance so they know when they have reached success or are successfully progressing toward it. According to Hattie (2012), "Two powerful ways of increasing impact is to know *and* share both the learning intentions and success criteria of the lesson with students. When students know both, they are more likely to work towards mastering the criteria of success, more likely to know where they are on the trajectory towards this success, and more likely to have a good chance of learning how to monitor and self-regulate their progress" (p. 75). During the first two stages of the direct instruction model, it's critical to include and clarify these intentions—along with success criteria—in your unit and lesson planning. During subsequent stages, share them with students at strategic points in the unit.

Stage 3: Set the stage and articulate the goal.

This initial stage of student interface involves preparing students for the learning that is about to take place by capturing their interest so they feel compelled to engage in the work ahead. Examples can include sharing a brief story or scenario (What if...? Suppose...), presenting an analogy, showing pictures or realia (i.e., objects used in teaching, such as a fossil, model, or costume), playing a song or video clip, tapping into students' current interests (e.g., referencing or featuring popular music, sports teams, or technology), or presenting a riddle or conundrum. So that the purpose and objective of the lesson are clearly established, pose and post a guiding question (in student-friendly language) so students are aware of the lesson goals. Set the stage for the upcoming learning by connecting what students already know to the new information and by providing a rationale that explains why this work is important. This stage is fairly brief.

Stage 4: Model or demonstrate new material.

Students need to visualize and see firsthand what they are expected to do and learn. This stage is similar to Step 1 of the gradual release of responsibility approach. It involves presenting new material by modeling or demonstrating a clearly delineated series of steps while keeping in mind the final outcome or goal (i.e., what constitutes success). Use text passages, charts, tables, graphic organizers, pictures, student writing samples, or any visual that aids in showing what is to be learned, what students are expected to do, and what mastery looks like.

When modeling, share your thoughts aloud (i.e., Think Aloud strategy) so students hear a thought process they should emulate when they work on the activity themselves. Clear explanations, relevant examples, and appropriate pacing allow students to process each step. In addition, solicit input and allow appropriate wait time for students' responses; ideas for quick formative assessments are listed in Step 1 of the gradual release model discussed earlier in this chapter. Conducting these assessments will help you check for understanding and keep students engaged. Plus, eliciting student participation and feedback will provide information about how well students are grasping the content and about the need to differentiate instruction. Model and demonstrate the new material until most students have a general understanding of the steps required to complete the task, and then move to the next stage.

Stage 5: Engage in guided practice.

This stage, which is like Step 2 of the gradual release model, allows time for students to begin mastering the skill, strategy, or process under your guidance so they can later be successful on their own. First, consider how students performed during the previous stage, arrange them in different grouping configurations, and scaffold your instruction and the group activities so all students are working toward proficiency. Orchestrate learning experiences for each group so students can practice the new learning (subsequent chapters include a variety of practical activities you can use to this end).

In order to guide students in the right direction, this stage requires even more formative assessment so you can fully grasp each student's level of understanding—and plan differentiated instruction accordingly. Students should also monitor their own learning and self-assess so they can contribute to their own improvement. As students are working, it's important to observe and interact with individuals and small groups to give feedback and ensure they are performing accurately. Repetition and review might be in order as students grapple with something new. By contrast, there may be students who are more advanced and need you to challenge them so they can go further. This differentiation is a critical step in both models, so be attentive and responsive to your students' needs, and you'll be able to guide them effectively.

Stage 6: Provide closure.

At this point, signify to students that the lesson has come to an end so they have an opportunity to reflect on what was taught and make sense of it. Provide closure at an important point in the lesson, too. This is a time "to help to organize student learning, to help to form a coherent picture, to consolidate, to eliminate confusion and frustration, and to reinforce the major points to be learned" (Hattie, 2012, p. 205). Before students set off on their own and apply the new learning independently, stopping to answer questions or clarify specific details can provide a sense of closure that fuels a confidence to continue. You might conduct any of the formative assessment sugges-tions mentioned earlier for modeling or demonstrating; however, this time, look for evidence of major learning of the objective rather than a beginning understanding. Alternatively, consider issuing exit cards if students are working on independent prac-tice the following day. Some versions of the direct instruction model reverse Stages 6 and 7.

 ## Exit Cards

Assign exit cards—or ticket-to-leave cards—during the last three to five minutes of a class period. On these cards, students write a brief response to a question or prompt that you pose. Allowing students the opportunity to take some time to reflect on what they learned and share their thinking is an effective teaching technique. Collect the cards and organize responses into three piles: one for stu-dents who clearly understand, a second pile for those who seem unsure, and a third stack of cards for students who are apparently confused or off track. With this information, gather together individuals or small groups of students to pro-vide additional and necessary support.

The possibilities for this task are endless. Keep in mind that this is a quick check to ascertain which students are learning and who is falling short, so keep the task manageable.

- You might ask students to respond to a text-dependent question about key details or provide a two-sentence summary of an idea from the text.
- You could ask these kinds of questions: "What confused you at the beginning of class, and what did you come to realize? What two questions do you still have about _____?"
- If you are using exit cards before independent practice, you might pose both of these prompts: "What questions or clarification do you have before independent practice? Briefly explain your understanding of what you just learned."
- Some teachers issue exit slips each day and write useful comments on them. The slips are returned to students so they can study them and prepare for a summative assessment.

· · · · · ·

Stage 7: Apply new learning through independent practice.

This stage is similar to independent practice for the gradual release of responsi-bility model. During both guided and independent practice, students should be given frequent opportunities to try out the new learning in novel ways. For example, if a lesson centers on analyzing the development of the central idea in one text, students need to apply the same skill with proficiency in an altogether different text. Often, teachers model something and then have students apply that skill in the same situation (i.e., with the same passage of a text). If students cannot transfer the skill, they are not demonstrating competency; rather, they are showing an ability to regurgitate what the teacher has modeled.

Once students show they have a grasp of the new skill, strategy, or process in guided practice, this stage is designed for them to reinforce that learning—independently. I share many relevant suggestions for how to do this in later chapters of this book, so choose assignments that connect to your specific learning goals and provide students with an opportunity to practice and show their own growth and proficiency. These tasks can be completed in class or as homework assignments. Continue to observe and monitor students' work to correct misconceptions and verify that they are on the right track and can independently apply the new learning.

What Is an Example of Direct Instruction in Action?

What follows is a lesson example using direct instruction that focuses on researching and culling salient facts for a biography that students will write. It can be adapted across content areas and is mostly suitable for upper-elementary and middle school students.

Stage 1: Identify learning intentions.

Direct instruction begins with clearly identifying what you want students to know, understand, and be able to do for a particular lesson, which resides within a unit of study. For this particular lesson, here are the KUDs and guiding questions:

- **Knowledge:** I want students to know relevant versus superficial facts, supporting details, evidence, and the purpose of the writing task.
- **Essential understanding:** Biographies provide information about noteworthy individuals; however, some facts contribute to keen insights about the individual and address the task, whereas others are merely superfluous and unnecessary.
- **Skills:** (1) Discern between essential and nonessential facts. (2) Choose relevant facts that support the writing task.
- What is the difference between relevant and nonessential (or unimportant) facts? How does the writing task help determine which facts I need?

Stage 2: Determine the criteria for success.

The following is a student writing task that can be used for a biography. This prompt can be tailored and used in various content areas since students can write a biography about a hero, a modern-day political leader, a historical figure, a mathematician, a scientist, an entrepreneur, and so forth. To differentiate, allow students to identify the subject for their biographies and use appropriately challenging resources to collect pertinent information. Consider providing a list of possible individuals as options.

> After researching informational text about your chosen individual, address these questions in a well-structured and developed biography: How did this person's accomplishments or innovations affect society then and now? What political, social, economic, or religious obstacles did this individual face, and how did he or she overcome them? How did individuals, events, or other factors influence or inspire this person? Include proper citations and a works cited document. Use the student checklist (or rubric) as a guide while writing.

Prepare a rubric for scoring the finished piece and a checklist that aligns to it. Students can assist in creating the rubric or checklist; however, you need to make sure it is aligned to standards and complete. Review and distribute the checklist (or rubric) so students can use it as a guide while they write.

For this specific lesson, the focus is on identifying certain kinds of facts that can be culled and used to support the biography writing assignment. During guided and independent practice, students demonstrate proficiency when they select relevant (rather than unnecessary) facts that address the writing task and serve to develop the topic. Of course, other evidence can be used for supporting details, and you should mention that statistics, examples, anecdotes, quotations, and other information are also fair game for evidence that can be used in their papers. This lesson, however, is focused on salient facts. What students learn in this lesson can be applied to other forms of evidence as the goal is for them to select the most relevant and salient pieces of information to satisfy the task.

Stage 3: Set the stage and articulate the goal.

To engage students, begin the lesson by sharing facts about a popular musical artist, sports figure, or actor, and ask them to ascertain whether the facts are relevant or irrelevant. Set the stage for learning by reminding students what you have covered in the unit and identifying the purpose for the day's lesson. Say something like "At this point in our unit, you're aware that you'll each be writing a biography and now have the writing prompt and checklist to guide you while writing. Today we will focus on the guiding question 'What is the difference between relevant and irrelevant facts?'"

Point out the aligned and pertinent line items on the student checklist to emphasize the purpose for learning. Reread the biography writing prompt so students are clear about the task. Say, "Let's pretend that the subject for your biography is Taylor Swift. I am going to read several facts about her. For each statement I read, hold up one finger if the fact is interesting but not necessarily important, two fingers if the fact is relevant, and a fist if you are unsure. I'll read each fact twice and then ask you to signal at chest level to show your responses. Please do not hold your fingers in the air or to the side for others to see so you are not influenced by your peers. Your signaling gives me good information about how I can best teach you, so your personal responses are important for me to see."

Use facts such as the following for this informal assessment. This active participation exercise is meant to be brief, lay the groundwork for the day's lesson, and serve as a starting point for collecting information to differentiate accordingly.

- Taylor Swift began writing songs at age 12.
- In 2012, *Forbes* magazine ranked Swift as the highest-paid celebrity under age 30 with a $57 million salary.
- Swift's zodiac sign is a Sagittarius.
- Swift shows a philanthropic spirit by funding the $4 million Taylor Swift Education Center at the Country Music Hall of Fame in Nashville.
- Swift went to Hendersonville High School.
- Swift has had a slew of celebrity romances that all have ended amid swirls of rumors.
- Swift's high-profile romances have been the inspiration for many of her popular songs, such as "Dear John" and "We Are Never Ever Getting Back Together."

Stage 4: Model or demonstrate new material.

Return to the facts you presented and use modeling and think alouds to explain the difference between unimportant versus essential facts. To do this, read selected facts and verify whether or not each is fluff—and should be excluded in a biography— or salient and worthy of inclusion in the paper. During your detailed explanation of how you determine which facts to include in a biography, refer to the writing task and the student checklist to be clear about the purpose and expectations. A sample of the internal monologue that you make audible to students might sound like this:

> I know I need to address these questions within my paper: "How did this person's accomplishments or innovations affect society then and now? What political, social, economic, or religious obstacles did this individual face and how did she overcome them? How did individuals, events, or other factors influence or inspire this person?"

> Since the subject of my biography is currently alive and not a historical figure, I'll alter the questions for present tense. I think two facts show evidence of Taylor Swift's accomplishments as an artist and therefore are relevant: <u>In 2012, Forbes magazine ranked Swift as the highest-paid celebrity under age 30 with a $57 million salary, and Swift shows a philanthropic spirit by funding the $4 million Taylor Swift Education Center at the Country Music Hall of Fame in Nashville.</u> The second fact shows her positive impact on society through her

willingness to make a difference in people's lives. I'll need to find more information about her influence, but this fact is a good starting point.

This fact seems irrelevant: <u>Swift went to Hendersonville High School</u>. However, I need to focus on obstacles that she might have suffered and overcome. If she were the victim of bullying or had difficulties with teachers while in high school, that might be a social obstacle. I can't include this fact, though, if I don't have more information about her high school years or if they presented any strife for her.

Stage 5: Engage in guided practice.

Students will now begin to apply what you modeled and explained using facts about an individual who is pertinent to the current subject matter. Use the same writing task so they can return to it to verify which facts address the assignment. For this activity, arrange students into small groups and distribute a set of sentence strips to each group. (As an example, see Figure 2.6 for facts about George Washington.) Instruct students to sort the strips into two groups: Unimportant Facts and Relevant Facts. Walk around the room and observe students as they sort. Listen to their conversations. If some students show clear understanding and others do not, assign the more proficient students the role of ambassador. In this capacity, they can work with their classmates who need further explanation or modeling. Concurrently, you can work with struggling students who need support so everyone can be ready to move on to the next stage together.

Stage 6: Provide closure.

Lead a brief discussion to recap the new learning using these or similar questions: "What is the difference between relevant and irrelevant facts? What type of facts should be included in the biography? How do you know this?" If this lesson takes more than one day, you can have students answer these questions on an exit card. Carefully review their responses before class the following day to inform your instruction. For students who still need support, reteach the skill before they begin independent practice so they are prepared to work on their own.

Stage 7: Apply new learning through independent practice.

At this point, students conduct research and cull facts about their chosen individual using what they learned during your instruction about collecting salient, relevant facts. Explain to them that the next lesson will focus on other types of evidence they will need to write a fully developed biography (e.g., anecdotes, quotations, examples). Tell them that during their research to find facts, they might naturally discover other forms of evidence they will want to use. If so, encourage them to use sticky notes or a notetaking device to flag these parts of their research in preparation for the next lesson.

George Washington Facts

1. Washington was the only U.S. president to be unanimously elected.
2. Even though Washington owned a lot of land, he did not have a lot of cash in 1789. As a result, he had to borrow money to get from his home in Mount Vernon to New York City, the place of his first inauguration.
3. Washington is the only state named for a president.
4. Washington had hoped he would be alive in the new century and joked with friends that they'd all live to see 1800. Unfortunately, he died on December 14, 1799, and missed that milestone.
5. Although never pierced by a bullet, two of Washington's horses were shot while he was riding them, and he later discovered four bullet holes in his clothes.
6. Throughout his life, Washington owned dozens of dogs. Some of their names were Captain, Forester, Jupiter, Maiden, Mopsey, Pilot, Singer, Sweetlips, and Tarter.
7. The story that Washington threw a silver dollar across the Potomac River, which is 1 1/4 miles wide, is untrue.
8. Washington lost more battles than he won during the Revolutionary War.
9. Washington was born on February 22, 1732, to a Virginia planter family.
10. The story of Washington chopping down a cherry tree when he was a young boy and uttering the famous "Father, I cannot tell a lie" line is fictitious. It was invented by one of his early biographers, Mason Weems, to add details about his childhood since so little was known about Washington's youth.
11. Washington suffered from chronic toothaches, so he had all of his teeth extracted at age 57. He then wore a kind of composite false teeth made from ivory and animal and human teeth.
12. Instead of wearing a powdered wig, which was fashionable during the late 1700s, Washington braided, tied back, and powdered his own reddish-brown hair.
13. Every Friday, Martha Washington hosted a tea party during her husband's presidency, and any well-dressed person was welcome to attend.
14. At 6'2" and 200 pounds, Washington was one of our country's largest presidents.
15. Washington felt that the British manipulated and used the colonists, and the regulations they imposed on colonists restricted them. He carefully and firmly spoke out against the injustice.
16. When Washington was 26, he married widow Martha Dandridge Custis, who had two children, Jackie and Patsy. Martha and George never had their own children.
17. Among his favorite dishes were cream of peanut soup, mashed sweet potatoes with coconut, and string beans with mushrooms.
18. George Washington was president for eight years, beginning in 1789.
19. Washington attended school at age 6 and had to leave at 15 to work as a surveyor since his mother couldn't afford to send him to college. At 16, he helped survey Shenandoah lands for Thomas, Lord Fairfax.
20. When Washington served as a Virginia delegate to the Second Continental Congress, he was elected Commander in Chief of the Continental Army.

Source: Adapted from information found at http://www.scholastic.com/teachers/article/7-fun-facts-about-george-washington and https://www.whitehouse.gov/1600/presidents/georgewashington

How Flexible Are the Models?
What Are Differentiation Suggestions?

In the gradual release of responsibility model, all four steps of the process are necessary when students are introduced to a new skill, concept, or strategy—including collaboration—since working with peers at strategic points in the process is vital. In direct instruction, the same applies, so the overlapping stages of the two models (i.e., Stages 3, 4, 5, and 7) are imperative for acquiring new learning. There is, however, some flexibility with regard to sequence, so do not feel obligated to progress lockstep through each stage in a rigidly linear manner. "Teachers often reorder the phases—for example, begin a lesson with an independent task, such as bellwork or a quick-write, or engage students in collaborative peer inquiry prior to providing teacher modeling... What is important and necessary for deep learning is that students experience all four phases of learning when encountering new content" (Fisher & Frey, 2014, p. 4).

Consider this example to illustrate how the steps or stages can be reordered. Purposefully prepare an expository paragraph that is missing the topic sentence and that includes details in the wrong order. Ask students to read the text and answer the following question: What is the author's main idea? Some students flounder and arrive at a variety of guesses without really knowing what the text is about. Others merely state that they have no idea. Allow time for a group discussion in which students will likely grope for a response. Then pose the guiding question that states the purpose for learning: What is the function of a topic sentence? Notice that the activity begins by propelling students to discover the absence of the target skill. In this example, the basic structure of both models is tweaked so that students work on a collaborative activity first, which is expressly orchestrated to prompt them to realize the objective for the day's lesson for themselves.

Timing is another area that can be adapted; each segment does not have to be neatly relegated to one class period. Sometimes a step or stage can take several class periods to accomplish; other times you might breeze through all of the stages in one or two class periods. For example, a lesson on teaching parallel structure in writing might take one or two classes for guided instruction, but a more complex lesson on extracting salient and sufficient evidence from researched sources may span a week. To determine how long to spend on a particular part and whether repetition is necessary hinges on how well students are mastering the new content. Therefore, assessment is the name of the game. Use the power of formative assessment to determine how best to differentiate for your students, and provide self-assessment opportunities so they can identify and communicate what they need to progress. Since students are at varying levels of readiness, some may require a considerable amount of support and even more time than some of their peers who might move to independence sooner. It's critical to differentiate individuals and groups of students appropriately (e.g., additional demonstration or modeling, extended or less time for practice, various types and levels of materials).

If students are reviewing previously taught skills or content, then an abbreviated version of either model can be implemented. You might find, based on your lesson goals, that it is prudent to delete a stage because it does not apply. However, this is only recommended when students have had prior exposure to and experience with what they are being asked to do. For example, after focusing the lesson, you could ask students to work individually and show evidence of proficiency. Then adjust teaching, as needed.

Since each learning situation is unique, you must use a critical eye to review the skills, strategies, and processes your students need to acquire and then plan your lessons accordingly. Decisions about whether or not to include each stage, the timing or repetition of each one, or how to sequence the segments are all made based on your specific learning goals, the familiarity students have with the lesson content, and the differentiated needs of your students.

Closing

Many educators and researchers have made it their mission to discover what works and what is most effective in raising student achievement. Therefore, as teachers, it behooves us all to capitalize on this research to plan our instruction and help our students. The instructional models of backward design, gradual release of responsibility, and direct instruction are all research-based approaches that have proven to be successful.

The backward planning philosophy is about beginning with the end in mind so that you first define what you want students to know, understand, and be able to do in a unit of study. Then determine what evidence you will accept from students that shows their mastery of targeted learning goals. With these clear intentions and criteria in mind, you are primed to develop or find lessons with selected strategies, activities, and assessments. Beginning with strategies and lessons does not provide the advantage of being able to see the overarching goals for an entire unit. You need to know where you are headed in order to take the necessary steps to get there.

Lynn Erickson and Lois Lanning (2014) write that "when teachers design learning experiences that employ KUDs and concept-based pedagogy, students will benefit because learning to think beyond the facts and transfer concepts and understandings through time, across cultures, and across situations expands the worldview of students, helps them see patterns and connections between new knowledge and prior knowledge, and provides the brain schemata to support lifelong learning" (p. 12).

The two lesson plan models discussed in this chapter—gradual release of responsibility and direct instruction—each provide a framework for developing sound lessons so any strategies you choose to use are embedded in a conscientious way for student improvement. Each model provides ample time for guided and independent practice and relies on differentiation so you can appropriately challenge each student.

3

Preparing, Prereading, and Exposing Students to Text and Its Structure

When planning instruction around complex text, close reading on your part is essential. This chapter is therefore dedicated to how you can prepare to teach complex text, the role of prereading, and some instructional strategies that can be embedded within a lesson to teach text structure and expose students to complex text.

Teacher Preparation for Close Reading

You might be familiar with the complex text at the center of your instruction because you have taught it in the past. Or maybe you are unfamiliar with it because it's a recent article or publication, something a colleague just shared with you, or a discovery from a search you conducted. If you have used it in your classroom before or were involved in the vetting process outlined in Resource B (or a similar undertaking), then odds are you're extremely acquainted with the text. However, many teachers do not take the time to thoroughly plan for teaching a text, which can compromise its effectiveness as a vehicle for student learning. With that in mind, here are some suggestions for how to approach a text so you can use it purposefully at the center of instruction. These recommendations, with the exception of the first, require more extensive explanations that I provide in other sections of this book where the respective topics are treated more fully. Consider this a heads up for what you will need to do to prepare for close reading encounters, and read the referenced chapters for more detail.

Divide the text into sections or passages. The author (or publisher) of a text has already divided the text according to his or her opinion of how it should be organized.

To teach the text effectively, though, you need to determine how many paragraphs, pages, sections, or chapters students should read at a time.

When encountering text for the first time, it might be hard to get oriented to the content. Therefore, to help students initially engage with the text and maximize comprehension, the first section should be relatively short. (Later on, students might be able to examine larger portions.) However, if the entire text is equally challenging (e.g., it includes archaic language, unfamiliar or sophisticated concepts, or complicated literacy devices), then each portion should be roughly equal in size. Other considerations for chunking text include the targeted skills of each lesson, individual student characteristics, students' developmental reading levels, and time constraints.

Identify general academic words. Domain-specific words—or Tier 3 words, as they are called in the CCSS—are those terms that content-area teachers incorporate into the curriculum. They often include medical, scientific, mathematical, or social studies terms. They are central to instruction for a particular unit of study and are critical to help students build knowledge of the subject matter. General academic words (i.e., Tier 2 words) are those that appear in texts across all disciplines and are included in the lexicon for relatively mature language users. Students need access to these words for reading comprehension, but many teachers do not typically concentrate on them because they instead focus on Tier 3 words.

However, these academic Tier 2 words can be particularly challenging because they sometimes change meaning according to context. For example, the word *commission* means something different depending on how it's used. For example

- The property owner commissioned a painting from a local artist so his artwork could be displayed in the lobby.
- After running the marathon, Michael was out of commission and in need of rest and hydration.
- Local environmentalists served on the commission dedicated to preserving the city's natural habitats.

Scour the complex text you will be using, and emphasize general academic words by underlining, highlighting, or somehow calling them out. If you cannot mark on the text directly, provide a separate list of these words. Within your instruction, plan to teach these words specifically since they carry rich meaning that can contribute to students' understanding of the domain-specific Tier 3 terms.

Chapter 4 is dedicated to a discussion of vocabulary and suggestions for how to identify words worth teaching and ways to teach unfamiliar words and terms.

Determine the core ideas of the text. It should go without saying that it's important for you to be aware of the key understandings and themes embedded in a text. Therefore, carefully examine and analyze any text you teach to realize the essence of it. It is not enough to state that the text is about a hero's journey, discrimination, the life cycle of a plant, or strategic military maneuvers. More attention is required to arrive at essential statements that you want students to eventually grasp. Write them in your own language and use them to guide the instructional experiences, just as essential understandings help drive your unit of study.

An example related to an article, a work of historical fiction, a documentary, a play, or a speech might be "Discrimination contributes to a splintering of communities, the collapse of values, and oftentimes reprehensible treatment of the most disadvantaged population." Standards can also reveal the core ideas that a text should entail, as in this example for a science text about natural selection: "Sometimes the differences in characteristics between individuals of the same species provide advantages in surviving, finding mates, and reproducing."

For more detailed guidance about how to develop these kinds of conceptual statements, see the material pertaining to text-dependent questions in Chapter 5.

Write or find text-dependent questions associated with each section of the text. Text-dependent questions are those queries or tasks that require students to use the text as the basis for a response. In doing so, it illuminates students' understanding of the text because these questions are fashioned in such a way that students must use the text as the source of information. In pointing them back to the text—for example, to examine the way an author uses text structure, a literary device, repetition, or style—students can make inferences, identify mood, or articulate an argument and sound reasoning to make sense of the text on a grander scale.

In Chapter 5, I present a comprehensive discussion of text-dependent questions, including definition and purpose, a step-by-step process for designing and redesigning questions for complex text, and practical examples. If you use text-dependent questions from an online or other resource, it's important that you know what text-dependent questions mean so that you can discern between questions and tasks that do not require text scrutiny and those that foster the kind of rigor required to challenge students appropriately.

Prereading Guidelines and Suggestions

Many wonder about prereading activities that are appropriate to use to sufficiently prepare students for reading complex text along with those that should be avoided. Generally speaking, frontloading information needs to help students dive into a text so they can begin to make sense of it themselves. Providing too much information can prevent students from deciphering the text on their own. For example, when a teacher summarizes a text in advance of reading it—or the publisher features a summary at the start of a text selection—students are not doing the job of figuring out what the content means for themselves.

David Coleman (2012)—contributing author to the CCSS for ELA—admits that it's tempting to orient students to the text by sharing a brief summary that grounds them in the basics of the material. Although this can be effective, he makes the point that when teachers provide a summary, students draw upon the teacher's words when they respond to questions later during group discussions or in writing. Instead of relying on what they've learned from the text on their own, students reiterate what their teacher has said. The bottom line is this: avoid offering summaries prior to reading a text; instead, have students summarize the text at intervals on their own to solidify learning and build knowledge.

Aside from summaries, consider the value of each prereading activity and whether it supports or detracts from the reading. For instance, a prewriting exercise in which students respond to a prompt about the theme of a text has the potential to prematurely reveal a discovery that students could make on their own. A better approach, therefore, might be to have students use evidence from the text to develop and articulate their impressions of emerging themes. In the end, they can verify the most dominant themes. Another prereading misstep can occur when teachers feel compelled to provide too much background information. Often, an author has included context clues and explicit material that students can piece together—given time and careful attention to details. For example, it is usually unnecessary to point out a country or other location on a map when there is probably sufficient evidence in the text to indicate the setting and other relevant locations. In short, avoid divulging what students are able to uncover on their own through dedication, time, and effort. More times than not, teachers provide an excessive amount of prior information that serves as an unnecessary crutch. Instead of students wrestling with the text to uncover content on their own, it is done for them. There are alternatives and guidelines to consider before jumping headfirst into assuming students need our help from the get-go.

There are exceptions, however. English language learners might benefit from prior knowledge—to level the playing field with their peers. And some texts do require additional information or frontloading at the outset of reading. Perhaps students have limited exposure to a particular historical setting, event, or cultural influence that serves as the basis for a text, and the text itself provides limited or no means for obtaining key information. To compensate for this lack of background knowledge, there is sometimes a sense of obligation to explain in detail what is missing. "If you think there is key information that students need to know before they read the text (something necessary for making sense of the text that isn't stated in the text), by all means tell it. If there is no pre-information necessary, then don't make such a presentation or discussion. If you are uncertain, then let the kids have a chance to make sense of it. If it goes well, fine. If not, then add the information before the second reading" (Shanahan, 2012, para. 10).

Let's return to that last point: "If you are uncertain, then let the kids have a chance to make sense of it." Perhaps before jumping in to provide what you think they need, help students engage in a productive struggle so they can figure out meaning or context on their own (or with your assistance). This route can yield valuable dividends by providing additional opportunities to practice reading skills and learn content that will enhance the complex text. The following examples provide concrete suggestions.

Use the text to provide background information. When I taught 8th grade language arts, students read either *Night* by Elie Wiesel, *All but My Life* by Gerda Weissmann Klein, or *The Diary of a Young Girl* by Anne Frank. Most students did not have previous knowledge of the Holocaust since it wasn't included in the social studies content standards for this grade level. Therefore, they needed orientation to appreciate the historical significance. To do so, I used the jigsaw strategy wherein each group of students was assigned a different nonfiction article to read (e.g., victims, perpetrators, bystanders, resisters, righteous gentiles). They then shared what they learned with others. In this regard, I orchestrated an activity in which students taught themselves the context of the texts they would soon read.

 Jigsaw

Jigsaw involves two groups. Students in the first group—referred to as the "expert" group—are each assigned a different text. They follow this sequence: (1) students in each group individually read the assigned texts (e.g., articles, poems, directions) and take notes on a teacher-prepared or student-generated graphic organizer; (2) group members discuss and compare their notes with one another; and (3) groups agree on the most important points they will share with others in the next grouping. The text each group reads is for an express purpose. When using Jigsaw as a tool to share background information, students read material to acquire foundational knowledge for the upcoming text. For example, as a prereading exercise, students might read a text to orient them to a particular historical context; each expert group focuses on an aspect of the time period and the key individuals or groups. In this instance, be careful to choose text to give necessary prior information rather than reveal too much about the mentor text that students will discover themselves. In another example, Jigsaw can be used to extend what students learn about a topic during or after investigation of the complex text. To do so, they can read speeches or essays that represent different points of view of an argument, or they can listen to song lyrics from an artist who has a similar or dissimilar style as that of the target text.

After expert groups have read and discussed their assigned texts, rearrange the class so that members of each expert group disassemble and form a new group. In this second group configuration, students teach others what they learned from the initial reading with the aid of the notes they took. After these groups meet, conduct a whole-class discussion and invite students to clarify points that need extra attention. You might have students write about their reflections and what they glean in a student journal or return to their graphic organizers and make additional entries based on what they learned.

The name *jigsaw* signifies the essential part that each student plays in studying text to share with others. Just like each piece of a jigsaw puzzle adds a new dimension and part to the whole picture, each student's contribution adds insight and understanding to complete the learning task.

· · · · · ·

Develop questions after a cold read. Sometimes teachers plan for students to read or hear a text cold. This invariably leads to many questions. After students read or listen to an excerpt, invite them to record and share their questions about the text. If the full text (and future lessons) will eventually reveal answers to certain questions, then put those questions aside to address when the time comes. However, if the text will not uncover answers to some questions, then you can use these questions to guide your prereading instruction. For example, you might have students watch a short video, read relevant articles, or conduct a formal activity to provide the necessary information and set the stage for reading. A cold read will only work effectively to generate questions if the text is at an appropriate challenge level. Otherwise, it could have an undesirable effect and produce frustration.

> If the text is selected to be at the right level for the reader, if it is the right length, and if the initial cold close reading generates enough sense of the content that the reader can ask some reasonable follow-up questions, then the cold close reading does precisely what it is meant to do—teaches students the value of struggling with text. But if the text is too hard, or too long, or too full of unknown words or about a topic that is too unfamiliar, then the reader quickly exhausts his or her initial willingness to struggle with it. Teachers refer to this as a deficit of stamina. It can just as easily be thought of as a collapse of motivation. (Snow, 2013, p. 19)

By this point, the message should be clear that you need to be thoughtful in the way complex text is introduced. Here are some prereading tips to guide your planning:

- Identify the title and author.
- For words that are critical for understanding a text, provide explanations and definitions if context clues do not reveal meanings.
- Set the stage for an upcoming lesson by posing a guiding question that identifies the purpose for reading (e.g., How do characters change over time? How do internal conflicts shape the plot? How do habitats differ? Are all habitats suitable for all organisms? Do artists have innate talent, or is talent cultivated?). Guiding questions should not give away the details of the text; rather, they are overarching

queries (as opposed to text-dependent questions) that ground students and pique their interest for the work ahead. Through various activities and assessments that propel careful scrutiny of the author's work, students will address these guiding questions.

- Invite students to get the "lay of the land" by skimming through the text to identify and peruse the various text features. Reading the subheadings, scanning the diagrams, and taking note of words and concepts in bold typeface can prepare them for what will come.
- Prepare students for complexity. A consistent dose of complex text is likely new to many students, so let them know that they should feel this is challenging work. That is expected. Explain that the ultimate goal is to help them read difficult text independently and proficiently so they are prepared for the next grade level and their future beyond school. Reassure students that you will guide them and provide the learning and practice they need to develop the necessary reading skills to understand complex text. Invite them to partner with you to ensure they are meeting learning targets and progressing along a continuum of reading more complex text competently and confidently.

Initial and Ongoing Exposure to Complex Text

After you introduce a text passage using the suggestions in the previous section, begin guiding students through the text. A student's first encounter with a text passage requires a unique strategy since it is essentially foreign material. This involves two separate exposures—through listening and silent reading or vice versa. You might elect to begin by reading the text aloud if it includes difficult cadence, archaic language, unfamiliar terms, or an unknown dialect. This can be done by you, by a capable student reader, or with a prerecorded audio version of the text. Alternatively, you can ask students to read it silently if you feel the text does not include the aforementioned conditions that would automatically impede comprehension. If you feel comfortable that students will actually read at home, you can assign silent reading as homework.

During these two exposures, instruct your students to annotate the text and begin to make sense of it. Students can then share their insights with peers and engage in an activity such as Turn-and-Talk or Think-Pair-Share. In these early stages of text initiation, consider leading a reciprocal teaching exercise to support student engagement with the new text. In all of these activities, students should get accustomed to using text evidence to support their assertions and impressions since they will be expected to do this throughout all of their speaking and writing experiences related to complex text. When interacting with nontraditional complex text, adapt the strategies, as needed, to appeal to the type of text under examination. For example, in lieu of making annotations on a written text, students can write their impressions in a journal.

Each time they revisit a text, students will delve deeper and uncover something fresh through your instruction, which should be built around both text-dependent questions and specific skills tied to learning goals. This chapter is focused more on the initial exposure to a text, even though some of the strategies mentioned can be used for ongoing examination. Future chapters include additional strategies, ideas, and assessments you can embed in your lessons for repeated reading.

 ## Annotation

Reading a complex text is a dedicated pursuit that requires thought and effort. "Since reading of any sort is an activity, all reading must to some degree be active. Completely passive reading is impossible; we cannot read with our eyes immobilized and our minds asleep. . . . One reader is better than another in proportion as he is capable of a greater range of activity in reading and exerts more effort. He is better if he demands more of himself and of the text before him" (Adler & Van Doren, 1972, p. 5). One way to read more actively and exert more effort is through annotation.

Of the many ways readers can engage with a complex text, annotation is among the more popular strategies. It is a vehicle for readers to make sense of what they read by stopping to notate parts of a text that are significant and need attention. The strategy involves two related parts. First, readers highlight, underline, or circle pertinent text. Then they write notes in the margin associated with what they marked so the connection between them is clear. Students can use sticky notes or a student journal if writing in the text is not an option, or if they are examining nontraditional text. In short, annotation is a two-step process: (1) flagging the text in some way, and (2) writing impressions based on what is marked. Merely highlighting, underlining, or marking in another way is incomplete; actively explaining what is flagged requires more thought and engagement with the text.

What is annotated can be student driven, or you can provide directions for students to annotate something in particular. For example, students can mark instances of repetition and state the effect of this rhetorical device, write about a character's personality trait and mark text that supports it, or place sticky notes on artwork reproductions that show evidence of an artistic movement and identify the consistent features (e.g., brushstrokes, palette). Students can also write annotations that pose questions they have while reading or make connections to other texts. Be careful not to overwhelm students by instructing them to annotate according to too many different directives. Providing excessive reading tasks all at once might interfere with students' enjoyment and comprehension of the text and might backfire as they end up skimming the text for cursory—rather than in-depth—observations.

To prevent students from engaging in a highlighting frenzy—where they indiscriminately splash color across pages of the text or underline a sea of text—it's critical to model this strategy. Conduct a direct instruction lesson to encourage students to be intentional about what they choose to flag, and then challenge them to think about and write what the emphasized text means. This skill takes practice, so model the process with different types of text and for different purposes (see Figure 3.1 as a guide to select examples). Show students that they do not have to flag whole sentences or paragraphs but should instead mark only significant words or phrases that reveal important information. Remember also to identify places where students might pose questions or need further clarification.

Although I've introduced this strategy for use during an initial exposure to a text, it's certainly possible to employ this strategy throughout reading. As students reread for different purposes, have them tackle another aspect of the text and annotate different notes. Suggest to them that they use different colors or symbols to represent separate targets for reading. For example, they could mark figurative language in one color and evidence for a personality trait in another. Alternatively, they could indicate main ideas in one color and key details in a second color, or they can use a combination of other marks, such as brackets, circles, clouds, triangles, or underscores. As students reread for different purposes, their subsequent annotations will be more introspective because they are capitalizing on what they investigated during previous reading experiences.

Use Figure 3.1 as a resource to select the kinds of annotations students should make. Since this list is fairly comprehensive, remember to be judicious in what you ask students to identify. Scaffold accordingly and use what you know about the text, your students, and the learning goals to determine what students should annotate. Allow them some measure of freedom in what they should annotate, and remember to keep the list of options short. In general, since complex text requires rereading, invite them to return to the text for a different purpose instead of overwhelming them with too many choices at once. When students approach a new text, they should have a relatively small selection of choices and focus on a manageable chunk of the text; then build from that point.

Consider creating a two-column chart like the example shown in Figure 3.2. (I made this using a two-column table and then copied and pasted text I found online.) Notice that the directions for this form indicate that students should annotate to one or two of the listed prompts. It is not mandated that they cover them all, so make this clear at the outset of the exercise or a similar one that you assign. By contrast, Figure 3.3 shows a different set of directions that expressly targets one aspect of the text—figurative language.

Yet another popular alternative is to use symbols as a precursor to note taking. During an initial exposure to text, you might prefer this kind of annotation.

FIGURE 3.1

Annotation Options

What to Mark *(Be careful to mark just the part of the text that applies to your notes.)*	Notes in the Margins *Write down . . .*
Vocabulary words and terms (mark both the word and any context clues)	what you think the word means (later you can verify the definition with classmates or a resource)
Specific words	the impact of the word on the text
Text that indicates the writer's style	the type of style represented (e.g., formal, informal, technical)
Text that indicates a historical era	the time period, event (e.g., Civil War, WWII), individual, or specific reference to an aspect of culture (e.g., language, government, religion, art)
Text that indicates tone or mood	the tone the author conveys or the mood evoked in the reader (e.g., sarcasm, anger, joy, melancholy)
Text that reveals information about the speaker or narrator	what you know about the speaker or narrator (e.g., gender, bias, political persuasion, religion) and the intended audience
Text that indicates the main idea	the main idea of a particular paragraph or the whole passage
Transitional words and phrases or places in the text where they are missing	alternative transitions that the author could have used that might be stronger
Text that shows some kind of repetition	the intended effect this repetition has on readers
Text that reveals the author's purpose, position, or major premise	the author's purpose, position, premise, or main argument
Reasons given in an argument	• a summary for each reason, or • an opposite viewpoint
Examples of unsubstantiated evidence	what the author might have done differently to convince readers of a position
Examples of rhetorical devices	your interpretation or impression
Steps in a process	the order of each step and provide a brief restatement of each one
Literary devices	the type of literary device used (e.g., symbolism, allusion, flashback, dialect) and your interpretation of it
Figurative language	the type of figurative language used (e.g., simile, metaphor, personification, imagery) and your interpretation of it

What to Mark *(Be careful to mark just the part of the text that applies to your notes.)*	Notes in the Margins *Write down . . .*
Text where there's an opportunity to make an inference	inferences you can make that are based on key details that you marked
Text passage	• the passage in your own words, or • a summary
Text passage	an analogy
Text passage	• questions you have about the text that confuse you or that you wonder about, • your reaction to the passage, • a connection between this text and another text you have read, or • a connection between this part of the text and another part of this same text
Text passage	a concept that represents this passage (e.g., fusion, diversity, collaboration, adaptation)
Examples of characterization	the personality trait(s) associated with what is marked (e.g., courageous, brutal, selfish, persevering)
Text that reveals features of a particular genre	• clues that reveal an art movement (e.g., brushstroke or subject of a painting indicative of an artistic movement) • clues that reveal a writing genre (e.g., suspect, witness, alibi, clues in a mystery; deities, supernatural powers in myths) • clues that reveal a musical genre (e.g., baroque, classical, folk, jazz)

Figure 3.4 presents some examples of symbol associations that students can use. As with other forms of annotation, it's important not to deluge students by asking them to use a multitude of symbols. If students have to identify too many aspects of the text at the same time, they'll end up preoccupied by a mere scavenger hunt and not at all be engaged with the text or its meaning.

The examples in any of the annotation figures can serve as a springboard for future annotations when students reread for different purposes to increase comprehension. Additionally, students' annotations are great launching points for partner, small-group, or whole-class discussions and written responses. Students can share their interpretations and inferences, gain new perspectives, and glean greater insights into the text. Included here are several annotation extensions.

Consider a combination of these approaches as students read and reread. For example, students can begin by conducting a partner annotation and then, after they have grasped more of the text, engage in collective annotation.

- **Partner Annotations:** Students first conduct their own annotations, then work in pairs; they designate who is Partner A and B. Partner A shares a section of the text he or she highlighted, circled, or underlined without stating the notes associated with what was marked. Partner B then suggests what Partner A might have written in the "Notes" column. Partner A shares what he or she did in fact write, and the two discuss their impressions together. Both students should then make revisions, additions, or deletions on their own sheets based on this conversation. Have students switch roles and continue the process; partners should go back and forth until all of the annotated text on their papers is discussed.

- **Collective Annotations 1:** Arrange students in small groups of about four—all of whom have read and annotated the same text. They should pass their annotations clockwise so each student reads another group member's annotations before adding his or her impressions. Papers continue to be passed around the circle so all students have a chance to provide input on each. When each set of annotations is returned to its rightful owner, there should be the same number of comments as there are group members. Students review their own papers along

FIGURE 3.2

Annotation Example for "Eleven" by Sandra Cisneros

Directions: Read the text passage. In the "Notes" column, respond to one or two of the following prompts.

- Write down the main idea of the paragraph.
- Make any inferences.
- Record ideas or questions you have.
- Write any reactions you have.
- Interpret figurative language.

Make sure to underline or highlight just the parts of the text that are associated with your notes.

Text Passage	Notes
What they don't understand about birthdays and what they never tell you is that when you're eleven, you're also ten, and nine, and eight, and seven, and six, and five, and four, and three, and two, and one. And when you wake up on your eleventh birthday you expect to feel eleven, but you don't. You open your eyes and everything's just like yesterday, only it's today. And you don't feel eleven at all. You feel like you're still ten. And you are—underneath the year that makes you eleven.	

with comments from their peers. Group members can then discuss their collective impressions and share with the whole class. Even if groups have read different texts, there is an advantage to this whole-class sharing, especially if the texts are linked by topic or theme.

- **Collective Annotations 2:** This strategy is similar to the previous one in that students work in groups of four; they each annotate individually first and then collect comments from others. However, in this version, the whole class is focused on the same text, and each group rotates its sheet among all groups instead of just within its own cluster. Here is how it works. Group members discuss what they each annotated. A selected scribe creates a master copy of the annotations based on the collective input from the group. The group then passes this master copy to another group, which discusses and adds additional impressions. The point here is for each group to expound on the ideas of other groups in order to foster new insights and connections. Have groups continue to pass the annotations around until each group has discussed and made additions to each. Consider asking each group to use a different-colored pen or pencil to track remarks. When each group receives its original annotation back, discuss the collective input. You might also instruct students to write a reflection in their journals based on what they each gleaned and how their impression of the text changed as a result of this exercise.

FIGURE 3.3
Annotation Example for *Tuck Everlasting* by Natalie Babbitt

Directions: The author uses figurative language (imagery, simile, metaphor, personification) to help portray the setting throughout this passage. Underline examples of figurative language from the text in the left column. In the right column, explain how the author uses it to present a picture in the reader's mind. An example is provided to help you with your annotations.

TEXT PASSAGE Underline or highlight examples of descriptive language.	AUTHOR'S PURPOSE What picture is the author presenting?
<u>The sky was a ragged blaze of red and pink and orange,</u> and its double trembled on the surface of the pond like color spilled from a paintbox. The sun was dropping fast now, a soft red sliding egg yolk, and already to the east there was a darkening to purple. Winnie, newly brave with her thoughts of being rescued, climbed boldly into the rowboat. The hard heels of her buttoned boots made a hollow banging sound against its wet boards, loud in the warm and breathless quiet. Across the pond a bullfrog spoke a deep note of warning. Tuck climbed in, too, pushing off, and, settling the oars into their locks, dipped them into the silty bottom in one strong pull. The rowboat slipped from the bank then, silently, and glided out, tall water grasses whispering away from its sides, releasing it.	The author wants the reader to picture the sun setting and the sky filled with vibrant, vivid color.

FIGURE 3.4
Options for Symbol Annotations

Teachers: Be careful about overwhelming students with too many prompts. Therefore, use this figure as a resource to create an annotation sheet tailored to your text that includes a short list of symbols and associated prompts.

Symbol	What It Can Mean
*	• Something important you want to remember • Words and phrases you think are most important • The main idea or premise of the text
+	• Ideas you agree with or that you like • New information or ideas • Strong evidence or support
−	• Ideas you disagree with or that are against your way of thinking • No evidence or support provided
?	• Parts that confuse you and need clarification (or an explanation) • Neutral on this idea • You don't know what to think yet • You are unsure if something is valid, substantiated, or true
!	• Evokes some kind of strong feeling (e.g., anger, fear, happiness, surprise)

· · · · · ·

 # Turn-and-Talk

Turn-and-Talk is a simple strategy that has a real benefit in the classroom as students talk with a partner (or a trio or small group) about what they read or in response to a prompt. You might have students turn and talk to one another after a think aloud or modeling exercise. They can also turn and talk after they have read a particular passage or watched a video segment. Discussing their ideas prior to writing or moving on to a new passage gives students a chance to voice their thinking so they can quickly refine, extend, or clarify it.

You would be wise to set parameters for this strategy so that the time is limited and the task is clear. To announce Turn-and-Talk time arbitrarily without giving clear directions or a focus will not be productive. Rather, it would be more effective if you provide students with a prompt to facilitate their conversations. For example, consider asking students to turn and talk in response to a text-dependent question or annotations they already made about a section of text.

· · · · · ·

Think-Pair-Share

As students engage with complex text, it is usually important to give them ample time to process the information individually before they collaborate with others. Think-Pair-Share is a strategy that accomplishes this (Lyman, 1981); it's related to Turn-and-Talk but has an extra step. It is a timed, focused exercise that allows you to maximize students' time on task while engaging with text. By thinking and then collaborating about content, students are afforded opportunities to examine complex text more closely.

Think: Pose a question and allow time for students to read and determine their responses individually. Consider students' exposure to the text as you arrive at an appropriate prompt (i.e., Is it the first or second time reading the passage? Is it a reread based on a particular purpose?). There are innumerable possibilities. Students could make inferences or predictions, respond to a text-dependent question, identify multiple-meaning words, locate and interpret figurative language, or find a counterclaim and defend it. By allowing this valuable commodity of time, students have the freedom to formulate their thoughts, avoid speaking in haste, consider options they might not have had the chance to make otherwise, and think independently without being swayed by others' input. Allow anywhere from ten seconds to five minutes for this step, depending on the task and whether students are expected to take notes or just ponder some options.

Pair: After independently considering what they think, students turn to a partner to share. Plan in advance for how students will work together so there is a seamless transition between these steps. You can assign pairs, create a seating arrangement in which students turn to their neighbor, or allow students to choose a nearby classmate. Give students frequent opportunities to work with different partners; as they discuss their ideas with others, they will clarify their thinking and resolve any misunderstandings or confusion they might have. Additionally, the intimacy of working with a partner helps reluctant students build self-confidence before they share with the whole class. (Often, those students who are reticent to share in a whole-class setting are less intimidated by working with only one partner.) This part takes five to ten minutes. If needed, consider limiting the time for each partner to share so there is equal opportunity for discussion.

Share: After partner conversations, students share with others in some fashion. (1) Have partners turn to another pair and discuss the highlights of their discussion before writing their individual responses in a student journal. The strategy then becomes Think-Pair-Share-Write. (2) Ask students to report out to the whole class the major insights that they and their partners made. You can invite volunteers to share or go around the room and ask each pair to give input. When reporting out, remind students to listen to others' contributions and avoid duplications.

Encourage them to link their comments to those of previous speakers. You might offer reminders or train them on the kinds of transitional phrases to use, such as, "We had a similar response; however, we also considered _____." "We also talked about _____, but then we realized that _____."

Conduct a Think-Pair-Share session after initially reading a new complex text or when rereading it for a specific purpose. The sequence goes like this:

1. Explain to students how the text will be divided for a series of think-pair-share conversations. Display an abbreviated form of the process for students to follow.
2. Present the relevant section of text.
3. Pose a prompt or text-dependent question, or present a problem. For example, "You have just finished reading (or listening) to the beginning of an argumentative essay titled _____. On your own, think about a response to this question: What is the author's position that he or she wants readers to adopt?"
4. Pause for at least ten seconds to allow time for students to formulate individual responses. If the question or prompt is particularly challenging and thought provoking, give each student a chance to jot down some notes or even complete a graphic organizer. The strategy then becomes Think-Write-Pair-Share (see Chapter 6 for more on this strategy).
5. Announce when it is time for students to confer with others. Reiterate the focus so they are clear about the basis for their conversations. Encourage students to return to the text during their discussions to find evidence for their assertions and, when needed, clear up inaccuracies.
6. Solicit volunteer partners to share highlights of their discussion with the whole class.
7. Repeat the sequence for the next section of text.

This strategy is appropriate for a wide variety of classroom experiences across content areas. Examples include solving math problems, discussing opposing sides of an issue, defining terms, studying a sewing pattern, identifying methods of characterization, making informed predictions, and proposing solutions to problems. When conferring with others and listening to input from the whole class, students might arrive at new realizations, dispel misconceptions, or consider other viewpoints—all in the service of the text.

· · · · · ·

Reciprocal Teaching

Reciprocal teaching is an instructional strategy designed to help students engage in orchestrated dialogue so they can grapple with complex text (Palincsar & Brown, 1984). It relies on students constructing meaning through a scaffolded series of steps that requires them to dialogue with one another by asking and answering questions, clarifying and summarizing a portion of the text, and making predictions. Hattie (2009) cites an effect size for reciprocal teaching of 0.74, which is quite high and indicates a strong correlation to student achievement. To put this figure in perspective, an effect size of 0.40 is considered a benchmark "where the effects of innovation enhance achievement in such a way that we can notice real-world differences" (Hattie, 2009, p. 17). As with most of these activities, the targeted text can be print or nonprint. For example, students can read written material; listen to a speech, guest speaker, or audio recording; watch a video clip or demonstration of a process; or study a model or artwork.

There are different ways to lead a reciprocal teaching exercise. I'll discuss two scenarios here. Figure 3.5 outlines the first sequence students can follow and use during their dialogues in which they all work in partnerships or small groups. For large groups or the entire class, refer to Figure 3.6. Both situations require a great deal of interaction among students and opportunities to take active speaking roles as they work toward meaning making. Determine which version is appropriate, based on the text students will examine, the number of encounters they have had with the text (i.e., initial or subsequent read), and the differentiated needs of your students. The particular grouping configurations can be differentiated by readiness or interest; use your professional expertise and knowledge to designate appropriate groupings and texts.

Sometimes, it makes sense to begin with a whole-class situation (the scenario featured in Figure 3.6) and then ask students to work in pairs or small groups once they are more familiar with the text. A combination of situations can also apply. For example, it might be that three pairs of students are able to work on their own while you lead the rest of the class in a choreographed sequence. Later in the year, possibly more pairs or small groups can be accountable to lead their own sessions. Again, making the decision about groupings and implementation of the more suitable reciprocal teaching version are contingent upon your students and the texts.

Although these prescribed sequences seem rather scripted, students should eventually be able to lead a reciprocal teaching scenario without the aid of the articulated steps. However, provide the support outlined in Figures 3.5 or 3.6 until they are ready to engage in a meaningful way without this structure.

FIGURE 3.5

Reciprocal Teaching Student Sheet for Pairs or Small Groups

Reciprocal Teaching involves these four reading comprehension strategies: questioning, summarizing, clarifying, and predicting. The ultimate goal is for you to become so familiar with these strategies that you use them on your own when reading difficult text to help you understand it better.

With your partner or small group, select someone who will be the Leader. Later, you will exchange or rotate roles so everyone has a chance to be the Leader, based on a different passage of the text. Follow the discussion pattern outlined below. In your conversations, remember to use textual evidence to support your responses.

Leader (Questioning)	• Read one paragraph or section aloud to your partner or small group. (Alternatively, your teacher might ask that everyone reads the text silently.) • Use the text to formulate one literal and one inferential question about the selection. Ask your partner these questions.
Participant(s)	Answer the two questions using textual evidence.
Leader (Clarifying)	Identify one or two places in the text that might need clarification or further explanation. Indicate why you chose these spots (e.g., unknown vocabulary, complicated concepts, challenging figurative language).
Leader and Participant(s)	Discuss the reading selection together, focusing on areas that need clarification.
Leader (Summarizing)	Summarize the reading material for the participant(s).
Participant(s)	Do any of the following: • Verify that the summary is complete. • Add to the summary. • Correct any part that is not quite right.
Leader and Participant(s) (Predicting)	Predict what will happen next, using text evidence to support your predictions.
Read a new section of text. Exchange roles and repeat so another student assumes the role of Leader.	

To introduce reciprocal teaching, prepare students by modeling the sequence and expectations with a sample text passage. Additionally, if they are unfamiliar with how to question, summarize, clarify, and predict, then lead a formal lesson in which you present the characteristics and examples of each strategy. Hattie (2009) states that "the effects were highest when there was explicit teaching of cognitive strategies before beginning reciprocal teaching dialogue, showing the importance of modeling and practice as well as giving instruction in the use of the strategies close to the time students used them. The explicit teaching of cognitive strategies and deliberative practice with content when using these strategies makes a major difference" (p. 204).

FIGURE 3.6
Reciprocal Teaching Resource Sheet

Students can keep a journal or notebook for Reciprocal Teaching. Use this format, which explains the teacher's and students' roles in response to complex texts that students read, hear, or watch (e.g., lectures, guest speakers, presentations, performances, demonstrations, videos). Consider adapting this sequence to a nontraditional text, for example a piece of artwork, sculpture, model, diagram, or photograph. Have students create a heading with a title and date for each entry.

Teacher	• Present a paragraph or section of content via read aloud, silent read, lecture, guest speaker, presentation, or video. • Ask students to create two questions about the content. Be specific as to the types of questions, such as one literal and one inferential. • Invite students to share their questions. Record and display selected ones for the whole class to see. Avoid duplication of questions. • Give students time to accomplish the following tasks.
Individual Students	• Select and record questions in a notebook or journal. • Write answers to those questions you can answer using textual evidence.
Student Partners	• Turn-and-Talk: Turn to a neighbor and review answers to your questions. Verify that the textual evidence is correct; add additional evidence, as needed. • If you and your partner disagree about an answer, underline or highlight it. Be ready to pose the question(s) to the class.
Whole Class	• Discuss confusing questions and arrive at collective answers. • Ask for clarification. • Predict what will happen next in the reading, if applicable.
Teacher	• Summarize reading material for the class. Ask students to write a brief summary.

For questioning, teach students how to pose different kinds of queries so they don't rely on literal questions only. Explain and show examples of literal versus inferential questioning. In addition, identify parts of the text that provide good opportunities to ask questions. An effective summary involves just the main idea and key details. Students tend to be too verbose, so model how to write a brief summary that consists of only the most salient information. Clarification is important, especially for students who have difficulty with comprehension. Identify points in the text that might present a problem for students, and model situations in which readers likely get confused and need clarification (e.g., problematic vocabulary, difficult concepts). Finally, don't fall into the trap of thinking that only narrative text is ripe for making predictions. Indeed, students can predict a subsequent event in history or the way a historical figure might react. Later, they can confirm whether their predictions were correct. Predictions can also be made based on expository text as students anticipate what topic, structure, or text feature (e.g., subheading, diagram) an author will introduce or cover next. For any response that you model, remember to include evidence from the text.

Sometimes teachers want more tangible evidence of on-task behavior and gleaning from the text beyond observations of students' discussions. If this is the case, during or after their partner, small-group, or whole-class exchanges based on the reciprocal teaching sequence, ask students who work together to complete and submit the graphic organizer shown in Figure 3.7.

FIGURE 3.7
Reciprocal Teaching Graphic Organizer

Directions: Complete this graphic organizer during or after you participate in a reciprocal teaching exercise.

Text title: _____ Page # (if needed): _____

Create or Copy Questions	Respond to Questions

Make Predictions

Summarize

As a more comprehensive means of individual formative assessment, students can demonstrate understanding in any of the following ways:

- **Dialectical (or double-entry) journals:** Ask students to make a T-chart. They choose one particular quote from the text, enter it on the left side of the chart, and use it as the basis for a response. On the right side, they respond to their selected quote in any number of ways, such as rewriting it in their own words, making an inference, connecting it to another text, explaining its significance, or creating an analogy. Chapter 6 provides a thorough description of and recommendations for the types of quotes students can use as the basis for their responses.
- **Exit cards:** During the last few minutes of class, have students write brief responses to a salient question(s) or prompt(s) related to relevant content. Chapter 2 provides a more detailed explanation of this strategy along with suggestions for prompts.

You might want to conduct a version of reciprocal teaching that involves a less formal means of participation—through oral prompt responses in pairs or small groups (see Figure 3.8). Encourage students to lead the discussion by using one prompt from each section at a time that serves to explore a passage of the text at the center of instruction. After students respond to the oral prompts, consider issuing a writing exercise to check for understanding.

Reciprocal teaching is just one strategy you can use to support students as they tackle a complex text. Use a combination of the different approaches presented in this section based on your students and their specific needs. Also consider coupling this strategy with others (e.g., annotation, graphic organizers) from this and other chapters in this book.

· · · · · ·

Text Structure as a Vehicle to Bolster Comprehension

To position students so they can effectively tackle complex text, it is beneficial to conduct explicit instruction around text features. Therefore, this section features a thorough explanation of text structure and a variety of lesson ideas to teach skills related to this topic. Identifying the organizational structure an author uses not only helps facilitate comprehension but also aids in retention of information and provides models for students' own writing. As such, it's a good idea to conduct lessons around text structure early so students are aware of the critical connection between structure and comprehension. Like reading strategies, text structure lessons should be conducted in conjunction with a text so there are opportunities for direct applicability.

FIGURE 3.8
Oral Prompts

PREDICT	SUMMARIZE
1. Based on the cover or title, I predict this book will be about _____ . 2. Based on this visual (drawing, graph, chart, picture), I predict that _____ . 3. After reading the part about _____ , I think _____ will happen. 4. This sentence or word gives me a clue that _____ will happen. 5. I can predict _____ will happen because _____ .	1. This paragraph or section is about _____ . 2. This story is about _____ . 3. The author is making this statement: _____ . 4. The author wants readers to understand that _____ . 5. Provide a brief summary of the passage.

CLARIFY

Choose one or more ways to clarify what is challenging about a selected passage and discuss new insights.

1. Reread a sentence or section.
2. Break down a long sentence into parts, paying attention to the punctuation.
3. Define unfamiliar words by looking at root words, prefixes, and suffixes.
4. Use text features such as bold type, captions, glossary, or visuals.
5. Use a reference.
6. Ask a classmate or the teacher.

QUESTION

Pair question words with helping verbs to frame questions. Then answer them using evidence from the text.

Question Word	Helping Verb
Who What Where When Why How	do/did/does can (cannot) should (should not) will (will not) might (might not) has/have/had

VISUALIZE

1. When I read/hear this passage _____ , I can visualize _____ .
2. Seeing _____ in my mind helps me understand _____ .
3. I learn more about _____ because I can visualize _____ .
4. I can draw a picture of _____ after reading _____ .
5. This part about _____ looks a lot like _____ .

The power of teaching students the structure strategy is that it enables them to a) follow the logical structure of text to understand how an author organized and emphasized ideas; b) use processes parallel to these structures to increase their own learning and thinking (e.g., comparing, finding causal relationships, looking for solutions to block causes of problems); and c) use these text structures to organize their own writing, such as written summaries, recalls, and essays. (Meyer & Ray, 2011, p. 128)

Text structure refers to the way in which content is organized. Authors choose a particular structure based on how they feel they can best communicate their ideas. At a young age, students are exposed to narrative fiction—fairy tales, contemporary realistic fiction, fantasy, and so forth. These genres include classic elements of literature (e.g., setting, characters, etc.) and are organized by a plot structure that includes a central conflict, rising action toward a climax, and ultimately a resolution. More sophisticated forms of fiction can incorporate subplots and literary devices such as foreshadowing or flashbacks that might make following the overarching plot more challenging and intriguing. Nevertheless, a plot forms the major structure of a narrative. When we are aware of this kind of text structure for fiction, we expect a particular pattern. We anticipate that there will be some tension as suspense builds and that the author will resolve the central conflict. It is this knowledge of text structure, coupled with an understanding of the genre, that helps readers make sense of the overall work.

Works of fiction are usually fairly straightforward since the story structure is familiar. This is not always the case with informational text, which can include material such as articles, essays, technical manuals, how-to guides, government documents, textbooks, and so forth. This kind of text often includes difficult concepts and ideas that might be unfamiliar to readers. In fact, research shows that although expository text is much more difficult for students to read than narrative text, elementary and middle school students are only getting between 7 to 15 percent exposure to this kind of instructional reading (CCSSI, 2010a, p. 3). One way to ensure that students are more comfortable with this material and can grasp an author's meaning is to introduce various text structures and associated words that signal certain organizational patterns.

Figure 3.9 outlines these most common structures, although there are others (e.g., question and answer, categorical):

- compare-contrast
- problem-solution
- cause-effect
- sequence
- description

Each structure serves a different purpose, so authors intentionally choose a particular one based on why they are writing, how they can best organize a coherent message, and the audience they intend to address. Aligned to each structure are transitional words and phrases that help readers navigate the text, follow an author's train of thought, and facilitate comprehension. For example, when experiencing a text in which an author is comparing and contrasting two topics, readers can more easily distinguish between them with words such as *alternatively, by contrast, conversely, the same as,* and *similarly.* When students learn, practice, and hone the skill of recognizing these structures and signal words, they will eventually internalize them and use them

FIGURE 3.9
Text Structures and Signal Words

	Expository Text Structures*	Underlying Structural Patterns**	Signal Words
Compare and Contrast	Relates ideas according to similarities and differences; complexity can be increased by the number and detail of issues compared. The main ideas are organized to compare, contrast, or provide an alternative view (e.g., political speech).	comparing two ideas, events, or phenomena by showing how they are alike and different	*instead, but, however, alternatively, whereas, on the other hand, on the contrary, in contrast, in opposition, not everyone, all but, conversely, nevertheless, however, while, compare, in comparison, alike, like, unlike, likewise, act like, look like, just like, have in common, similarities, similarly, share, resemble, more than, longer than, less than, despite, although, difference, differentiate, different, either/or, in the same way, the same as, just as, yet, rather than*
Problem and Solution	Relates responding ideas; complexity can be increased by the identification of causes of the problems and ways to reduce them. The main ideas are organized in two parts: the problem (or question) part and the solution (or answer) part, which responds to the problem part (e.g., popular science articles, medical information).	identifying problems and hypothesizing solutions	**Problem**: *problem, trouble, difficulty, hazard, need to prevent, threat, danger, puzzle, can hurt, not good, bad, dilemma is* **Solution**: *to satisfy the problem, ways to reduce the problem, so solve these problems, protection from the problem, solution, in response, recommend, suggest, reply*
Cause and Effect	Relates ideas causally; complexity can be increased by embedded cause-and-effect paths and causal chains and can be reduced by similarity to familiar narratives. The main ideas are organized into cause and effect parts (e.g., directions, explanations, economic or science texts).	proposing the reasons or explanations for various phenomena	*cause, because of this, led to, bring about, originate, produce, make possible, owing to, by means of, accomplish by, since, due to, as a result (of), because, in order to, reasons, why, if/then, on account of, in explanation, effect, affects, so, consequently, as a consequence of, thus, therefore, so that, so, accordingly, for the purpose of, for, hence, this led to*

	Expository Text Structures*	Underlying Structural Patterns**	Signal Words
Sequence	Relates ideas via time. The main ideas are the steps or history presented (e.g., recipe steps, history books, biographies).	• Chronological: describing a series of events in the order they happened in time (as in a historical account) • Temporal: presenting a sequence of actions for doing something (a process that always happens in the same way)	*later, after, afterward, after a short while, then, subsequently, as time passed, following, continuing on, to end, finally, year(s) ago, at the start of, first, second, third, 1, 2, 3 . . ., next, primarily, early, before, previously, preceding, to begin with, more recently, again, finally, the former, the latter, not long, soon, now, immediately, today, meanwhile, steps, stages, time line, history, sequence, development, during, while, concurrently, simultaneously,* (actual dates)
Description	Relates ideas by elaboration of attributes, specifics, or setting information. The main idea is that aspects of a topic are presented (e.g., newspaper article).	using language to provide details and form images so readers can determine how something looks, moves, tastes, smells, or feels	*attributes of, characteristics are, for example, for instance, in describing, marks of, namely, properties of, qualities are, specifically, such as, that is, is like, including, to illustrate, in fact,* (descriptive words)

Sources: *From "Structure Strategy Interventions: Increasing Reading Comprehension of Expository Text," by B.J.F. Meyer and M.N. Ray, 2011, *International Electronic Journal of Elementary Education, 4*(1), 127–152. Copyright © IEJEE.
**From *Genre Study: Teaching with Fiction and Nonfiction Books,* by I.C. Fountas and G.S. Pinnell, 2012, Portsmouth, NH: Heinemann.

as models for their own writing. As adults, many of us do this instinctively as we figure out how a text works and then anticipate what might come next in terms of organization and content.

Following is a list of ideas to use as the basis for instruction when teaching students to identify and use text structures. You can differentiate by arranging students in various grouping configurations (e.g., individuals, pairs, small groups) and assigning different text passages based on readability levels. Consider using a combination of activities, as appropriate.

- **Comparing and contrasting:** To identify the type of organization an author uses, ask students to read several short passages that employ the same text structure. Pose the following questions: What similar (or recurring) pattern do you notice in how these passages are written? What do you think this pattern is called? How does it help you understand and remember the text better?

  Your goal is to have students discover on their own the similar structural characteristics specific to a text pattern and then name it rather than you merely stating, "I'm distributing text passages that all have the compare-contrast structure. Find evidence of the similarities." Later, identify longer works that follow the same structure to demonstrate that text structure is merely an organizational feature regardless of the length of the text.

  Once students are familiar with different text structures, create cards with short passages that are based on the same topic but utilize different structures. Have students sort them by text structure, and then ask them to compare and contrast the different structures they can identify: Which form of organization best conveys the information? Alternatively, have students compare different topics that utilize the same text structure to illustrate how various authors present content. This is helpful for teaching literacy across the content areas.

  Another approach could be to conduct a text scavenger hunt. Prepare a variety of text formats, such as magazines, newspapers, and books. Have students choose a text and determine its structure. They can use sticky notes to label the structural elements and indicate signal words. Then ask students to compare, contrast, and discuss their findings with others.

- **Predicting:** Have students read up to a certain point in an expository text passage. Then ask them to make predictions based on the text structure, content, and text features. Use the following questions: What will the author discuss next? What text structure and features will the author use? What evidence from the text informs you of what you might expect next? After a group discussion, read the rest of the text and see if students can confirm their predictions.

- **Identifying signal words:** Distribute an expository text and ask students to identify signal words. Pose these questions: How do signal words indicate text structure? How do particular words emphasize a point or change a direction? How do signal words lead to comprehension? How do these words signal a relationship between and among ideas?

Alternatively, find a text, delete all of the signal words and phrases, and distribute it to pairs of students. Ask them to read the text and identify its structure. They will likely have difficulty, so lead a discussion asking them to articulate why they cannot determine the structure. Then provide a variety of signal words (see Figure 3.9) and instruct pairs to choose and insert the ones they think are appropriate in certain places. Have partners team up with another duo and read their revised versions, compare them, arrive at a consensus about the clearest one, and together identify its text structure. Come together as a class to discuss the purpose and value of signal words and phrases.

- **Using graphic organizers:** Organizers can represent a visual display of a particular text structure. With that in mind, provide a series of graphic organizers that depict several different kinds of structures. As students read complex text (or listen to you read it aloud), have them choose an appropriate graphic organizer that mirrors the structure of the text. They can complete it using the content of the text to demonstrate understanding. Point out how knowing the structure and selecting the right graphic organizer that is aligned to this structure facilitates notetaking and helps to enhance comprehension. Figure 3.10 includes a list of online resources for downloadable and printable graphic organizers. Choose those that are suitable for this activity; others can be used for prewriting and various comprehension tasks.

For another way to use organizers, identify a specific structure—such as compare and contrast, cause and effect, or problem and solution—and ask students to create a blank graphic organizer that could be used for each type. Have them compare their organizers and explain their rationale for the ones they created. Provide examples to show that there can be several different graphic organizers that are versions for the same text structure.

FIGURE 3.10
Online Resources for Graphic Organizers

- **edHelper.com** (www.edhelper.com/teachers/graphic_organizers.htm)
- **Education Oasis** (http://www.educationoasis.com/curriculum/graphic_organizers.htm)
- **Freeology** (http://freeology.com/graphicorgs)
- **Houghton Mifflin Harcourt Education Place** (www.eduplace.com/graphicorganizer)
- **Teacher Files** (http://www.teacherfiles.com/resources_organizers.htm)
- **TeacherVision** (www.teachervision.com/graphic-organizers/printable/6293.html)

Closing

Before you begin to design lessons around complex text, it's important to scrutinize the reading material carefully and plan for teaching it. Specifically, it is critical to divide the text into manageable chunks, tease out vocabulary that will be the focal point of instruction versus words that simply need to be defined, identify the core ideas of the text, and plan for text-dependent questions. In short, there are ways to expose students to text effectively that need to be understood. This due diligence is essential for smooth lesson design.

When introducing a new complex text, there are suggested guidelines to consider with regard to prereading so you do not reveal too much about the text before students have a chance to read it. The overarching premise here is to let the text speak for itself. Therefore, minimal introduction is warranted. Allow students to dive into the text as early as possible to begin close reading experiences. Let them discover on their own what the author intended. However, if a text requires prereading, be careful in how much information to frontload.

When students first encounter a text, there are specific strategies that you should employ for this initial exposure. Many of these concrete and practical strategies can also be adapted and used when students critique and analyze a text at a deeper level during subsequent reads. Within your instruction, it's important to orient students to various text structures; awareness of a text's organization directly contributes to comprehension.

04
Vocabulary

As mentioned in the previous chapter, a prerequisite for teaching complex text is determining which words to target during your lesson. There is longstanding research to support the strong connection between vocabulary and reading comprehension (National Reading Panel, 2000). This should not be surprising, considering the more words one knows, the more accessible the text. Since students encounter challenging texts across content areas, direct and explicit instruction in vocabulary is paramount so they can grasp the content. "The research on the effectiveness of direct vocabulary instruction is strong. Direct instruction about a targeted set of vocabulary terms helps students learn new words and gain the vocabulary knowledge they need for success in school" (Marzano & Simms, 2013, p. 11).

Although direct instruction leads to success, it is not the only way that students acquire new words. In fact, there simply is not enough time to use this strategy to teach all of the words students will confront and need to know. Therefore, extensive reading provides additional opportunities for students to learn new words on their own since the amount of reading students do correlates to a positive boost in vocabulary knowledge (Texas Reading Initiative, 2002). This includes all types of text that students read—and listen to—for a variety of purposes, such as magazines and books students read independently for enjoyment, books that teachers read aloud, complex text that is part of an instructional program, and so forth. This combination of reading material contributes to students' exposure and mastery of new words because if a text is too difficult for students to read, they will not be able to comprehend it or learn new words. Likewise, if it is too easy or below their grade level, there are not enough new words for them to learn. A variety of texts and strategies, then, is key to teaching vocabulary acquisition: direct instruction, extensive and diverse reading, and discussions about words and their parts.

This chapter includes a concentration on vocabulary, including pertinent standards; an overview of vocabulary categories; research highlights and other salient information; vocabulary activities, strategies, and assessments; lessons for how to use context clues to define unknown words; and lessons for teaching words when context clues are weak or nonexistent.

Standards That Address Vocabulary

The CCSS stresses the importance of regular practice with complex text and academic vocabulary. Students need consistent support to build their vocabulary throughout the school year and between grades so they can have greater access to complex text. The CCSS uses a hybrid approach in which some similar standards appear in more than one strand. Vocabulary is such an example since word acquisition is included in both the Reading and Language standards, as shown in the following College and Career Readiness Anchor Standards. Vocabulary should not be handled in isolation—its utility extends across reading, writing, speaking, and listening.

- Reading Anchor Standard #4: Interpret words and phrases as they are used in a text, including determining technical, connotative, and figurative meanings, and analyze how specific word choices shape meaning or tone. (CCSS.ELA-LITERACY.CCRA.R4)
- Language Anchor Standard #4: Determine or clarify the meaning of unknown and multiple-meaning words and phrases by using context clues, analyzing meaningful word parts, and consulting general and specialized reference materials as appropriate. (CCSS.ELA-LITERACY.CCRA.L4)
- Language Anchor Standard #6: Acquire and use accurately a range of general academic and domain-specific words and phrases sufficient for reading, writing, speaking, and listening at the college and career readiness level; demonstrate independence in gathering vocabulary knowledge when encountering an unknown term important to comprehension or expression. (CCSS.ELA-LITERACY.CCRA.L6)

Other states and provinces include vocabulary in their standards documents as well. In Virginia's Standards of Learning, expectations around word meaning are replete throughout grades K–12 (Virginia Department of Education, 2010). For example, a reading standard for 6th grade states, "The student will read and learn the meanings of unfamiliar words and phrases within authentic texts." Grades 9–12 include this standard: "The student will apply knowledge of word origins, derivations, and figurative language to extend vocabulary development in authentic texts." Some specific skills aligned to this standard include "a) Use structural analysis of roots, affixes, synonyms, antonyms, and cognates to understand complex words; b) Use context, structure, and connotations to determine meanings of words and phrases; and c) Discriminate between connotative and denotative meanings and interpret the connotation" (Grade

9, Standard 9.3). Likewise, the Texas Essential Knowledge and Skills include this partial list of knowledge and skills expectations under Reading/Vocabulary Development for 5th grade: "Students understand new vocabulary and use it when reading and writing. Students are expected to (a) determine the meaning of grade-level English words derived from Latin, Greek, or other linguistic roots and affixes; (b) use context to determine or clarify the meaning of unfamiliar or multiple meaning words" (Texas Education Agency, 2011).

Word Categories/Tiers

Beck and her colleagues devised a three-tier system to classify words based on their usage and roles in language. The aim was to aid educators in determining which words to focus on as the basis for instruction (Beck, McKeown, & Omanson, 1987).

Tier 1 words are basic, high-frequency words used in everyday speech and conversation that most native speakers acquire when they are young. Types of words in this category are sight words and commonly used nouns, verbs, and adjectives, such as *boy, table, chair, walk, take, pretty,* and *blue.* Because they are widely and frequently used, explicit instruction is usually unnecessary for native English speakers.

Closely related to text complexity and inextricably linked to reading comprehension is a focus on Tier 2 words, also called academic vocabulary. Words classified as Tier 2 appear in a variety of content areas and in all kinds of text—informational, technical, and literary. They have multiple meanings based on how they are used within a discipline (e.g., *parallel, differentiate, angle, itemize,* and *relative*); therefore, they can be confusing to students (see Figure 4.1). They also include words that express different connotations, such as *meander* and *stroll.* Sometimes teachers ignore these words because they are paying more attention to Tier 3 words, which are specific to a content area and require in-depth instruction. However, these Tier 2 words are vital to reading comprehension—particularly in complex text—and should be a major focus during your instruction since they are often overlooked, frequently found in written text, and indicative of literate language users. In addition, context clues are sometimes nonexistent for academic vocabulary, so students cannot determine accurate meanings while reading. Knowledge of Tier 2 words also supports students in successfully making inferences and analyzing text so they fully comprehend what they read in general. In short, determine and teach appropriate Tier 2 words that are essential for students to learn so they have greater access to complex text.

Finally, Tier 3 consists of words and terms related to a particular discipline and are often referred to as domain-specific words. Examples include *mitosis, digestive system, partisanship, global economy, gymnosperm, syllogism, allusion,* and *figurative language.* The CCSS does not focus on Tier 3 words because a content-area text is usually replete with text features that help to teach them (e.g., boldface or highlighted words, labeled diagrams, glossary terms), and because teachers address these content-rich words, which are integral to instruction during a particular unit of study. "Because Tier Three words are obviously unfamiliar to most students, contain the ideas necessary to a new topic, and are recognized as both important and specific to the subject area in which they are instructing students, teachers often define Tier Three words prior to students encountering them in a text and then reinforce their acquisition throughout a lesson" (CCSS, 2010b, p. 33). In fact, instruction around Tier 2 words will aid in the understanding of Tier 3 words since academic vocabulary is regularly used to define and explain the domain-specific words.

FIGURE 4.1
Examples of Tier 2 Words

Ignite	System
• Pockets of methane gas **ignited**, resulting in a fiery blast that caused people to run for their lives. • The passions of Patriots and Loyalists **ignited**, which pitted one group against the other and ultimately led to war. • When a driver puts his or her key in the **ignition**, it starts the car. • Their love was **reignited** when they spotted each other again at their 10-year high school reunion.	• The digestive **system** makes it possible for the body to break down and absorb food. • The mother pointedly told her disruptive child, "Have you finished your tantrum? Now that it's out of your **system**, please apologize to everyone." • The solar **system**–which was formed 4.6 billion years ago– is composed of the sun, eight planets and their moons, and other nonstellar objects. • The teacher **systematically** taught the steps in the writing process to help students produce their best work. • There was no evidence that racism was **systemic** among the company's board, so the one culprit was voted out of his position.

Words Worth Teaching

As I mentioned before, Tier 3 words are emphasized within a unit of study since conceptual understanding centers on students knowing those words to grasp content. Tier 3 words are often defined or explained using general academic words, so attention to Tier 2 vocabulary is critical to help boost reading comprehension. Choose words that are worth learning across the content areas, and plan your instruction around acquiring these words. Select from the complex text at the center of instruction and that support comprehension of it. However, sometimes a word is not integral to comprehending a particular passage, but learning the word would enrich understanding of it (e.g., it helps to make inferences or determine tone). By contrast, some unfamiliar words do not inhibit comprehension or play a significant role in the text. These words can be defined and discussed quickly in order to spend more time on words that are more valuable to teach.

To determine if a word is a candidate for direct instruction, consider the following guidelines (adapted from Beck, McKeown, & Kucan, 2002, 2013). If you answer *yes* to most of these questions, put the word on your list.

1. **It is useful and appears across texts.** Is the word Tier 2? Is it useful enough to warrant attention and teach students? Will it appear across many texts in other domains that students will encounter? Is it indicative of words used by mature language users?
2. **It increases sophisticated word choices.** Are there words similar to the target one that are familiar to students? If so, learning this new word is beneficial since it would extend their inventory of vocabulary to include more expressive and specific words. This does not mean merely adding synonyms to words already in their lexicon. It is about providing students with new words that are more precise or that are complex versions of the familiar words they already use. For example, if students know *salesperson,* then learning the word *merchant* widens their choice of conceptually related words.
3. **It aids in comprehension.** Does knowing the word enhance comprehension? Does the word serve an important function within the context of the text? Does the word contribute to meaning making? Without it, are important concepts lost or confusing?
4. **It connects to other learning.** Does the word relate to other concepts that students are studying, perhaps in this subject or in another content area? Does the word have the potential for students to build representations of it and connect to other words and concepts?

Vocabulary Exposure

Repeated exposure to a word in a variety of ways and contexts helps to cement meaning. When students first encounter a word (even with its definition or usage), they will not automatically be able to use it with fluency and accuracy. Instead, it is a gradual and incremental process from initially learning that word to full ownership. Therefore, it's important to provide students with multiple opportunities to hear, see, and use a word in multiple contexts. During direct instruction, plan for varied and consistent exposure by asking students to use new words in their writing, incorporating the words into your casual conversations and formal instruction, pointing out the words in various texts, and encouraging students to use the words in their discussions with peers and presentations. In addition, you might want to suggest that students use the words outside of school so they can internalize the words further. A research study showed that when students have 12 encounters with a word (versus only 4), they show increased comprehension of texts where the word appears (McKeown, Beck, Omanson, & Pople, 1985).

So when is it best to introduce words to students—before, during, or after reading? There are valid reasons why teachers might teach new words at various points surrounding a text. Beck, McKeown, and Kucan (2013) provide some direction and assert that the optimal time to teach a word is when it appears in the text. This way, it is taught within a specific context for an express purpose. When teaching it in the moment, it furthers comprehension of the content.

However, sometimes it makes sense to frontload students and preteach words that are critical to comprehension but are presented without context clues. When doing so, use direct instruction and be cautious about how many words to teach. If there are too many, it is unlikely that students will retrieve their definitions when they read the words within the passages in which they appear. It's important not to overwhelm students with too many words before reading. By the same token, be careful if there are numerous words you plan to teach during reading that could interfere with comprehension. In all, Beck and her colleagues (2013) suggest teaching six to ten words over the span of five to nine days. The point here is to be judicious in your word selection and timing.

The caveat to preteaching words is when there are enough context clues for students to figure out the meaning on their own. If this is the case, wait until the word appears and teach how to use context clues to define unfamiliar words while reading. When students are proficient with this skill and can do it well, give them the reins to define words with ample context clues on their own.

There is still one more scenario: teaching words after they have read the text. Beck and her colleagues (2013) address this strategy as well: "Words that you want to provide instruction for and that appear in a text being read—but that are not essential for comprehension—can also be introduced after the text is read" (p. 41). In short, these are words that are useful to teach but do not impede comprehension. Even though the words may be unfamiliar, students can still understand the content.

Effective Vocabulary Instruction

As I mentioned, various findings support the premise that direct and explicit instruction for vocabulary, as well as extensive and varied reading, are critical components for increasing students' word banks. Research conducted by Robert Marzano (2004) uncovered the following list of eight research-based characteristics of effective vocabulary instruction:

1. Effective vocabulary instruction does not rely on definitions.
2. Students must represent their knowledge of words in linguistic and nonlinguistic ways.

3. Effective vocabulary instruction involves the gradual shaping of word meanings through multiple exposures.
4. Teaching word parts enhances students' understanding of terms.
5. Different types of words require different types of instruction.
6. Students should discuss the terms they are learning.
7. Students should play with words.
8. Instruction should focus on terms that have a high probability of enhancing academic success.

The following lesson sequence, inspired by Marzano and Pickering (2005), has been adapted for teaching words associated with a complex text at the center of instruction and can apply when introducing words either before or after reading the text. To teach new words appropriately, Marzano and Pickering suggest conducting the first three steps in the lesson sequence that follows in succession. In doing so, you can ensure that students have an accurate formal introduction to the target word. The writing and speaking activities (Step 4) can be conducted over time and used to provide multiple encounters with the word so students are afforded regular practice.

Rely on your professional judgment to determine how you might adapt these steps and be mindful not to disturb the flow of reading and meaning making. For example, you might provide a brief definition to support comprehension and then return to the steps so students can fully experience the word. However, if the word is central to understanding the text, you might elect to go through the steps carefully at the moment it is presented. Note that "word" refers generically to *word, term,* or *phrase.*

Step 1: Preassess and Introduce the Words

If preteaching words, preassess during this step to discover which words students already know, which they don't know, and which they think they know. If students have an incorrect perception of a word, now is the time to ensure that you set them straight. See Figure 4.2 for a sheet you can distribute to preassess words that appear in a text you are about to read. It is inspired by these four levels of word knowledge (Dale, O'Rourke, & Barbe, 1986):

- I never saw it before.
- I've heard of it, but I don't know what it means.
- I recognize it in context; it has something to do with . . .
- I know it.

Providing students with a definition of a new word will not help them learn the word; likewise, asking students to look up a new word in a dictionary is no better (Beck et al., 2002; Marzano & Pickering, 2005). The rationale for this is that dictionary definitions tend to be artificial, and words with multiple meanings are confusing so students don't know which usage aligns to the relevant text. Once students participate in a series of activities, develop their ability to draw on available context clues, and are more familiar with the target words, using a dictionary to verify meanings can be helpful. To begin to learn the word, though, students need a more authentic and natural launch point, such as a description, an explanation, or an example. You can introduce the word by telling a story or providing an example related to the text. Alternatively, personalize the word by explaining how you would use it in practical conversation or correspondence. There are many possibilities, but the main point is to avoid a sterile dictionary definition, and be sure to articulate and pronounce the word clearly so students hear it correctly.

A useful resource for examples (rather than unclear definitions) is the Collins online dictionary (www.collinsdictionary.com). Access the tab "English for Learners" to find entries similar to this one for *cultivate*: "(1) If you cultivate land or crops, you prepare land and grow crops on it. (2) If you cultivate an attitude, image, or skill, you try hard to develop it and make it stronger or better. (3) If you cultivate someone or cultivate a friendship with them, you try hard to develop a friendship with them." Another excellent resource that also provides useful examples and explanations, as well as definitions and other tools, is www.vocabulary.com.

Step 2: Ask Students to Restate the Meaning of the Word

So that students learn the word correctly, make sure they explain what they think it means in their own words. Encourage students to give their own examples instead of ones you provide. Restating gives students the opportunity to try out the word and also provides you with the assurance that they are beginning to master the word as it's intended to be used. Original descriptions, explanations, and examples allow you to verify that they are acquiring the appropriate meanings. Make sure, too, that they are pronouncing the words correctly. This step can involve a lot of conversation as students talk to one another about words and meanings.

Step 3: Ask Students to Create a Representation of the Word

Not everyone has confidence drawing, so allow students to represent the word using other nonlinguistic means, such as through clip art, tear art, graphics, cartoons, or symbols. Provide as many resources as possible, such as art utensils, magazines, Internet access and appropriate websites, and so forth. Model different kinds of nonlinguistic representations so students have ideas of what they are expected to do. Allow them to work in pairs to discuss the representations they will each create or how they might collaboratively complete a task, such as a mini-poster or cartoon strip. Invite students to share their finished products with others in small groups or as a class.

FIGURE 4.2

Vocabulary Preassessment

Directions: Please complete this chart to give me an idea of your knowledge of these words before we begin our next unit. If you know the word, complete the prompts in column 4. This preassessment will not be graded, so try your hardest to answer what you can. See the example in the first row to help you.

Word	1 Write an *X* if you've never seen the word before.	2 Write an *X* if you've heard the word but don't know what it means.	3 *Complete this prompt:* "I recognize this word in context; it has something to do with . . . "	4 I know the word.		
				Provide a definition and/or examples.	Write a sentence showing you know what the word means.	Write other forms of the word.
constructive				"helping to improve" *Examples:* • constructive feedback • constructive criticism • constructive conversation	Mark asked for constructive feedback on his essay so he could make it stronger before presenting it to the class.	*construct* *constructed* *constructs* *constructing* *reconstruct* *reconstructive* *reconstruction* *unconstructive*

Step 4: Conduct Various Writing and Speaking Activities

The CCSS expects that students will engage in various activities around word work. "In alignment with the standards, materials should also require students to explain the impact of specific word choices on the text. Materials and activities should also provide ample opportunities for students to practice the use of academic vocabulary in their speaking and writing" (Coleman & Pimentel, 2012, p. 18). Several activities are provided in the next section that you can assign to provide multiple exposures to words. Choose those that help illuminate your text and align to unit goals. Consider augmenting your activities with any of these points:

- **Text Focus:** Keep the text as the focus for instruction, and make sure students understand the context and content in which the words appear. Emphasize that words are not used in isolation but rather are a vehicle for authors to convey meaning. Pose text-dependent questions around the words to help students fully appreciate the text and the impact specific words or combinations of words can have on meaning (see Chapter 5). Discuss how proficient readers use the author's words to make inferences and interpretations.
- **Differentiation:** Differentiate instruction by allowing students to choose an activity from among a list that you provide. This chapter is replete with activities, and you likely have some you have found effective as well. In addition, you might provide students with different vocabulary lists based on the results of a presassessment, such as the one featured in Figure 4.2. If students are reading different complex texts based on interest or readiness, tailor their vocabulary lists appropriately. Some activities featured in this chapter might need to be modeled or examples provided. For instance, if students are expected to complete a writing assignment that embeds vocabulary on a regular basis (e.g., content summaries, ongoing journal entries), then show them how to approach this assignment and provide examples and expectations of what "quality" entails. For these particular routine activities, there is no need to model or show examples each time students work on the task unless you need to provide additional support to modify or extend the assignment for certain students.
- **Routine Vocabulary Binder:** As students learn new words throughout the year, they need a place to house them so they can refer back to and continuously reinforce them. To this end, have students keep a three-ring vocabulary binder where they can insert and accumulate pages with new words throughout the year. The binder can be divided into sections according to parts of speech or another category (e.g., descriptive words, technical words). It can serve as an ongoing resource where students can add information to existing entries (e.g., synonyms, examples, sentences) and continue to insert new words. There are many graphic organizers available online that you can download for this purpose. One such resource is Education Oasis, which has a wide selection of graphic organizers specifically for

vocabulary development that students can use as a template for their resource binders (http://www.educationoasis.com/curriculum/GO/vocab_dev.htm).

Context Clues

Students repeatedly hear the term *context clues* and are asked to identify and use them. Not all writers offer context clues, but when they do, students must be able to use them to their benefit. Without formally teaching students how to look for specific clues, they will not have the self-agency to define unfamiliar words independently. In fact, Tier 3 (domain-specific) words contain far more contextual clues that students can access to define them, which isn't the case with the more pervasive Tier 2 words that are used across texts. "Aligned materials should guide students to gather as much as they can about the meaning of these words from the context of how they are being used in the text, while offering support for vocabulary when students are not likely to be able to figure out their meanings from the text alone" (Coleman & Pimentel, 2012, p. 11). Even in states where the CCSS was not adopted, teaching to identify and use context clues is a necessary skill.

Many social studies and science textbooks use various context clues to define domain-specific words. What is tricky is to use these clues to decipher meanings of Tier 2 words that are not so apparent. It is not critical that students memorize each type of context clue and are able to put a name to each. Rather, it is more important that they come to understand that authors give hints in a variety of ways to help readers decipher unknown words. Therefore, they must be alert to these devices, which are featured in Figure 4.3.

The following series of steps focuses on using context clues to derive meaning of unknown words where they appear in a text (inspired by Goerss, Beck, & McKeown, 1999). Research findings have shown positive student achievement using this proposed direct instruction sequence: "Over the course of the study, students showed strong improvements in being able to identify relevant information from contexts and using that information to develop reasonable hypotheses about a word's meaning" (Beck et al., p. 123). Once teachers lead students through this sequence, they will have a bank of new words they have just begun to learn. Instruct students to put these words in their vocabulary binders, and conduct various activities around the words so they have the repeated exposure necessary to command them fully. Later, use text-dependent questions and tasks (the focus for the next chapter) around these words to illuminate salient passages of the text.

1. **Read and paraphrase the excerpt.** Read an excerpt that has an unfamiliar target word and highlight, circle, or underline it. Stop to identify its location in the text. Reread the entire excerpt again. Paraphrase the excerpt, putting emphasis on the unknown word.

FIGURE 4.3
Types of Context Clues

1. Word Parts: Break down the different parts of the word–prefixes, suffixes, base or root words–to figure out what it means. For some words, like *discrimination,* analyzing the word parts might be confusing or misleading because the prefix has multiple meanings. Therefore, it is best to read the context where the word appears and see what makes most sense. When in doubt, verify the word's meaning with another source.

- **Discrimination:**
  - *Dis-:* not, opposite of, reverse, deprive of; apart, away
  - *crimin:* verdict, judicial decision; judgment
  - *-tion:* indicates the word is a noun

2. Definition/Explanation: Look for a definition or an explanation within the sentence.

- **Discrimination** or *unfairly targeting one or more groups by those who perceive themselves to be a superior group* can cause distress.
- **Vulnerable** people are oftentimes *in need of protection under certain laws so others cannot take advantage of them.*

3. Synonym: words next to the unknown word can be a clue that there is a synonym.

- **Discrimination** or *bias* can cause distress toward the targeted group.
- When people know they are **vulnerable** or *defenseless*, they tend to protect themselves to avoid harm.

4. Example: providing examples of the unknown word can give readers a clue to meaning.

- *Like shunning smokers in restaurants by making them satisfy their habit outside,* **discrimination** targets a perceived undesirable group.
- **Vulnerable** people, *such as young children, the elderly, or handicapped individuals,* might have protections under certain laws.

5. Antonym/Contrast: opposite information about the unknown word can be offset by words and phrases such as *unlike, as opposed to, different from.*

- **Discrimination**, *as opposed to fairness for all people,* can have damaging effects on a targeted group.
- **Vulnerable** people, *unlike those who can stand up for themselves,* tend to be the target of unethical or dangerous individuals.

6. Analogy: comparisons of the word help to determine what it means.

- The ill effects of **discrimination** are *like black, evil tendrils gripping the heart.*
- **Vulnerable** people can be *like fragile glass in need of care and attention.*

7. Appositive: look for the grammatical structure of appositives which can provide a definition, synonym, or example.

- **Discrimination**, *the act of showing bias to one group,* can have damaging effects.
- *The elderly and handicapped*, a **vulnerable** group of individuals, have laws to protect them from unethical individuals.

2. **Establish meaning of the context.** Explain that this process is not just about determining the meaning of one word. Emphasize the point that by defining the word, readers can have a better understanding of the passage as a whole. Ask and answer questions such as "What is happening in this passage? Is someone talking? If so, what is he or she saying? What is the author trying to convey?" This dialogue helps to form a relationship between the context and the unfamiliar word.

3. **Identify what the word might mean, along with a rationale.** Provide some sense of what the word could possibly mean. Explain why this is so. If a definition is not forthcoming, return to the second step and find out what is going on in the passage.

4. **Consider further possibilities.** Talk about how there could be more than one possible meaning for the word within the context it is used. Make educated guesses about a few possible definitions.

5. **Summarize.** Review the possible meanings and try them out within the context of the text. Reread the passage and verify if it makes sense. If unsure, consult a print or online resource to verify the word's meaning. If students skip this step, then they might be learning the wrong definition of a word and possibly be misguided in understanding the text passage where the word appears.

Vocabulary Activities and Strategies

This section includes several activities around word work that can be embedded in a lesson sequence for teaching new Tier 2 (e.g., *determine, parallel, commission, angle, itemize*) or Tier 3 (e.g., *mitosis, digestive system, filibuster*) words and reinforcing words students are just starting to acquire. As students engage in these tasks, have them add to and revise their vocabulary binders by including nonlinguistic representations, examples and nonexamples, antonyms and synonyms, word part coding (e.g., underline root word, circle prefix, put a square around suffix), and definitions for each word.

Mini-poster

Students choose a magazine or catalog picture and associate a vocabulary word with it (that is drawn from a list of provided words that appear in the complex text). They then create a mini-poster for each word. Here is a suggestion for how you can conduct an activity to help students create their own mini-posters:

1. Prepare a word list with words drawn from the complex text. Figure 4.4 provides an example of one you might create. Provide a part of speech, definition, explanation or example, and the text excerpt where the word appears. Since some words have

multiple meanings, make sure the definition and examples you provide match the one that is used in the text.

2. Distribute the list to students. Consider dividing the list so pairs of students work on different words.

3. Review each word with students. Discuss each one and try to build real-world connections by interjecting a relevant personal story or current event that relates to the word.

4. Instruct students to create a mini-poster for each word that includes the following items. If necessary, display an example so students know what their finished products should look like (see Figure 4.5).
   - the word
   - its part of speech
   - a representative picture (can be original art or an image clipped from a magazine or from a website)
   - a caption (an original sentence that includes context clues so someone unfamiliar with the word can determine its meaning)

5. Hang the finished mini-posters in your classroom (placing related posters near one another). Extend the activity by asking students to walk around the room and compare posters that are focused on the same word to see their similarities and differences. Pose questions to reinforce meaning (e.g., Which posters have similar pictures? Do they both depict the word well? What other graphics could have been included?). Also encourage students to identify the similarities in certain words, determine which words are opposites, or identify words that could belong to the same category.

When students work on this project, expect that there will be chatter as they share their pictures and ideas with one another while flipping through magazines and discussing how a word might apply. This is productive talk, so welcome it. Circulate around the room and discuss the words and pictures students select to ensure they are learning the words correctly. Read some examples of sentences aloud as you walk around if students give permission to do so. Clarify and redefine words to specific students, as needed, by providing more examples and explanations.

Part of Speech Tests

Students must know how to use unfamiliar words correctly; therefore, identifying a word's part of speech is critical. Point out that knowing how words function in a sentence is an issue of grammatical construction. To know and use a word well requires a combination of grammar and meaning. Here are a couple of useful rules for teaching adjectives and nouns:

FIGURE 4.4
Word List Example

Word	Part of Speech	Definition	Explanation/Example	Text Excerpt
agitator	noun	one who stirs up others to further a political, social, or other cause; one who urges others to rebel or protest	• An agitator might give a fiery speech to rile up or anger a crowd into action. • Patrick Henry's "Give me liberty or give me death!" speech agitated those who were loyal to British rule and urged those against Parliament to fight for independence.	He was an agitator who caused trouble by riling up the crowd and arousing negative feelings.
inscription	noun	written dedication or message	• Inscriptions are words of dedication carved, engraved, or written on a tombstone, book, coin, or sculpture. • Tombstone inscription example: "In loving memory of . . ." • Emma Lazarus's poem is an inscription on the Statue of Liberty's pedestal.	The inscription on the soldier's statue was appropriate and touching. Those who walked by read it with an intent look on their faces.
rebellion	noun	revolt, uprising, upheaval; resistance to a government or ruler	• Most armed rebellions seek to establish a new government in place of the old one. • Examples: French Revolution, American Revolution, Warsaw Uprising, Arab Spring	The American Revolution was a rebellion in which Patriots fought to overthrow King George so they could become an independent nation.

- **Adjectives:** If a word can fit into this frame, then it is an adjective: the very _____ man (or other noun, such as *cat*). The only exception to this rule is numbers, which can be adjectives (and also nouns) but don't fit in this sentence frame. Have students rattle off a list of adjectives while you record them on the board. Check that each fits into the frame. Although students might be able to use adjectives correctly by applying this rule, they must still understand the word's meaning and context in order to use it well. Therefore, it's important to explain that adjectives answer the question "What kind?" (e.g., the *diabolical* witch—What kind of witch? *Diabolical*.) With this in mind, students can hunt for familiar and unfamiliar words that are adjectives.
- **Nouns:** If a word can fit in this blank, it is a noun: _____ is/are enjoyable. Some suffixes also indicate that a word is a noun (e.g., *-ness, -tion, -sion, -ism*).

To introduce a rule, conduct an activity in which you write one of the sentence frames on the board. Invite students to contribute words while you keep a running list. After a hearty list of entries, have students spot check to see if the words fit in the frame correctly. Once the words are verified, point out that all words that fit in the frame share a common part of speech. Ask students to name the appropriate part of speech and write it at the top of the list. You now have a list for a word wall (if age-appropriate) that students can continue to add to when they acquire new words that belong to this category. Remind them to apply this rule to new vocabulary words in order to help them identify words and use them correctly. Encourage students to put these rules and new words in their vocabulary binders or notebooks as a handy reference.

FIGURE 4.5
Vocabulary Mini-poster Examples

serene (adjective)	*nomadic* (adjective)

The serene and peaceful beach is a favorite spot for people who like to relax by the calm waters and feel the warm tropical breeze.	The nomadic man always has a suitcase in one hand and a briefcase in the other since he constantly travels from one city to another.

4-Square Graphic Organizer

The 4-Square graphic organizer is incredibly versatile and can be used in a variety of ways to meet different lesson goals. Here, let's look at how it can be used for vocabulary reinforcement after students have been introduced to words associated with the text. To begin, ask students to draw a graphic organizer with four squares and a small center rectangle on a blank sheet of paper. Instruct them to write the following words (or others—such as nonexamples, synonyms, or antonyms—as you see fit) in the corner of each square. Alternatively, you can prepare a graphic organizer for them.

1. definition
2. symbol/picture
3. sentence
4. examples

Figure 4.6 shows what the prepared organizer should look like. Notice that the words are in small letters to leave room for writing in the empty squares.

FIGURE 4.6
4-Square Graphic Organizer

Definition	Sentence
Symbol/picture	Examples

Once the organizer is ready, instruct each student to write one word in the center of his or her organizer and then wait for further directions. Make sure each student has a different word, or if you have a large class, two students can have the same word. This is a formative assessment to check for understanding so these should be words the class has been studying during the unit and appear in the complex text. Tell students that soon they will take their organizers and circulate around the room to find four separate people who will each fill in one square. Before they set out to complete the task, provide the following guidelines:

- If you choose to write a **sentence** on someone's organizer, it must include a context clue. For example, for the word *elaborate*, it is not good enough to write "The woman's outfit is elaborate." You must add more detail, such as "The woman's outfit is elaborate because it includes different hemlines, colorful beads, and several textures."

- If you choose to complete the **examples** quadrant, enter at least three. For instance, if the target word is *transportation,* you might enter any of these words: *submarine, subway, car, airplane, feet, bicycle.* Examples for the word *intolerable* could be someone who snores, clipping toenails in a public place, or having an uncontrollable tantrum.
- Make sure the **definition** is thorough (as opposed to a one-word synonym) and your **symbol** or **picture** is somewhat detailed.
- Let's say a classmate approaches you and his or her organizer is entirely blank. If you can't remember the word, you can pass. If, however, the organizer has two or three quadrants filled in and you are fuzzy on the word, use the quadrants that are completed as context clues to make an educated guess on filling in the blank quadrant.

When students' organizers are complete, instruct them to return to their seats. Since there is no guarantee that students have entered correct information onto one another's organizers, have them review and edit their 4-squares with a partner. If they need support, encourage them to use resources to do this step, such as a textbook, an online dictionary, or your own assistance. Once they have checked their 4-squares for accuracy, ask students to place a star at the top and submit their graphic organizers to you for review. Make necessary edits, and return the papers for them to put in their vocabulary binders. An adaptation of this exercise is for students to sit in table groups to complete one another's organizers as they pass their papers among group members instead of circulating around the room.

You can also conduct a follow-up activity. To do so, review the graphic organizers and make any edits. Instead of returning the papers, though, prepare for a tactile exercise designed to reinforce the same words by cutting along the lines of each organizer so there are five pieces—the word and four quadrants. Combine the pieces for several words and place them in an envelope. Return them to students to reassemble the next day. One envelope can have up to four word puzzles, so there might be twenty pieces to assemble. Differentiate the number and actual words students have in their envelopes accordingly.

It is possible to reverse the order of these two activities. To do so, create graphic organizers for words aligned to the complex text that students are reading (using the examples in Figure 4.7 as a guide). Cut out puzzle pieces from your teacher-prepared organizers, and instruct students to assemble the pieces. After this tactile activity, have students participate in the kinesthetic group activity described earlier where they walk around the room (or circulate the graphic organizer in a small group) soliciting others to complete their organizers. Any way will work.

As mentioned before, this activity (or versions of it) is used to check for understanding and reinforce vocabulary words. Another benefit is that it not only provides more exposure to the words but also gives students an opportunity to use context clues.

FIGURE 4.7
4-Square Graphic Organizer Examples

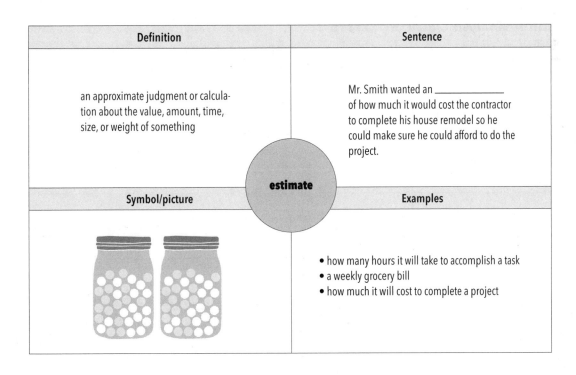

Definition	Sentence
to ascertain or make a conclusion in answer to a problem, situation, or question after careful consideration, observation or reasoning	Ted wanted to _____ how he might solve the problem, so he weighed his options to help him decide what to do.

determine

Symbol/picture	Examples
	• decide the correct answer to a math problem • choose an influential individual who deserves a special award • figure out which character changes the most during the course of a story • decide which tools to use for a science experiment

Definition	Sentence
an approximate judgment or calculation about the value, amount, time, size, or weight of something	Mr. Smith wanted an _____ of how much it would cost the contractor to complete his house remodel so he could make sure he could afford to do the project.

estimate

Symbol/picture	Examples
	• how many hours it will take to accomplish a task • a weekly grocery bill • how much it will cost to complete a project

Semantic Feature Analysis

A semantic feature analysis can be used for vocabulary acquisition and comprehension of complex text as students examine, analyze, and make connections between words and various aspects of content. For this activity, examples (e.g., events, people, characters, objects, locations, ideas, concepts) are listed down the left-hand side of a grid or chart. Features, criteria, or characteristics are entered across the top. (The reverse is also fine.) Students should write a plus symbol in a cell to signify an association between an example and an intersecting feature. If there is no relationship between the two, they should enter a minus symbol. It is acceptable to put both symbols in a cell for certain situations. When the chart is complete, students analyze it and discuss similarities and differences among the examples and features. Figure 4.8 provides an example for the novel *Outsiders*. Note that there are blanks for students to add more personality traits and characters. Since characters, historical figures, and other topics change over time, students can create more than one graphic organizer to reflect this development. Even though Figure 4.8 shows a partially completed chart, students can create one from scratch.

There are endless possibilities for what can be entered on the matrix in any content area, so refer to your learning goals and text to focus the activity. For example, in

FIGURE 4.8
Semantic Feature Analysis *Outsiders* Example

Directions: Add additional characters and personality traits to this table. Place a + symbol in cells where a character exhibits a personality trait and a – symbol where a character does not show this trait. If you are unsure, you can leave a cell blank. Be ready to support your analysis with evidence from the text.

	influential	rebellious	insightful	vulnerable	mature	unrefined	perceptive			
Ponyboy Curtis										
Darry										
Johnny Cade										
Sodapop										
Cherry										

a language arts or social studies class, you can list various characters in a novel (as in Figure 4.8), historical figures, or individuals in the first column and then enter personality traits across the top row (e.g., *persevering, parsimonious, carefree, resourceful, diligent, controversial, egotistical*). In a science class, the matrix can be used to organize content knowledge and find associations. For example, list various biomes (e.g., tundra, taiga, temperate deciduous forest, tropical rain forest, temperate rain forest, grassland, desert) in the first column. Across the top, include items such as different plant or animal adaptations or climate conditions. The features do not have to be one word but can be a longer phrase or even a sentence.

Either you or your students can generate items for the chart. In pairs or small groups, students work on the task and can return to their texts to help them complete the chart. Collaboration is key as students discuss whether plusses or minuses belong in various cells. Encourage students to return to the text to defend their responses if there are disagreements. After they finish their charts, allow time for whole-class sharing and discussion using evidence from the text. You might ask students to create a summary based on the grid and their discussions. If students have not worked with a semantic feature analysis grid before, make sure you model how the exercise is to be done, along with a think aloud explaining each step.

Routine Writing Tasks

Consider assigning a variety of short writing tasks in which students self-select words from a list as the basis for their assignment. Figure 4.9 shows three different options that can be assigned as an in-class or homework assignment; any can also be featured on an exit card. Consider adapting tasks so students use the words expressly associated with the targeted complex text. For example, the Word Connections task can be revised to state, "Select two terms and write a sentence that explains the connection between them using a situation individuals or groups faced based on the historical events in the section we are reading. Make sure your sentence shows an understanding of the historical context in which these events took place." The tasks for Examples and Nonexamples can be a writing task or merely a listing of items connected to the text. Model how to complete any of the tasks to show how detailed you expect the responses to be before students begin. Determine if students can work individually or with a partner.

Another option is have students engage in a comprehensive writing task. Ask them to self-select words from their weekly or lesson lists to use in a writing assignment, such as a short story, descriptive paragraph, or a summary of steps in a process based on the text. Figure 4.10 features two student samples. You can assign this assessment on a weekly basis. For easy reference, ask students to underline each vocabulary word in their writing. Some students might elect to write a continuous piece by writing a chapter or section each week. Alternatively, to connect to the complex text students are reading, they can write a continuous series of short summaries of chapters or sections of the text.

FIGURE 4.9
Short Writing Task Options

Word Connections	Select two terms and write a sentence that explains the connection between them. Examples: • *intolerable/compromise*: The situation between the twin boys became so intolerable that their parents demanded they go to their bedroom until they could reach a compromise. • *ostentatious/wary:* Mr. Smith's banker was wary of the ostentatious shoes his client was wearing because he knew that his bank account could not support such a lavish lifestyle.
Quick Writes	Choose the sentence frame that best fits each word you select, or create your own frames: • _____ makes me think of a time when . . . • _____ makes me think of the color _____ because . . . • _____ reminds me of _____ because . . . • _____ is used to describe _____ because . . . • If I were to paint a picture of _____, I'd paint . . .
Examples and Nonexamples	Create examples and nonexamples of your selected words. Examples for *diversity*: • The United States is home to people from different cultures and backgrounds. • The United Nations is comprised of representatives from all over the world. • A mall's food court includes food from different countries. Nonexamples of *diversity*: • An all-women's school • A board of directors for a company composed entirely of one gender or race • Before Civil Rights laws, public schools in the South admitted only white students.

Word Construction and Deconstruction

Research shows that "as students' understanding of word parts and word construction increases, so does their vocabulary knowledge. . . . For confident readers who have reached a level of automaticity with decoding longer words, understanding roots and affixes can help them remember words they have learned and figure out the meaning of unfamiliar terms" (Marzano & Simms, 2013, p. 29). To assist with learning word parts, make individual cards with a different root, suffix, or prefix on each one. Have students construct different words using various combinations of the cards and then use a print or online resource to define them. An Internet search will yield many lists that you can use to make these cards.

You can also give a couple target words to pairs of students and ask them to make a list of as many morphological derivatives of a target word they can find, such as *decide, decision, undecided,* and *decisive.* Students then study all of the words in each family to note how many word forms they can construct. Partners then share their lists with another pair of students to notice the similarities and differences within these word families. Foursomes can compete with other groups to see how many versions of a target word they can create.

FIGURE 4.10
Student Vocabulary Writing Samples

Another Game of Basketball

It was noon as my basketball team, the Lumberjacks, sprinted onto the court. We came here with seven wins, and hopefully we will leave with eight. Our team manager wanted to <u>advertise</u> the game and bring an NBA scout to <u>analyze</u> how well we all played. Thankfully, the scout showed up and took a keen interest in player number 11, Bobby Johnson. With <u>candor</u>, we stated that we wanted him off the team. Our honesty didn't bother Bobby, though, because he would much rather play in the NBA than our college basketball team. But Bobby knew the <u>pitfalls</u> of playing in the NBA, which include not playing as much and–when playing–not scoring any points.

The referee threw the ball into the air and the game started. <u>Criticism</u> and cheering were heard by fans, but we had to focus on one thing: where to play on the court. Luckily, the ref had to <u>compromise</u> about a call he made and how he would repay it and give us the ball next time. Then as Bobby took a shot, a <u>ravenous</u> fan shouted, "Lemonade and peanuts. I'm starving over here!" Bobby shot an air ball and blamed it on the fan. There was shouting, and the ref had to <u>mediate</u> the fight.

At the end of the game, the score was 120 to 67 with us the winners. We all <u>lauded</u> Bobby as the scout told him he would play with the Miami Heat the following season. I was so surprised he got on the team even with the airball. However, the NBA players wanted to <u>inaugurate</u> him onto their team anyway.

The Menacing Morning

I woke up shocked and in a fright because the <u>menacing</u> alarm clock read 7:20 a.m. and the school bus comes at 7:35 a.m. So I threw off my covers and sprang out of bed. My room was so <u>bedraggled</u> because my covers were off the bed, <u>shards</u> of pencil tips littered the floor, and my clothes were piled on the dirty carpet. It was in such a state of <u>squalor</u>–like a pig sty. I sprinted out of my room into the kitchen, and my mom was looking at me with a <u>penetrating</u> look because I was so late. She felt <u>despondent</u> thinking I would never make the bus. With speed, I stuffed toast in my mouth and ran outside to the bus stop. Relief washed over me as I sank into the last seat on the bus.

Appositives

Some context clues are embedded in the grammatical construction of an appositive. Prepare several sentence strips with appositives that expressly define words that are likely unknown to students. Do not reveal the pattern; allow students to discover this for themselves during this hands-on activity. Here is how you conduct it: Distribute one sentence at a time to a student pair. Instruct students to read each sentence and circle the unknown word. Ask them if they can figure out what the word means and provide a rationale for how they determined that definition. Finally, have them underline the part of each sentence that provides clues about the meaning of the word. Chances are they underline the appositive.

Have students repeat this exercise with several sentences. When they finish circling unknown words and underlining the appositives, ask them to compare all of the sentences they read and see if they notice a pattern. Once they do, provide them with the proper name of this structure—appositives—along with its definition and the examples featured in Figure 4.11. Using this pattern to guide them, ask student pairs to create their own sentences using appositives as context clues to define words. Invite them to share these sentences with their classmates.

FIGURE 4.11
Appositives

Definition

An appositive is a noun or noun phrase that identifies, explains, or renames a noun or pronoun right beside it. Typically, an appositive appears after the word it explains or identifies, but sometimes it can precede it. The appositive can be a short or long combination of words that help to define unknown words, terms, individuals, or events.

Examples

See these examples for how appositives, which are in boldface type, serve as a valuable context clue for the underlined words:

- Discrimination, **unfairly targeting one or more groups by those who perceive themselves to be superior**, can cause distress.
- Discrimination, **the act of showing bias to one group**, can have damaging effects.
- **Typically frail and white-haired,** octogenarians have laws to protect them from unethical individuals.
- A metaphor, **a type of figurative language that is a comparison between two unlike objects**, does not use the words *like* or *as*.
- A civil war, **a feud between groups of people within the same country**, began in 1861 in the United States.
- The United States is a democracy, **a form of government in which the authority is derived from the people.**

Appositives are a trigger for a context clue. They can also improve sentence structure since one way to fix short, choppy sentences is to write an appositive to combine them. Figure 4.12 shows examples of how appositives can be used to improve sentence fluency. Although this is not a vocabulary activity, it complements the previous exercise, so share this figure. Ask students to review their writing and apply what they learned.

· · · · · ·

Closing

Teachers must include vocabulary acquisition in their instructional programs since the connection between word knowledge and reading comprehension is intimately intertwined. Domain-specific (Tier 3) words are regularly taught in the class and get attention. However, general academic (Tier 2) words are high-utility, cross-domain words that must also be taught in a robust instructional program so students can examine complex text deeply.

FIGURE 4.12
Using Appositives to Combine Sentences

Short Sentences	Combined Using Appositives
Kathy is from Indianapolis. The capital of Indiana is Indianapolis.	Kathy is originally from Indianapolis, the capital of Indiana.
A civil war is a war between groups of people in the same country. A civil war began in 1861 in the United States.	A civil war, a feud between groups of people within the same country, began in 1861 in the United States.
A metaphor is a type of figurative language that is a comparison between two unlike objects. A metaphor does not use the words *like* or *as*.	A metaphor, a type of figurative language that is a comparison between two unlike objects, does not use the words *like* or *as*.
The telegraph was a faster form of communication than the Pony Express. The Pony Express became obsolete because of the telegraph.	The Pony Express became obsolete by a faster form of communication, the telegraph.
Samuel F. B. Morse invented the Morse code. It was a form of communication using groups of short and long signals that signify letters of the alphabet.	Samuel F. B. Morse, the inventor of Morse code, created a form of communication using groups of short and long signals that signify letters of the alphabet.

Students increase their inventory of words through a combination of efforts. Direct instruction has proven to be an effective method for teaching students new words. Reading a variety of texts is another vehicle for increasing vocabulary. Although direct instruction for vocabulary knowledge and a hearty dose of reading have proven effective, they are not the only methods—given the vast number of words that need to be learned. Students must also use context clues, when an author provides them, since explicitly teaching each unfamiliar word encountered is not necessarily practical.

Context clues make words more transparent because they offer information that help readers infer meaning to define unknown words. Direct instruction is used to teach specific words and is also an effective way to learn the process for finding and using context clues. "Practicing the procedure of inferring meaning from context helps readers develop a sensitivity to the relationship between a novel word and the context in which it appears. It is important for students to understand the relationship between words and the broader context; the word has to make sense within the context and that words bring meaning to the context" (Beck et al., 2013, p. 132).

To devise appropriate vocabulary instruction, determine a list of words that are worth teaching. Identify which words you'll preteach and those that can be defined during and even after reading. In addition, identify words that include context clues for students to define on their own and those you should frontload if the text does not provide any hints to meaning. Whichever new words students confront, they need to have repeated exposures to those words so they can internalize and commit them to memory and retrieve them easily on their own for different purposes. Students should get in the habit of using these words throughout the day; therefore, provide opportunities and encouragement so they practice these words during activities, informal conversations, collaborative discussions in group work, and any presentations they conduct.

5
Skilled Questioning Techniques

Effective learning experiences around questioning can have a meaningful impact on student achievement. Hattie's work on visible learning (2009) catalogs various research studies, which reveal the not-so-surprising finding that "overall effects of questioning vary, and the major moderator is the type of question asked—surface questions can enhance surface knowing and higher-order questions can enhance deeper understanding" (p. 182). In addition, he cites evidence that there are gains in student achievement correlated to teacher training in questioning skills (e.g., types of lower- and higher-level questions, purposes for using each type) and attention to monitoring how we use questioning. Another effective use of questioning is when students craft and use questions to facilitate their own learning.

Hattie's work also discusses the salient distinction between monologic and dialogic discourse. The monologic teacher is concerned with imparting information, uses a recitation/response/response form of discussion, and checks for understanding from only some of the students. This kind of pedagogy revolves around whole-class instruction with the teacher at the front of the class, talking and asking questions that evoke brief responses from students. By contrast, in a classroom where dialogic discourse dominates, teachers set the stage for students to engage in worthwhile discussion. "Dialogic talk aims to promote communication with and between students, to demonstrate the value of the views of the students, and to help participants to share and build meaning collaboratively" (Hattie, 2012, p. 82).

Once students have begun to make sense of the text, it's time to use questioning techniques wisely and elicit dialogue among students to contribute to deeper learning. In this chapter, you'll read about three types of questioning that yield positive effects on student achievement and promote an environment that values student involvement. The first type includes text-dependent questions—a central focus and catalyst for delving deeply into complex text—which have received a great deal of attention, especially with the introduction of the CCSS. Through these types of questions, you can and should facilitate rich learning experiences that compel students to ruminate over salient parts of the text that might otherwise go unnoticed. These questions—and the necessary time for students to respond to them—are critical not only to do justice to a worthwhile text but also to model how to approach a text and uncover its core message. As I've explained, text can have a rather broad meaning, so by all means prepare questions around whatever complex text is aligned to your subject area.

Questioning does not solely have to be teacher generated to make a positive impact on student learning. Students can also take the helm to craft and lead their own discussions with queries they generate and use as the basis for meaningful discourse. When students are charged with developing their own questions, they have to work hard to determine appropriate questions to ask. This helps them cultivate the intellectual habits of careful reading and meaning making. Text-dependent questions that you share can serve as models for students as they transfer what they've learned to build their own questions. Therefore, the Socratic approach—in which students develop and pose their own questions—is a valuable type of questioning that provides opportunities for critical thinking and growth. This represents the second form of questioning discussed in this chapter.

Finally, I'll introduce a strategy for framing questions that can be used in a Socratic dialogue or adapted for another purpose that is ostensibly a strategy for designing levels of questions. Regardless of who creates the questions, the emphasis needs to be on generating salient ones that are worthwhile to address. Equally essential as a learning opportunity are, of course, the answers that students provide using text evidence as the basis for their responses.

Refer to your complex text and unit goals to determine how best to plan for instruction using the questioning techniques and strategies presented in this chapter:

- Text-Dependent Questions
- Socratic Method
- Question Formulation

Text-Dependent Questions

Definition and Purpose

Since analysis of complex text is pervasive and emphasized across reading standards documents, you need to plan for and facilitate close reading of complex text so students can comprehend it at a deeper level. To accomplish this goal, it's important to design learning experiences around introspective queries referred to as text-dependent questions. Such questions are intended to illuminate the material and address various standards that call for interpretative and critical reading (on top of evidentiary analysis). Rather than rely on personal opinions or experiences as the basis for a response, students are required to use the text as the information source.

When students respond to text-dependent questions, they must use material found in the text to support their assertions through written or oral discourse. It is not good enough for students merely to support what they say because it is a personal opinion. Rather, what they provide as support needs to originate from a credible print or digital source they can actually identify and cite.

If you were to ask a question that could be answered without reading the text, then it does not qualify as text-dependent. For example, suppose students are reading *Tuck Everlasting* and are asked, "How would you conduct your life if you were granted immortality?" Does that question require students to dive into the text and arrive at a conclusion or assertion based on a character's actions or beliefs? No, it doesn't. It might be a question related to the theme of the novel, but students can respond without having read a single page. By contrast, suppose the question were "How does immortality change Tuck's view of the world and his interactions with his family and Winnie?" To answer this, students have to delve into the text and find evidence to respond adequately. As a result, they are provoked to examine the text more carefully and engage in text analysis.

There are plenty of questions that teachers can ask—and have asked—that allow students to skirt the text to respond. Some students are masters at circumventing the text, reading it quickly, or skimming it only to arrive at weak answers that do not help them seek deeper knowledge or do justice to an author's work. In a nontraditional text, students can be equally evasive and glance at a finished industrial arts project or halfheartedly watch a drama performance. Your job, then, is to ensure that meaningful questions guide students back to the text for closer examination and greater insight. It's important to note, however, that text-dependent questions begin with more simplistic and concrete queries that lay the groundwork for questions that facilitate deeper meaning making. Still, even these foundational, literal questions must require students to use the text for their responses. Therefore, a combination of both is warranted. Take a look at Figure 5.1 to see examples and nonexamples of text-dependent questions.

Review the following questions independently or with a colleague to consider which qualify as text-dependent. In other words, which demand reference to the text "To Build a Fire", and which do not?

1. What details does Jack London use to indicate a bitterly cold setting?
2. What is it like to experience extreme cold? How would you prepare for it?
3. Does London use limited or omniscient point of view? Provide evidence from the story to support your answer and provide reasons for his preference.
4. The author titles the story "To Build a Fire." What kind of stories might have this title?

5. Why do you think the author selected the title "To Build a Fire"? What evidence supports it?

FIGURE 5.1

Text-Dependent and Non–Text-Dependent Questions

Not Text-Dependent	Text-Dependent
In "Casey at the Bat," Casey strikes out. Describe a time when you failed at something.	What makes Casey's experiences at bat humorous?
In "Letter from a Birmingham Jail," Dr. King discusses nonviolent protest. Discuss, in writing, a time when you wanted to fight against something that you felt was unfair.	What can you infer from King's letter about the letter that he received?
In "The Gettysburg Address" Lincoln says the nation is dedicated to the proposition that all men are created equal. Why is equality an important value to promote?	"The Gettysburg Address" mentions the year 1776. According to Lincoln's speech, why is this year significant to the events described in the speech?

Source: From www.achievethecore.org

Question 1 requires students to use London's words and phrases to describe the bitter cold, so it is dependent on the text. Students cannot merely choose arbitrary words associated with winter. Rather, the goal is for them to see how London uses imagery and strong word choice in "To Build a Fire" to capture a particular mood. The next question is a free-for-all as students can easily respond based on their personal experiences—and maybe not even firsthand encounters with cold. For example, they could live in Florida and merely describe what they have seen in a movie set during a snowy winter. Question 3 asks students not only to demonstrate their knowledge of point of view but also to go even further than simply identifying it as third-person omniscient. It requires them to cite passages, such as the examples that follow, in which the man and the dog have impressions of the severe cold. They must then examine the perspectives indicated by the quotes to make an assertion of why London chose this point of view and its impact on the story as a whole.

- "Once in a while the thought reiterated itself that it was very cold and that he had never experienced such cold. As he walked along he rubbed his cheek-bones and nose with the back of his mittened hand. He did this automatically, now and again changing hands. But rub as he would, the instant he stopped his cheek-bones went numb, and the following instant the end of his nose went numb" (London, 1982, p. 179).
- "The dog was disappointed and yearned back toward the fire. This man did not know cold. Possibly all the generations of his ancestry had been ignorant of cold

of real cold, of cold one hundred and seven degrees below freezing point. But the dog knew; all its ancestry knew, and it had inherited the knowledge. And it knew that it was not good to walk abroad in such fearful cold" (London, 1982, p. 182).

It is probably evident at this point as to why Question 4 is not text-dependent. Question 5, although written simplistically, creates an opportunity for students to demonstrate key understandings of the text and cite pertinent quotes to support them.

During your lessons, require students to return to the text repeatedly to respond to questions and tasks. Each time students return to the pages, speech, or appropriate text for a content area, they uncover a richer meaning. Think about your own experiences with a challenging text. You might need to reread passages because you want more information or need material for work-related reasons. Often, your impression is entirely different after revisiting the text two or three times; in short, rereading complex text yields new information you don't always glean the first time through.

Posing text-dependent questions enable you to design and orchestrate a richer reading experience. The following sections include specific suggestions and examples for writing or redesigning questions and tasks. Keep the following in mind:

- Questions (or tasks) should be designed in a way that requires students to read the text in order to respond. Questions that do not require students to refer back to the text for information are not dependent on the text.
- Students must cite specific and relevant textual evidence to support their responses.
- The first questions you pose can be foundational and literal and then should build in complexity.
- Questions ought to be tailored to a specific text and designed to align to learning goals.

Questions and Tasks for Analytical Reading

Designing a series of text-dependent questions and tasks requires skill, practice, and attention. There are useful resources to support you in developing them and also various lessons with examples of questions that can be used immediately.

Sites such as Edmodo (www.edmodo.com)—see the Basal and Anthology Alignment Projects—and Achieve the Core (www.achievethecore.com) have rich repositories of text-dependent questions and tasks and accompanying lessons for traditional forms of text that you can use at no charge. Although valuable resources abound online and in print, it is imperative that you feel empowered to create your own text-dependent questions and tasks. For one, there are undoubtedly complex texts you wish to use across content areas and grades where questions and lessons are not available. Second, because there are a plethora of resources available, knowing about text-dependent questions allows you to competently critique them and ascertain whether a particular question is truly quality driven. Third, if you teach a class that uses nontraditional text, you'll need to know some pointers for how to fashion such questions. Therefore, what follows is a step-by-step guide to creating text-dependent questions and tasks so you can be knowledgeable about what they entail. It is a synthesis and adaptation of various books and documents (e.g., Fisher, Frey, & Lapp, 2012; Glass, 2013). From the resources I've cited throughout, the information that follows, and your own professional judgment, my hope is that you will have a variety of tools to confidently build questions around complex text.

As you create questions in accordance with these different steps, be mindful of standards and include relevant questions that align to these expectations. Also, if you write a solid question and are unclear about which step it addresses, do not be overly concerned. Consider these steps as a guide to ensure that you have a wide variety of appropriately challenging questions. Furthermore, when writing or redesigning the questions, it's important to customize them to the text—rather than overuse generic questions.

Step 1: Uncover the Core Ideas of the Text

Critically read and annotate the text you expect students to experience prior to beginning a unit around it. While reading, determine key insights and themes, and then verify that these core ideas are implicit in the text when you finish it. Create thematic statements that encapsulate what you want students to understand as a result of their own reading. When you do the work up front to figure out the essence of the text, you put into practice a backward design approach that begins with the end in mind. Specifically, the point is to read and determine key understandings so you can be sure to fashion a series of questions that drive learning experiences toward the essence of the text. Plus, you'll use these core ideas to create an appropriate culminating assignment for the entire work.

For example, if students are reading a social studies text about religions of the world, a key idea you want all students to understand could be "The evolution and spread of religion can affect communities by influencing social structures and political beliefs." Another example—for an autobiography students are reading in language arts—might be "Writing about personal experiences can help authors heal from a detrimental situation and provide insight and guidance to readers." For a performing arts class, a core idea for using a dance performance as the text could be "Dancers choreograph a sequence of artistic and expressive movements that incorporate technical expertise and convey meaning." More than one key takeaway might emanate from a work, so consider creating several such statements. This step in the process is akin to the essential understandings that are discussed in Chapter 2.

Step 2: Identify Key Details

To prepare students to address sophisticated questions and deeply examine the text, write a series of text-dependent questions about factual details to orient students. You'll pose these kinds of questions—that typically begin with *who, what, where,* and *when*—to elicit surface and foundational knowledge about the text. Examples include "What is the solar system? What are the main objects in the solar system? Where are different types of water found and in what form?" In answering these questions, students can build confidence that will put them in good stead when grappling with more complex ones.

Step 3: Focus on Vocabulary, Syntax, and Structure

This step provides students with practice that helps prepare them for future reading encounters that contain challenging words, sentence structures, and text features. Find Tier 2 vocabulary words and fashion questions that require students to connect these words to a deeper meaning about the text's conceptual ideas. Furthermore, bring attention to words in the text that carry meaning and, as such, need further examination to illuminate the text. Here are some examples of text-dependent questions pertaining to the way an author uses words and what readers might glean from them:

- Reread this sentence from Andrew Carnegie's (1889) article about wealth: "It is well, nay, essential for the progress of the race, that the houses of some should be homes for all that is highest and best in literature and the arts, and for all the refinements of civilization, rather than that none should be so" (para. 2). Why does Carnegie insert the word *nay*? What impression is he attempting to leave on readers? How does he distinguish houses from homes? What connotations do these words carry?

- Consider the following example: "Sudden gray phantoms seemed to manifest upon inner room walls where a curtain was still undrawn against the night, or there were whisperings and murmurs where a window in a tomb-like building was still open" (Bradbury, 1951). What does the image of "gray phantoms" evoke in this sentence? What other words and phrases does the author use to create a consistent mood? Identify that mood.

- How does the word *pervasive* add dimension to the quote that follows? Would another word convey the point better? "He blamed politicians who catered to racist votes, newspaper editors who fueled the racial tension, and church and business leaders who refused to take responsibility for the pervasive racial hatred in the city" (McKinstry, 2013, p. 74).

- What does the author's word choice of *disheartening* imply in this sentence? What other word contributes to the same impression? "The bleak line of shore surrounding the gray harbor was a disheartening contrast to the shimmering

green and white that fringed the turquoise bay of Barbados which was her home" (Speare, 1986, p. 1).
- The blueberry cheesecake bar recipe uses the verbs *stir*, *whisk*, and *beat* for certain ingredients. What is the difference between these techniques? How do they contribute to the final product? What would happen if a baker did not heed these directions?

Sentence syntax refers to the grammatical arrangement of words in a sentence. Sometimes syntactical difficulties can trip readers up and interfere with understanding an author's meaning. Therefore, highlight complicated passages, and develop questions that help students decode these complex sentences. In addition, entertain questions that lead to a discussion about why the author crafted such seemingly convoluted sentences. Text excerpts with possible text-dependent questions associated with syntax are featured in Figure 5.2.

FIGURE 5.2
Text-Dependent Questions Related to Sentence Syntax

Text Excerpt	Examples of Text-Dependent Questions
"But different men often see the same subject in different lights; and, therefore, I hope it will not be thought disrespectful to those gentlemen if, entertaining as I do, opinions of a character very opposite to theirs, I shall speak sentiments freely, and without reserve." (speech by Patrick Henry)	Divide Patrick Henry's sentence into simpler parts and explain what each part means. Then state the author's overall message.
"It is a melancholy object to those who walk through the great town or travel in the country, when they see the streets, the roads, and cabin doors, crowded with beggars of the female-sex, followed by three, four, or six children, all in rags and importuning every passenger for an alms." ("A Modest Proposal" by Jonathan Swift)	Rewrite this sentence in your own words. What mood does Swift evoke?
"The Earth's crust, on which we live and depend, is in large part the product of millions of once-active volcanoes and tremendous volumes of magma (molten rock below ground) that did not erupt but instead cooled below the surface." (*Volcanoes of the United States* by S. Brantley)	Divide this long sentence into individual sentences that explain its meaning. Change or delete words that do not contribute to the meaning.
"As to the second mode, that of leaving wealth at death for public uses, it may be said that this is only a means for the disposal of wealth, provided a man is content to wait until he is dead before it becomes of much good in the world. . . . The cases are not few in which the real object sought by the testator is not attained, nor are they few in which his real wishes are thwarted." ("Wealth" by Andrew Carnegie)	Rewrite Carnegie's last sentence in the paragraph so that it isn't a double negative. In other words, put it in the positive! Alternatively, explain what the last sentence means.

Finally, craft questions that direct students' focus to the overall structure of the text, including text features that are prevalent in both nonfiction (e.g., subheadings, bold text, graphics) and fiction (e.g., pictures, timelines). Instruct students to preview the text before reading and pay attention to these text features. While reading, ask how these features contribute to comprehension. You might use the following kinds of frames as a starting point to design specific questions related to this aspect of a text:

- How does the _____ (diagram, graph, chart, table) on page _____ allow readers to (understand, identify, recognize) _____?
- Summarize the information from the _____ (diagram, graph, chart, table) on page _____ of _____, including the relationship between the information presented.
- Review the (topographical, physical, political, climate) map on page _____ of _____. How does it reveal specific information about an aspect(s) of (culture, government, religion, politics, economy)?
- Compare two maps of the same region from different time periods. What does the information reveal about the people or culture of the area?
- Notice the distance between _____ and _____ on the map on page _____. How does the distance affect the people of the region in terms of (religion, economy, social interactions)?
- Study the (picture, diagram, graph, chart, table, map) on page _____ and answer this question: _____?
- Using the (picture, graph, chart, table, map) and corresponding text, what inferences can you draw about reasons for _____?
- Rewrite the (headings, subheadings, captions) to support readers in understanding the main idea and key details of the text.
- Create a sidebar for a salient part of the text that provides succinct and interesting information.
- After reading _____, create a timeline that includes important events in chronological order and the cause-and-effect relationships of each.
- Review the timeline on page _____. Add events that you feel are missing and defend your reasoning for why these events are important enough to include.
- Create an alternative plot structure to this narrative and explain why this version is clearer or more compelling than the author's.

Step 4: Illuminate Challenging Text Passages

Create questions that compel students to grapple with challenging areas of the text and thereby provide opportunities for deep examination and analysis. These could be questions that require identification and interpretation of figurative language (e.g., metaphor, simile) or literary devices (e.g., tone, mood, allusion, flashback) and their impact on the work. Alternatively, these questions might ask students to make inferences or draw logical conclusions, identify evidence of the author's writing style and purpose, decipher syntactically difficult sentences—which can overlap with questions in Step 3—or grapple with a conceptually dense part of the text.

Here are some examples:

- "The Pedestrian" is replete with figurative language, specifically imagery, metaphors, and similes. Identify Bradbury's most vivid use of figurative language and explain why it is a strong representation of the story's tone.
- In "The Pedestrian," how does Bradbury use the police car to symbolize progress and Mr. Mead's humanity?
- In *Freakonomics,* authors Levitt and Dubner (2005) state, "But it isn't so much a matter of what you *do* as a parent; it's who you are." Explain the difference between what a parent does versus who a parent is, using examples from Chapter 5 of the book.
- "When a governor or president, who has the power to pardon, refuses to use it in favor of a condemned prisoner, he could then be said to affirm the judgment of the guilt and the sentence. But in *The Sunflower* the narrator had no such power. His refusal to say anything in response to Karl's plea for forgiveness has, therefore, the character of a purely neutral act." Do you agree with Konvitz's conclusion in this quote? Does he make a logical comparison?
- Based on Steinbeck's initial description and interaction of the two characters on page 1 of *Of Mice and Men,* what do you infer about the relationship between these men?
- Explain how geography contributed to the development of Rome.
- How do the small and large intestines differ in function and structural appearance?
- How does a hybrid car engine compare with a traditional car engine?

Step 5: Ensure Standards Are Addressed

Review your grade-level standards. Make sure you write questions that address pertinent standards and serve to illuminate the target text. For example, during a history unit, students might read and compare *A Proud Taste for Scarlet and Miniver* by E. L. Konigsburg with various nonfiction texts about Eleanor of Aquitaine, King Henry II, Thomas Becket, the Crusades, Medieval feasts and tournaments, Constantinople, and other topics related to this time period. Text-dependent questions could address this 7th-grade standard: "Compare and contrast a fictional portrayal of a time, place, or character and a historical account of the same period as a means of understanding how authors of fiction use or alter history" (CCSSI, 2010a, RL.7.9). Alternatively, they could align with this 6th-grade standard, since the historical fiction text includes four characters who provide commentary about the protagonist: "Analyze how an author develops and contrasts the points of view of different characters or narrators in a text" (CCSSI, 2010a, RL.7.6).

Consider all relevant standards, as applicable, such as those related to pertinent content areas and those within all categories and strands of English language arts standards. Examples of standards- and text-based questions for the aforementioned historical text might include the following:

- Respond to these questions based on the novel *A Proud Taste for Scarlet and Miniver* and the nonfiction articles and textbook passages: "How did the relationship between King Henry II and Thomas Becket change through the years? Why was Eleanor opposed to Henry's appointment of Becket as Archbishop of Canterbury?" Compare and contrast your responses based on these different sources.
- After discussion based on the previous questions, address these: "What liberties with history does Konigsburg take and why? What different accounts do the various informational texts provide about the relationship between the historical figures? What can you infer to be the truth based on evidence?"

Step 6: Determine the Sequence of Text-Dependent Questions

At this point, you should have a compilation of questions that represent all different aspects of the text as well as levels of questioning. Consider the best order for how to present these questions so there is a natural progression of understanding. The goal is to build a set of questions that allow students to first develop foundational knowledge about details that are explicitly stated. Then pose more complex questions and tasks that lead to keener insights and analysis, requiring students to examine how those details fit together and impact the work as a whole. Therefore, review all the questions you have designed in the various steps and arrange your finished list of text-dependent questions in a choreographed sequence—possibly aligned to how the text unfolds.

Step 7: Create a Culminating Assessment

Create and assign a final assessment that students will complete independently to demonstrate an understanding of the text. Make sure that this task links to the key ideas of the text (established in Step 1), aligns to relevant standards, includes writing, and—as with responding to text-dependent questions throughout instruction—asks students to use evidence from the text. Following are examples. When assigning tasks, provide students with the criteria against which they will be assessed. For a more detailed discussion and examples of other writing tasks, checklists, and rubrics, see Chapter 7.

- Explain why "The Pedestrian" is an appropriate title for this story or if another would be more suitable. Be sure to cite evidence from the text to support your response.
- Write a detailed letter from the point of view of the large intestine to the small intestine showing appreciation for how you work together for proper digestion. Use detailed evidence from the text about functionality and structure to illustrate the result of successful collaboration.
- Identify a personality trait that describes Auggie at a strategic point in *Wonders*. Using evidence from the text, write a paragraph to explain this trait. At another point in the story, provide a different trait and answer this question: What contributing factors cause Auggie to change?
- Create a graphic organizer that details the major causes and effects of events leading to the American Revolution. Include dates, notable individuals, and a brief synopsis of each event.
- Based on what you read about fitness, develop a personal fitness plan that includes goal setting; the frequency, duration, and intensity of specific exercises; and a means for monitoring your progress. Include a paragraph that answers this question: How can physical activity affect your physical, mental, emotional, and social health?
- After reading and listening to the lyrics of "Strange Fruit" by Billie Holiday, write an essay that discusses how the ballad exemplifies the political, social, and cultural climate of the South during the time it was written. Use evidence from the text to support your thinking.
- Create a multimedia portfolio to share with classmates about an art movement (e.g., Impressionist, Art Nouveau, Pointillism) highlighting the works and techniques of key artists during the era, along with the cultural, religious, or political influences of the time.

Text Connections

There are three kinds of text connections that students are usually asked to make while reading: text to self, text to text, and text to world. Simply put, text to self is when students relate what they read to their own lives and personal experiences. In the CCSS, no explicit mention is made of text-to-self connections. The expectation is that the reading, writing, and speaking that students are asked to do rely on evidentiary support from literary and informational text. "The Common Core emphasizes using evidence from texts to present careful analyses, well-defended claims, and clear information. Rather than asking students questions they can answer solely from their prior knowledge and experience, the standards call for students to answer questions that depend on their having read the texts with care" (CCSSI, 2010d, para. 7).

There are other reasons for keeping teaching experiences wedded directly to the text. For one, it maximizes instructional time when conversations revolve around the text at hand. Since you operate within a very rigid schedule, focusing the lesson on the text itself encourages students to learn skills in the service of the text, such as finding evidence, making inferences, analyzing a literary device, or identifying alternative perspectives. Thus, text-centered discussions and activities serve to illuminate the content and extract deeper meaning. In addition, if you ask questions predicated on personal connections and some students have no personal experience with the subject matter, they are precluded from participating in meaningful discussions. Furthermore, some text-to-self questions allow students to bypass the text entirely when responding; in other words, they are not text-dependent.

Consider these examples: (1) The text highlights heroes who overcome obstacles. When was a time that you overcame obstacles to achieve something? (2) In "Harrison Bergeron," Vonnegut begins with this quote: "The year was 2081, and everyone was finally equal. . . . Nobody was smarter than anybody else. Nobody was better looking than anybody else. Nobody was stronger or quicker than anybody else." What would life be like in this kind of society?

With all this in mind, review potential text-to-self questions critically and perhaps revise some to become text-dependent. It is doubtful that any of us is immune from this practice because even the "best" of us has designed questions that don't require careful reading of the text. However, do not be so quick to scrap questions that spur personal connections. Even though they should not be used as the primary form of instruction, they still have value *after* students have thoroughly examined the text. In fact, questions that let the imagination soar or foster personal connections make for lively discussions. Posing such questions later, though, when students have a firm grasp of the text, can provoke them to refer back to and reexamine the text in a new light. Making personal connections, blended with what they gleaned from the text, can result in richer conversations.

> You're trying to define questions that not only are text dependent but worth asking, worth exploring, that deliver richly, that as you look at the text more closely you see more and more in it because that's the true source of excitement and interest. And I would say, to be clear, that once you've . . . immersed yourself in that, then it might be very interesting after such a close encounter to then say, "How does that resemble or not resemble what I've experienced or seen in others?" (Coleman, 2012)

When relating the text to another text, students can draw parallels in all sorts of ways. For example, they can link similar themes, ideas, concepts, procedures, features, literary devices, characters' and individuals' motivations and interactions, community problems, governance, and so forth. Similarly, they can make different connections by identifying and discussing dissimilarities among texts. "Text" here can literally mean another written work or be used more broadly to refer to works such as a speech, film, photograph, artwork, song, or website. With respect to disciplinary literacy, making text-to-text connections can also involve comparing two diagrams, car engines, dance performances, sports plays, and so forth.

As students read critically, they develop their inventory of information and their intellect; hence, each text they read makes a deposit in their "bank" of knowledge and contributes to their growth. Where pertinent, it is altogether natural and even encouraged that they refer back to previously read text to support an assertion or provide further information. Making text-to-text connections deepens their understanding of the targeted text and allows them to capitalize on what they've already learned. Furthermore, when students conduct research, it is imperative that they compare multiple sources for a variety of reasons, such as verifying facts, cross-referencing and synthesizing information, uncovering bias, and so forth.

Eliciting text-to-world connections occurs when students consider how the topics, concepts, or ideas in the text share commonalities with the past, present, or future world in some way. This could be the local community, a state, the entire country, or a region of the world. Text-to-world connections require students to consider what is going on around them both in close proximity and across the globe, in the present and in the past, and then forging connections (e.g., one idea or theory is similar to another) or disconnections (e.g., this idea or theory is contrary to another). They can examine recurring situations, ideas, or philosophies in the real world for similarities or differences to the text under consideration. Viewing a text through the lens of local and global events and current and past figures, ideas, and innovations—and defending the connections they make—will help students comprehend and strengthen their understanding of the text and broaden their perspectives.

Whenever you incorporate connections as part of your instructional program, your students must be guided to analyze how such connections bring them back to the targeted text to further illuminate it. Tangential responses that divert their attention away from the text should be avoided; students must return to the text at hand and use it as the basis for linking various concepts and ideas.

 ## Cubing

Cubing is a strategy in which pairs or groups of students roll one die or a pair of dice (or cubes) with prompts written on each face as the basis for an oral or written response. There are limitless prompts that can pertain to content across disciplines, so this strategy is extremely versatile.

Any of the text-dependent questions discussed in this chapter can be featured on a cube, or more generic prompts can be used for different texts. If using general questions—What key details lead to an inference? How does a graphic further your understanding of the text?—be sure to augment text-dependent questions throughout instruction around the target text. Since text-dependent questions can be used for diverse text forms, use them across content areas to formulate cube prompts that are aligned to any number of texts (e.g., graphs, photographs, food products, videos, choir performances). When students participate in this instructional strategy, they must use textual evidence in their responses. Even if a prompt fosters a *yes* or *no* answer, referencing the text should still be mandatory (e.g., "Yes, because the text states . . .").

Word your questions and prompts so different responses can apply; otherwise, the activity will be brief if there is only one correct response. For example: "Find a simile and interpret its meaning." Notice that even if this prompt is rolled more than once or twice, each student should still be able to locate and explain different passages with fresh responses.

Cubing can be an informal or formal formative assessment, depending on how students are asked to participate. To conduct a cubing exercise, a student rolls and responds to a prompt orally and then invites others to add to that response or ask for clarification. These conversation exchanges are a means of informal assessment. After discussion, students can produce a written piece that can be used as a more formal assessment. Both oral and written responses should be used to inform instruction. This strategy can be differentiated by assigning students to read different texts based on their interest or readiness. Arrange them in homogeneous groups, and provide cubes with appropriate prompts. If using particularly introspective prompts, consider asking pairs of students to first discuss their impressions and then extend the conversations by instructing each pair to form a foursome and compare and discuss their responses.

Aside from using Cubing as an engaging strategy to discuss and write about a complex published text, consider crafting prompts around strong and weak student writing samples in an attempt to compel students to carefully examine different pieces of writing. This type of exercise can prepare students for their own writing. They can compare and contrast the texts to help them recognize a consistent pattern in the structure and characteristics of a particular genre and focus on areas of the writing that are either weak or strong. Students can examine the writing samples with generic prompts (such as those that follow) for an argumentative, informational, or explanatory piece of writing, and then use text-dependent questions to delve deeper into these student samples. Consider fashioning prompts for types of poetry or fictional narrative as well, such as historical fiction, myths, legends, science fiction, and so forth. Remind students that any *yes* or *no* response must be followed by an explanation citing specifics from the text.

- What is the writer's opinion? Is it clearly stated?
- What is the writer's purpose for this piece?
- Who is the intended audience?
- What strategies does the author use to organize ideas or information?
- Is the thesis appropriate for the whole text?
- Is the thesis statement in the right place?
- What reasons support the author's position? Are they sound?
- Do the topic sentences support the thesis?
- Is the evidence relevant?
- Is there sufficient evidence?
- Is there an appropriate counterclaim?
- How strong is the counterclaim?
- What facts, definitions, quotes, or other information does the writer use to develop the topic?
- Show where sources are cited. Are they correctly cited?
- Is the conclusion complete? What might be missing?
- Point to transitional words and phrases. Are they effective?
- Replace or add transitions, as needed.
- Is the writer's style appropriate for the task?

Cubing can also be used to teach and reinforce vocabulary. Here is a partial list of prompts around vocabulary acquisition:

- Find a word in the text that is unknown to you. Use context clues to define it.
- Identify a context clue the author uses to define a word.
- Replace a weak word with a stronger one.
- Select a word that includes Greek or Latin roots and define it.
- Find a word related to the content. What are examples of it?
- Find a word related to the content. What are nonexamples of it?
- Use a content-related word in a sentence that shows you know what it means.
- Find a word that has multiple meanings. Create different sentences that show these various meanings.
- Find a word that is essential within the context of a passage. Explain its importance and why another word would not work.
- Are any words repeated? What is the effect?
- What words and phrases create mood? Identify the mood.
- What words and phrases create tone? Identify the tone.

In terms of logistics, wooden cubes are available for purchase from teacher or art supply stores. Print prompts onto mailing labels and affix one to each side of the cube, or write the prompts on paper and attach them using double-sided tape.

Alternatively, paper cubes are available through online templates; however, these are not as durable or long-lasting.

. . . . . .

Socratic Method

The Socratic method has proven to be a powerful strategy for eliciting critical thinking. Hattie (2009) specifically refers to this approach as being particularly effective: "As the work of my colleagues and I on the Socratic questioning in the Paideia project has demonstrated, structuring class sessions to entice, teach, and listen to students questioning of students is powerful" (p. 183). This section on the Socratic approach is organized in the following way:

1. Overview and Purpose
2. Appropriate Texts
3. Roles and Responsibilities
4. Lesson Sequence
5. Assessment
6. Resources

Overview and Purpose

Socrates's approach to philosophy and instruction involved responding to his students' questions with a series of continual queries, which encouraged them to think for themselves, clarify their ideas, and seek to arrive at the truth.

In today's classrooms, you can utilize this method in any grade or subject area as a way for students to explore values, issues, and ideas emanating from a specific text. This student-centered pedagogy allows students to be actively engaged in their own learning in a collaborative way to spawn rigorous thought. It is a powerful learning opportunity that has a host of benefits. By engaging in analytical dialogue around a complex text, students can develop critical thinking skills, clarify their own impressions and ideas, engage in divergent thinking, appreciate different points of view, and arrive at new insights and deeper understandings. It also fosters communication skills, since students are taught and encouraged to listen attentively, acknowledge others' comments respectfully, and use transitions to bridge ideas. In addition, students can conduct (text-aligned) research to support their views, which fosters introspective reading of the central and ancillary texts.

A key feature of the Socratic method is that it is predicated on collaboration, discussion, and dialogue to produce a shared understanding. It does not focus on debate and competition, which can be oppositional. High value is placed on open mindedness and receptivity to others' contributions. You can orchestrate either a Socratic circle or a Socratic Seminar. The goal of either configuration is for participants to use questioning as a means of intellectual pursuit to examine and understand ideas, issues, values, and principles emanating from a source text. Socratic circles involve an inner and outer circle; those in the inner circle participate in discussion while the outer circle members observe and coach. Midway through the activity, participants switch roles. This arrangement mimics a fishbowl strategy and lends itself to larger classrooms so students can have a greater opportunity to contribute to the discussion.

Seminars might be more conducive to smaller groups in which all students can participate equally in a scholarly discussion and sit in one circle or square facing one another. In either situation, the main premise is to have students lead a fruitful and intellectual discussion around a central text to gain more meaning from it and supporting texts. Here, I focus primarily on conducting Socratic circles; however, some suggestions can apply to either scenario. If your class is too small to accommodate this arrangement, lead seminars by relying on your own professional expertise to adapt the suggestions I provide. Alternatively, you might consider merging with another class or inviting in colleagues to participate in a circle.

Socratic Circles

In this version of the Socratic method, students form an inner and outer circle.

1. **Inner Circle:** These students engage in discussion for about 10–15 minutes. They should have the text along with their annotations or notes with them during discussion so they can refer to what they have written.
2. **Outer Circle:** These students silently critique the dialogue of the inner circle. They can record their observations on an electronic device or on paper. These notes can include symbols, such as + (strong), √ (good), or – (weak) next to original comments they jot down. Alternatively, teachers can prepare a form to guide them during note-taking, such as the peer observation sheet sample shown in Figure 5.3. At designated time(s), students in the outer circle provide feedback to those in the inner circle.
3. **Switch Roles:** Students switch roles so the outer-circle members become inner-circle members, and vice versa. The inner-circle members now have an opportunity to participate in the discussion while students in the outer circle take notes to share when the discussion ends.

· · · · · ·

Appropriate Texts

A focus text is an essential feature of Socratic discussions; students cull important information from it so they can engage in hearty dialogue. In the process, they stimulate and foster new ideas. Sometimes more than one text is used. For example, (1) two or more texts that represent different views on the same issue, (2) aligned views that can be expressed by different authors, (3) thematically linked subject matter featured in different genres or formats (e.g., a nonfiction article and a poem; a graphic novel and a biography), or (4) two films that are adaptations of the same novel.

FIGURE 5.3

Socratic Discussion Peer Observation Form

	# of Times	Notes
CONTENT PARTICIPATION		
Offers thoughtful and relevant interpretations, comments, or connections; stays focused on discussion.	1 2 3 4 5	
Asks a related, open-ended question.	1 2 3 4 5	
Cites evidence from the text to support or make a point.	1 2 3 4 5	
Augments discussion with relevant research findings.	1 2 3 4 5	
Incorporates relevant vocabulary.	1 2 3 4 5	
CONVERSATIONAL TECHNIQUES		
Shows attentive listening by maintaining eye contact with those who are speaking.	1 2 3 4 5	
Directs comments to the whole group and not just the leader.	1 2 3 4 5	
Speaks clearly and loudly, paces words, and uses proper grammar.	1 2 3 4 5	
Participates respectfully and avoids inappropriate language.	1 2 3 4 5	
Uses transitional phrases to connect to others' comments and acknowledge their contributions. *Examples:* • "I see your point (name), and I was thinking . . ." • "When (name) said . . . , it made me think that . . ." • "Since (name) brought up the point that . . . , shouldn't we consider . . . ?" • "I hear you, (name), and did you consider . . . ?" • "I'm not sure I get your point, (name), so I'd like to clarify. Did you mean . . . ?" • "I'm unclear about your interpretation, (name), so can you show me where in the text you got that impression?"	1 2 3 4 5	

The text or texts can be almost anything—fiction or nonfiction, poetry or prose—and can also include nonprint material, such as artwork, music lyrics, a dance performance, a video clip, and so forth. Since the Socratic method can be conducted across content areas, feel free to use pertinent text based on the subject you teach.

Appropriately challenging texts should be carefully selected so that they are conducive to fostering a deep discussion where there is no right answer but that relates to the concepts of the content area. Through the texts, students should be able to probe relevant issues and extend ideas; therefore, they need to be rich enough for such introspection.

Beside the central text or texts, students investigate other kinds of material (e.g., newspaper article, speech) and use this research to enhance the discussion. Any of these ideas—or certainly others—can contribute to and generate deep discussion.

Roles and Responsibilities

In the Socratic approach, the leader can be the teacher or a trained student. The interaction between the leader and the students is a shared dialogue in which all participants assume active roles. The leader, however, has a unique position in modeling conversational behaviors and insightful thoughts.

While making contributions during discussion, the leader should model how to communicate effectively and respectfully. Also, he or she should demonstrate how to solicit comments from others and bridge responses between contributors. For example, "I'm not sure Carla got to finish her thought. Can you continue, Carla?" "I am interested to hear what Jose has to say. Can you please share your thoughts?" "When Kim shared her idea, it reminded me of . . ." "How do Jorge's and Syd's comments relate to each other?"

When responding to students' comments, the leader might ask for supporting evidence or clarification while maintaining neutrality and avoiding personal opinions or interpretations. For example, "What I think you are saying is . . ." "Let me understand this correctly. I think I heard you say . . ." He or she can also focus attention back to the text by artfully posing challenging questions that might be open to interpretation or stimulate additional discussion around issues or values relevant to the text. The leader can also bring students back to the text as the primary source of information. For example, "What evidence from the text supports your comment?" "Can we bring our attention back to the text? What other ideas emerge from the text that we can discuss?"

The leader should help propel the discussion further by interjecting salient open-ended questions at strategic points to continue discussion where it is halted or needs redirection. He or she must be careful to avoid monopolizing the conversation but rather contribute something that will facilitate more productive discourse among students. Throughout the discussion, the leader must be cognizant and comfortable with wait time. It takes people time to think of responses and ruminate about a question or comment just posed, so it's important to give students the gift of time. Additionally, the leader should be mindful of time parameters so the discussion ends when necessary and with proper closure. Therefore, if students are expected to provide feedback, complete a written exercise, or engage in oral debriefing, the leader needs to budget time accordingly.

Although students observe one another and tally their classmates' involvement during discussion, it's still a good idea for leaders to take notes that will inform future instruction. For example, consider jotting down who contributes more than his or her fair share, who is nonparticipatory, and threads of ideas that didn't get developed (for a future group discussion). To assume this role responsibly, the leader must be intimately familiar with the text and prepare the questions in advance. In addition, he or she needs to be well versed in how to navigate dialogue among a group so ideas flow smoothly, participants maintain a respectful dialogue, and the oral discourse is both rigorous and insightful.

In Socratic discussions, students rotate among various roles: speaking, listening, coaching, and observing. When students are speaking and listening during the actual dialogue, they participate and learn when and how to interject a salient point, dovetail off of one another's comments, and use evidence from the text to support a point—in general, they learn how to engage in intellectual discourse. They should be encouraged not to raise their hands but rather to exchange comments by being cognizant of cues. Specifically, they should pay attention to one another's body language and eye contact and respectfully take turns, just as in an authentic conversational situation.

Other times, it might make sense to pair a student with a designated coach who evaluates his or her participation during discussion. In Socratic circles, you might assign one member of the outer circle with a member of the inner circle so they work together to critique and coach each other's participation. Coaches listen carefully and offer their partners oral or written feedback, such as suggesting additional research, making a new point, praising an insightful comment, or improving communication skills. Leaders can call for a break during the discussion for coaches to confer with their speakers, or they can permit brief consultations among these participants (in whispered voices) during the Socratic discussion.

Additionally, students can participate as keen observers for collective comments among the whole group. In this role, each observer might be assigned to keep track of a particular aspect of the discussion, such as the quality of comments, use of transitions, text evidence citations, honoring different points of view, and so forth. Observers can log these contributions on prepared observation forms or merely with tally marks. Later, they can share their impressions so classmates have tangible feedback on how to improve during future sessions. If some students do not participate in a way that honors the process—by monopolizing the discussion, for example—tally marks that keep track of how much they participate might help them be mindful to limit their input and allow others a chance to speak. The converse can also apply. Students who are reluctant to participate altogether can pay attention to tally marks and be more conscientious of their involvement in future discussions.

Lesson Sequence

Preparation

- **Seating:** In a Socratic seminar, students sit facing one another either in a circle or square with or without desks or tables. If it is a Socratic circle, arrange students' seats in two concentric circles—one inner circle and one outer.
- **Role Assignments/Grouping:** Determine what role each student will assume. For example, inner- and outer-circle members, coaches paired with speakers, or observers who tally or complete observation forms for designated skills. Assign roles, and determine which group will begin the discussion.
- **Schedule:** Post a schedule that shows the structure. For example, designate the amount of time devoted to discussion, coaching and conferring, more dialogue, and so forth.

Before Dialogue

- **Guidelines/Roles:** Review and post the schedule and guidelines, discuss how the seminar will flow, and assign roles to students. Distinguish between a debate and a discussion so students are aware of the focus for the Socratic approach. Distribute and review the information featured in Figure 5.4. Explain that this list contributes to a productive dialogue; with time and repeated practice and reflection, students will be able to hone these skills. Students should adhere to the following ground rules, which you should announce at the beginning of a Socratic discussion:
  - Only participate in a discussion if you have read the text(s).
  - Support your comments with evidence from the text or from research that supports the text.
  - Show respect for all participants.
- **Tools for Improvement:** Hattie (2009) cites goal setting and self-evaluation of how well a student meets his or her targeted goals as strategies that contribute to high achievement. Instruct students to use the items in Figure 5.4 to pinpoint areas of focus that they will particularly strive to achieve during the Socratic discussion. They enter goals at the bottom of the figure prior to beginning the discussion and later reflect on their participation. Another tool for improvement is a self-assessment sheet (Figure 5.5). As students engage in Socratic dialogue (and during any group discussions), instruct them to use Figure 5.5 to reflect on their participation aligned to specific communication skills. You can then share

your observations so they compare their self-assessments with your comments and make a plan for future improvement. In addition, students can use the peer observation form (Figure 5.3) to provide input to designated classmates. It is a companion piece to Figure 5.4, so students should be aware of these expectations.

- **Talking Chips** *(optional)*: All students are expected to participate in some capacity and be actively engaged. If warranted, distribute a certain number of talking chips to each student and explain how they are used. Each time a student contributes a comment, he or she gives up a chip. Once the chips are gone, he or she is finished speaking and then solely concentrates on listening. Those who are hesitant to participate can be encouraged to do so by making sure to use their chips. Determine if this tangible strategy is necessary (or feasible), based on the student composition in your classroom.
- **Reading:** All students are required to read the source text(s) that is the basis for discussion. Assign this text(s) prior to beginning the Socratic discussion. While reading, instruct students to annotate it or complete a graphic organizer. This initial reading and response serves to stimulate students' thoughts in preparation for the Socratic dialogue. Additionally, since the Socratic experience is predicated on a give-and-take discussion, students need to be prepared with not only their comments but also with relevant questions. Therefore, encourage students to devise questions they want to address during the discussion. They can also jot down questions if they need clarification or want to ask classmates about their viewpoints.
- **Preconference:** Allow students enough time to meet with their coaches and exchange ideas and plans in preparation for the discussion. Peers who are providing feedback to others (see Figure 5.5), can preconference to review what they will be listening for during discussion.

During Dialogue

To commence a Socratic session, the leader poses a question and posts it for everyone to see. Leaders, oftentimes teachers, typically provide the leading question. However, you might conduct a question formulation activity—described in detail in the next section—in which students generate, group, and rank questions to arrive at the strongest one to begin the discussion. The questions they generate can also be used throughout the dialogue. To craft the initial question or prompt, consider that it (1) is provocative enough to generate discussion and dialogue, (2) allows for open-ended responses, and (3) requires text evidence to answer.

Once the launch question is posed, participants return to the text and begin to respond and pose additional questions to classmates. The leader should strive for a natural fluid discussion to evolve; however, he or she can ask a prepared question if responses are not forthcoming and there is a hesitancy to get the dialogue moving.

FIGURE 5.4
Socratic Discussion

Effective participants . . .	Ineffective participants . . .	NOTES
CONTENT PARTICIPATION		
• Bring notes and text to the discussion to show proper preparation. • Offer thoughtful and relevant interpretations, comments, or connections; stay focused on the discussion. • Ask a related, open-ended question. • Consider different points of view. • Cite evidence from the text to support or make a point. • Augment discussion with relevant research findings. • Incorporate relevant vocabulary. • Ask for clarification, if needed. • Take notes during the discussion, if needed, to clarify ideas or remember certain points.	• Monopolize the discussion. • Fail to participate in discussion. • Make contributions that are off-topic. • Come unprepared to the discussion. • Lack evidence to support points. • Engage in debate rather than a collective discussion.	
CONVERSATIONAL TECHNIQUES		
• Maintain eye contact with those who are speaking. • Direct comments to the whole group and not just the leader. • Listen attentively. • Call other participants by name. • Speak clearly and loudly, pace words, and use proper grammar. • Participate respectfully. • Avoid monopolizing the conversation or interrupting a speaker. • Use transitional phrases to connect to others' comments and acknowledge their contributions.	• Interrupt a speaker. • Disagree (or agree) with others disrespectfully. • Talk out of turn. • Speak inaudibly or too fast so others cannot hear or understand their comments. • Initiate sidebar conversations. • Fail to acknowledge others' contributions. • Use foul and inappropriate language.	
GOAL SETTING		
Before: What goals will you focus on during this discussion?		
After: How well do you feel you met your goals?		

FIGURE 5.5
Self-Assessment

Reflect on how well you participate in group or class discussion by completing this self-assessment. Your teacher will review it and offer comments. Compare how you rate yourself with your teacher's comments to see if they match. At the bottom, identify a goal for the next time you engage in discussion with others.

	+	√	--	**Teacher Comments**
1. I ask questions that make others think carefully. *My comments:*				
2. I make thoughtful contributions to the discussion. *My comments:*				
3. I refer to others' comments when I speak. I use these or similar linking phrases: • *Although I think _____ made a good point, my thoughts are _____.* • *I agree with _____ when he/she says _____, and I also think _____.* • *I respectfully disagree with _____ because I think _____.* *My comments:*				
4. I encourage others to participate in the discussion. *My comments:*				
My goal for the next discussion:				

Symbol key: + *consistently;* √ *sometimes;* – *not much*

Each question or comment is intended to lead to further analysis, insight, and possibly research. Through generating and responding to questions, students process the information and arrive at a deeper level of understanding. Research might be required or suggested during the discussion as students investigate more support for a particular idea or point.

Coaches do their part during discussion to record information that provides useful feedback to their assigned partners. Again, coaches can use Figure 5.3 to record notes to share with their peers at appointed times during the discussion. You can also use this form to assign tasks to observers whose job is to track specific aspects of performance during the discussion (e.g., cite evidence, make transitions). Remember that roles rotate at designated points and then discussion resumes.

After Dialogue/Closing

At the end of the Socratic discussion, ask for volunteers to summarize the main points of the conversation or offer a salient overarching statement that expresses a synthesis of the various points that were raised. Pose evaluative questions that prompt students to share their opinions and observations in connection with the text and the ideas that emerged from the discussion. Leaders might pose the following kinds of questions:

- What different perspective do you have now versus at the beginning of the discussion?
- How did the process help you better understand the text?
- What major statement can summarize your impression of the topic?
- How do the ideas and issues we discussed connect to our world today or to another text?
- Do you agree with the author's perspective? In what significant way do you have a different impression of particular ideas?
- Why is it important that people are aware of these ideas or issues?

If there wasn't an opportunity during the discussion for students to share their feedback and observations, make sure to do so now at the end. Students need to be mindful of what they did well and recognize areas for improvement so they can prepare for future Socratic discussions. Finally, you might have students return to Figure 5.4 to reflect on or take notes on how well they accomplished their goals.

Assessment

As mentioned, students can self-assess to determine how well they participated in a Socratic discussion by paying particular attention to the goals they set at the start of the dialogue. You can also evaluate students' involvement using a combination of feedback: students' self-assessment, peer evaluation, and your own observations about students' communication (speaking and listening) and reasoning skills.

Additionally, students can write reflectively about their participation and include what they would do differently in future Socratic discussions. They can mention what they did well and how it contributed to successful participation in the process, along with perspectives for the ideas and issues that emanated from the text. This writing would be more comprehensive than the notes they recorded on Figure 5.4.

Resources

An Internet search will yield many valuable resources for Socratic approaches. In addition, I suggest using one or both of the following short videos from the Teaching Channel, which feature Socratic circles in a high school language arts class. Besides viewing them to gain professional expertise, use them as an instructional tool both to show students what a Socratic discussion looks like if they have not yet engaged in this strategy and to highlight a particular aspect of Socratic discussions that students might need help implementing. Although the videos are shot in a language arts classroom, the structure and skills embedded in these videos are adaptable to any content area and can also be modified for middle school or possibly upper-elementary grades.

- **"Patience & Practice" (7 minutes):** The focus for this seminar is on discussing the meaning and importance of poetic language. What is particularly noteworthy about this clip is how the teacher capitalizes on wait time to get results. She also explains and shows how to incorporate goal setting and rubrics so students can self- and peer-assess. As students become more proficient in Socratic participation, you can change their method of evaluation throughout the year to reflect growing expectations. (Link: https://www.teachingchannel.org/videos/bring-socratic-seminars-to-the-classroom)
- **"The 'N-Word'" (6 minutes):** This video is centered on the use of language in Mark Twain's *Adventures of Huckleberry Finn*. It clearly defines the various roles students play: speaker (inner circle having organic discussion around text), listener (coach assigned to specific student in inner circle, listening for comments; help at halftime to become a more effective speaker), and evaluators (various students count comments and track transitions, quotes, and thematic questions and ideas). The video clip shows how students rotate among these roles, orchestrate inner and outer circles, utilize half-time peer coaches, and focus on their participation. (Link: https://www.teachingchannel.org/videos/teaching-the-n-word)

 # Question Formulation

Typically, leaders launch a Socratic circle or seminar through a provocative question that is posed to the group. In addition, a list of relevant questions is prepared in case the participants reach a lull in the conversation and need stimulation to examine a new idea. These questions are also used in the event the conversation needs redirection. What is presented in this section is a suggestion for orchestrating a learning situation in which students generate a host of questions and then determine which ones they want to use as the basis for launching a Socratic discussion (or other task).

The following details feature an adapted sequence of the Question Formulation technique from the Right Question Institute, a non-profit organization that teaches a process for generating questions (Rothstein & Santana, 2011). By implementing this strategy, students not only learn a process for developing questions but also begin to engage with the text and choose areas that are of most importance and interest. Before students begin, provide a brief overview of the process and its purpose—creating and determining which questions to address in the Socratic discussion. If you are using this process for another purpose, then merely state how the questions will be used.

1. **Assign the text as the focus for developing questions.** Students should begin by reading the text that will be the focal point of the Socratic discussion. In addition to taking notes or completing a graphic organizer, ask students to record the questions they would like to address. Tell them they will have a chance to share these questions later.

2. **Option A: Brainstorm.** Instruct groups to brainstorm questions; tell them they can use those they individually crafted. During the brainstorming exercise, tell them to abide by the following rules (if they aren't familiar with them already):
   - Record every question exactly as it is stated.
   - Do not stop to discuss, judge, or answer any question that someone contributes.
   - Change any statement into a question.

3. **Option B: Roundtable.** Arrange students into small group of three to four. Instruct each group to write as many questions as they can that pertain to the text. Use a roundtable strategy in which there is one piece of paper per group and each student has a pen or pencil. The paper begins with a designated person and then rotates in a clockwise fashion. Each student writes down one question each time the paper comes to him or her. At some point, a student may say "pass" if he or she is out of ideas, but others may still contribute. For this exercise, it's a good idea to set a time limit.

4. **Share questions.** Orchestrate a whole-class session in which each group shares one question at a time. Record the questions on an easel, a whiteboard, or a sheet of chart or butcher paper; alternatively, type them on a computer that is projected for all students to see. Tell students to pay attention to each entry that is recorded so that when they report out, they do not duplicate another group's question. By the same token, if a group has a question that is similar to one already recorded but students think theirs is worded better, they should state it and let the class determine which version is strongest.

5. **Identify types of questions.** Students carefully review the class list and notate an *O* by each question that is open-ended and a *C* for those that are close-ended (i.e., can be answered with *yes* or *no*). If students are not aware of the difference between these types of questions, make sure to educate them. If one type of question appears significantly more often than another, ask students to produce more questions. Discuss why a variety of open- and closed-ended question types is needed.

6. **Prioritize questions.** This is a three-step process:
   - Students work in their groups to prioritize the class-generated list of questions based on what they consider to be the most important and interesting issues to discuss during the Socratic discussion. They can number the questions or merely circle the questions they think are most worthy of addressing—because answering them will illuminate the text and allow them to understand it more deeply. Of their top choices, ask them to put an asterisk next to the one question they feel would be best for launching the discussion. This needs to be a provocative and compelling question that requires text evidence and fosters a lot of discussion and ideas (as previously discussed in the preceding section on Socratic discussions).
   - Ask groups to report out to the class.
   - Together, compare students' collective input and rank the whole-class list to arrive at an agreement about which question should be used to launch the Socratic dialogue.

7. **Use questions.** Use the chosen question to launch the discussion. Save the other questions for the leader to use if there is a time during the dialogue when conversation is halted or needs redirection.

· · · · · ·

Closing

Strategies for initial exposure to complex text begin to get students primed for richer comprehension. The role of well-designed and facilitated questioning sessions around complex text allows students to delve deeper. Therefore, capitalize on different types of teaching and questioning techniques to generate meaningful dialogue that promotes deeper examination of the text. Through their participation, students develop new perspectives and insights, make inferences and draw conclusions, connect to other texts, cull evidence, and critique and examine aspects of the author's work—all in an effort to expand their critical thinking and store of knowledge. This is a lofty endeavor and orchestrated with clear sights on learning goals so the complex text—and the questions used to illuminate it—are part of a sound comprehensive program.

6
More Strategies and Activities for Teaching Complex Text

Up to this point, I've focused on various aspects of complex text, what it is, how to design lessons around it, and how to introduce and teach it. I've also shared several activities and strategies to teach salient words and terms, craft text-dependent questions, conduct Socratic discussions, and use text structure. This chapter focuses squarely on more instructional strategies, teaching methods, and activities to formatively assess. The subsequent and final chapter features various writing assignments—an essential element in a robust instructional program for diving deeper into a text to gain keener insights and demonstrate understanding.

Reading Strategies

Before discussing and presenting instructional strategies, it is important to touch on the role that teaching specific reading strategies plays within the curriculum. Some dedicate individual units of study to teaching a particular reading strategy, such as questioning, visualizing, or summarizing, throughout the school year. Sometimes there is no direct correlation between a reading strategy and the text at the center of instruction. The designers of the CCSS implore you to rethink this practice and avoid conducting isolated lessons on particular reading strategies. Instead, lead with the text as the focal point and intentionally determine which strategy best aligns with the work so students can use the newly learned strategy to gain access and deep meaning from the complex text. This approach enables a clear link and application between the strategy and the reading material.

Reading strategies should work *in the service of* reading comprehension (rather than an end unto themselves) and assist students in building knowledge and insight from specific texts. To be effective, instruction on specific reading techniques should occur when they illuminate specific aspects of a text. Students need to build an infra-structure of skills, habits, knowledge, dispositions, and experience that enables them to approach new challenging texts with confidence and stamina. As much as possible, this training should be embedded in the activity of reading the text rather than being taught as a separate body of material. (Coleman & Pimentel, 2012, p. 9)

Be conscientious about how to teach reading strategies, and incorporate only those that support comprehension of the text at hand. Eventually, students will have an arsenal of strategies at their beck and call, so when they encounter complex text on their own they can intuitively pull from that inventory. As you personally read, no one is formally teaching you how to clarify, ask and answer questions, or visualize. You know when a passage is difficult and automatically use applicable strategies to make sense of it. This is the goal for your students as well. Therefore, it's critical to help them build their competencies with reading strategies while experiencing a complex text—not as a separate unit before or even after a text is read. The text should serve as the vehicle to illustrate which strategies students use so they can master self-sufficient reading.

Strategies and Activities: Valuable Assessment Opportunities

Figure 6.1 provides previously introduced strategies and activities, along with others that appear in this and the final chapter. Notice the *X* inserted in different cells. This denotes options for flexibility in using a strategy at various points while reading or in various grouping configurations. For example, Annotation might be selected for initial exposure to a particular text and again while reading the text. Students can begin by annotating individually, share either with partners or in small groups, and finally report a synthesis of peer impressions with the whole class.

I haven't yet met a teacher who didn't have a plentiful supply of preferred strategies and activities. Nevertheless, in this chapter, I present several strategies and activities, which appear in the following list, that can be used at different points throughout a lesson. Many of them are appropriate for almost any subject, but some adaptations will likely be needed. If you teach technical subjects, keep in mind the broad definition of *complex text* and discussion of disciplinary literacy presented in Chapter 1.

- Think-Write-Group-Share
- Dialectical (Double-Entry) Journal

FIGURE 6.1
Strategies and Activities Organizer

Chapter	Teaching Strategies and Learning Activities	Initial Exposure(s)	During	After	Individual	Pairs	Small Group	Whole Class
2	Think Aloud	X						X
2	Modeling	X						X
2	4-Square Collaborative Graphic Organizer	X	X	X			X	
2	Exit Cards	X	X		X			
3	Jigsaw	X	X				X	
3	Annotation (Active Reading Notes)	X	X		X	X	X	
3	Turn-and-Talk	X	X			X		
3	Think-Pair-Share	X	X		X	X		X
3	Reciprocal Teaching	X	X			X	X	X
3	Text Structure	X	X		X	X	X	
4	Vocabulary • Preassessment • Context Clues • Mini-poster • Parts of Speech Tests • 4-Square Vocabulary Graphic Organizer • Semantic Feature Analysis • Routine Writing Tasks • Word Construction and Deconstruction • Appositives	X	X	(X)	X	X	X	X

Grouping/Collaboration Options: Individual, Pairs, Small Group, Whole Class

Chapter	Teaching Strategies and Learning Activities	Initial Exposure(s)	During	After	Individual	Pairs	Small Group	Whole Class
5	Cubing		X			X	X	
5	Socratic circles		X	X				X
5	Question Formulation		X	X	X	X	X	X
6	Think-Write-Group-Share		X		X		X	X
6	Dialectical (Double-Entry) Journal		X		X			
6	Graphic Organizers		X		X	X	X	
6	Manipulatives		X			X	X	
6	Diamanté Poem Adaptation		X		X	X		
6	Active Participation Strategies	X	X		X			
7	Writing Prompts		X	X	X			
7	Attribute Poem		X	X	X	X		
7	Complex Instruction		X	X			X	
7	RAFT		X	X	X	X		

- Graphic Organizers
- Manipulatives
- Diamanté Poem Adaptation
- Active Participation Strategies

For optimal efficacy, be deliberate in choosing each strategy and activity. In other words, before deciding which ones to embed within a lesson sequence (like those explained in Chapter 2), consider factors such as the target skill and purpose for reading, the type of complex text under consideration, which part of the text is the focus for instruction, your specific student population, and even time constraints.

Permit yourself to change a strategy or method if the one you are using doesn't produce the positive results you had intended. That means you have to be alert and aware of the impact (or lack thereof) that the strategy has on your students. Hattie (2012) asserts that educators shouldn't monopolize their time focusing on a particular method or strategy, such as cooperative versus individualistic teaching or homogeneous versus heterogeneous groups, and so forth. "Our attention, instead, should be on the effect that we have on student learning—and sometimes we need multiple strategies and, more often, some students need different teaching strategies from those that they have been getting. A strong message from the findings in *Visible Learning* is that, more often than not, when students do not learn, they do not need 'more'; rather, they need 'different'" (p. 93).

The strategies and activities that you select for students to engage in are all opportunities for formative and self-assessments. Collect, interpret, and use the evidence that students produce to make informed decisions about what happens next in the learning cycle, such as enrich, reteach, slow down, speed up, keep going, or practice more. You aren't the only assessors, though; students can and should be taught how to assess their own learning. When both teacher and student collaborate on what is working, what is not, where there is a sticking point, what needs to happen next, how will it happen, and so forth, there are actionable reflections and goals that foster dedicated learning. And do not feel compelled to grade everything; some work is merely intended as practice for honing a skill.

> Routinely grading formative or ongoing assessments predictably impedes learning in at least three ways. First, it misrepresents the learning process to students, leading them to conclude that making errors is cause for punishment rather than an opportunity to improve. . . . Second, it focuses students more on getting good grades than on learning. Third, it makes the classroom environment seem unsafe for many students—and would make it seem unsafe to more students if classwork were appropriately challenging for the full range of learners. (Tomlinson & Moon, 2013, p. 62)

Think-Write-Group-Share: Version 1

Think-Write-Group-Share, an adaptation of Think-Pair-Share can be used for students to use the power of collective conversations around a text to gain deeper meaning. Here is how this strategy works:

1. **Think:** After students read a section of text, pose a thought-provoking question, such as one that asks them to analyze the passage and make inferences, or identify a problem and some possible solutions. Allow time for them to consider responses independently.
2. **Write/Draw:** Students then record their impressions in response to the query, using writing or drawing to crystallize their thinking. They can write brief summaries or analogies; or draw graphics, symbols, or sketches.
3. **Group:** Instruct students to share and discuss their individual work with a small group. On a large sheet of paper, each group can craft a cohesive response that incorporates a collection of individual responses.
4. **Share:** When finished, small groups present their work to the whole class. Together, discuss similar threads of understanding, contrasting views, and insights.

· · · · · ·

 Think-Write-Group-Share: Version 2

In this collaborative learning strategy, students discuss and agree on the main idea and significant details of a text and articulate what they glean by producing either a summary or graphic representation. Students then compare the content and format of these products to extend and cement their learning. The specific details for how this activity can be conducted, along with a list of discussion questions for further introspection, are listed in Figure 6.2.

This exercise grounds students in the main ideas, details, and vocabulary of a text. It is conducted after two encounters with the text and students have taken notes or annotations specific to the text type (e.g., purpose or argument, evidence, key details). In the last step shown on the figure, students will be well positioned to engage in more sophisticated discussions guided by text-dependent questions where they can make inferences, compare and contrast ideas, apply concepts, synthesize information, and so forth.

· · · · · ·

 Dialectical (Double-Entry) Journal

In this strategy, students are given time for reflection based on a particular self-selected quote in a text. To begin, they choose a quote and write it on the left side of a two-column chart. They also include a reference to the passage, such as a page, paragraph, or chapter number. On the right-hand side, students respond by selecting one choice from a list of options. Once they finish, they are prepared to engage in a thoughtful discussion with others.

FIGURE 6.2
Think-Write-Group-Share: Version 2

Teacher	• **Overview to students:** Explain that this activity is conducted after at least two exposures with the text. 1. Review your notes based on previous readings of the text. 2. Confer with your classmates to confirm and improve your notes. 3. Work with others to produce either a summary or graphic organizer. • **Resources:** Text and students' notes • **End product:** Half of the student groups write a summary; the other half creates a graphic organizer based on the text.
Students Independently ↓	• **Step 1: Review and Edit Notes/Annotations** - Review your notes or annotations to confirm your impressions of the author's main idea, argument, evidence, supporting details, and so forth. Make sure to include any key terms and definitions. - Reread the text, as needed, to verify and refine your notes.
Groups ↓	• **Step 2: Share Notes and Arrive at a Consensus** - Share and discuss your notes about key aspects of the text, including terms and their definitions, with a small group. - Ask for or offer clarification, as needed. Use evidence from the text for verification. - Arrive at a group consensus; make adjustments to your notes based on the group discussion. • **Step 3: Create a Group Project** - Collectively write a paragraph summary or create a graphic representation of the content including vocabulary terms. - Transfer your work onto a large sheet of paper to post and share.

Whole Class ↓	• **Step 4: Share and Discuss**
	- Present the summary or graphic representation to the class.
	- Discuss using these questions:
	  • How do the summaries and graphic representations complement each other?
	  • Are the main ideas and details captured best in one form or another? Is it necessary to have both?
	  • Did groups create different graphic organizers? Does each appropriately convey the information and mirror the structure of the text?
	  • Is information missing, overdone, or incorrect in either piece? If so, what? Refer to the text to support your response.
	  • What conclusions can you draw from this exercise? How did it help enhance your understanding of the text?

Students	• **Step 5: Respond to Text-Dependent Questions** - Respond to text-dependent questions and tasks for specific purposes (e.g., compare-contrast with other texts or ideas, make inferences, predict, critique, etc.). - *Optional:* Return to the group summaries and graphic organizations to revise, as needed.

To differentiate, find appropriately challenging quotes for both struggling and high achievers; students choose one from among these preselected options as the basis for a response. You might think that a high achiever does not need support in choosing quotes; however, some do not work to their potential and quickly choose a quote they can easily respond to without exerting much effort. Therefore, it might be beneficial to find three quotes from the passage that will suitably challenge these particular students. For struggling learners, it might be overwhelming for them to select a quote, so providing them with two or three options narrows the field and makes the activity more accessible. Although these are worthwhile differentiation techniques, many students can self-select a quote that represents an appropriate challenge level without your support.

Following are suggestions for the kinds of quotes students can extract from the text and a list of response options. Consider adaptations that might be warranted. For example, a double-entry journal in which students record a quote about a historical event and discuss its implications might be more effective as a triple-entry journal. A third column can include connections to modern-day world events and how the political and social impacts were similar.

Types of Possible Quotes. The quote students select should be something they feel is significant in some way. Consider the learning goals of your lesson when explaining which quotes to target. These examples are some of the many possibilities; revise as necessary for your content area. The quoted excerpt

- Provides reasoning or evidence for an assertion.
- Raises doubt.
- Contains lofty ideas in need of interpretation.
- Shows an example of the concept.
- Includes figurative language (e.g., imagery, simile, metaphor).
- Includes a literary device (e.g., allusion, symbolism, dialect).
- Represents the main idea.
- Reveals information about a character, individual, or historical figure.
- Shows a continuation of a pattern (e.g., words, actions, motifs, images, behavior).
- Reflects a turning point or shift.
- Reflects the writer's style.
- Reveals an epiphany or phenomenon.
- Indicates a belief or value system.
- Is interesting, surprising, or confusing in some way.

Response Options. The selected quote, of course, will drive which response students choose and make. Examples can include any of the following or original ones you create. When giving students an option for how to respond, provide choices that illuminate the text and are appropriate for your student group; don't overwhelm them with choices. Students can respond to the quote by

- Explaining the author's meaning.
- Interpreting figurative language.

- Making a connection to another text or to the world (e.g., event, character, individual, situation, behavior, pattern).
- Explaining the impact of this quote on the whole passage.
- Explaining the political, economic, or social impact of the quote.
- Creating questions to explain why the quote is confusing.
- Identifying the literary device used and what it might mean.
- Restating the claim and providing a counterargument.
- Explaining faulty reasoning or evidence.

 Graphic Organizers

Graphic organizers are a visual representation of information that can be used as an effective instructional tool. There are all sorts of organizers intended for different purposes. Incorporating them into your lessons for reading, writing, listening, or speaking across content areas could prove a powerful learning tool. They represent a useful strategy to teach text structure (as discussed in Chapter 3); organize students' writing, presentations, and speeches; and connect to and make sense of concepts and ideas that students read, hear, or watch. Utilizing this strategy compels students to discern peripheral and irrelevant information from that which is salient and important. Creating an organizer can be an individual activity, a highly collaborative one, or a combination of both.

Graphic organizers are typically divided into four basic categories: sequential, cyclical, hierarchical, and conceptual. Sequential organizers, as the name denotes, depict a process, such as cause and effect, problem and solution, flowchart, chronology, or time order. Cyclical organizers, unlike sequential ones where there is a beginning and an end, reflect a sequence that is continuous. A hierarchical organizer has a main idea, topic, or concept with subordinate parts at different levels (e.g., subtopics, subcategories). Conceptual organizers feature a key focus concept and show how other concepts and ideas branch out from it—but not necessarily in a ranked, hierarchical order.

What follows is a sample of possible ideas for using graphic organizers. (Later in this section are some suggested activities aligned to them.)

- **Record information:** As students read text; listen to a presentation, lecture, or guest speaker; or watch a video or demonstration, have them complete a graphic organizer to make sense of the information. This can help them understand, retain, and use what they record for a future purpose. Students can create their own graphic organizers, or you can provide a blank one for them to use.
- **Collect and synthesize information:** Arrange students in groups and give each one a question that is associated with the text. For example, if students were studying about the Middle Ages in England, assign one of these questions to each group: How did feudalism develop in medieval England? How did feudalism affect

the economy of medieval England? How was feudalism in medieval England influenced by the physical geography? How did feudal relationships in medieval England contribute to political order or unrest? Instruct students to create a group graphic organizer based on the guiding question, using any structure they feel best captures their response to their question. For example, one group might decide to create a concept map, whereas another might complete a cause-and-effect organizer. When finished, each group passes its organizer to another group, who reads what is recorded and then makes additions or revisions without re-creating the structure the original group made. The organizers are passed to another group to repeat the process until all groups provide input on each one. Ask each group to use a different-colored pen so each contribution is distinguishable from another. After the organizers have rotated among the groups, return them to the original groups who will discuss all of the entries, cross out duplications or incorrect information, merge similar and related information, add any new insights, and agree that everything is based on evidence from the text. Then each group writes a summary statement that succinctly responds to the guiding question. As a class, compare the statements and arrive at a collective impression that conceptually captures the essence of the text.

- **Use as a prewriting tool:** Graphic organizers are excellent prewriting tools. Prior to composing their first drafts, students can create a graphic organizer and partner with another student to discuss the ideas they brainstormed and elicit peer feedback. Allow time for students to revise their brainstorming sheets based on classmates' input before they write their drafts.
- **Create a human organizer:** Clear out empty space in the classroom or go outside and let students create a human organizer. They can work in groups to organize information in some way using their bodies. For example, they can link arms or situate themselves in height order to represent a hierarchy. After groups display themselves in a particular way, their classmates should try to determine how the content fits their stances. (You might need to set safety parameters in the event, for example, students want to stand on each others' shoulders to mimic hierarchical relationships.)
- **Introduce plot structure through music:** Play music and instruct students to draw a visual representation of what they hear. They don't need to include words. I've used Tchaikovsky's *1812 Overture* for this exercise, which aptly mirrors a story's series of problems and high points leading to a climax and then slowly resolving. Then show the basic plot structure of an inverted check (see Figure 6.3), and explain how it is a graphic depiction of a basic storyline. Students compare their work to this graphic organizer and determine if they graphically represented certain plot elements, such as the suspense in a rising action or the climactic moment. Option: Review or show the basic plot diagram first, and then have students listen

to the music and draw an alternative diagram that still accounts for the plot elements. They should use the text (music, in this case) to show evidence of the central conflict, rising action, and so forth.

Inverted Check Plot Diagram

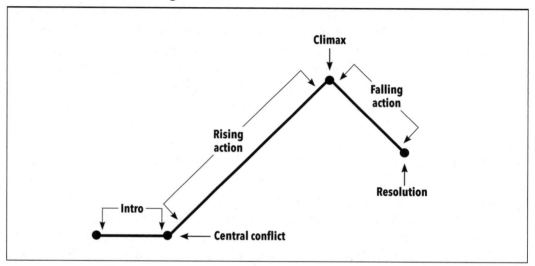

There are all sorts of ways to differentiate when using graphic organizers. Students can create their own organizers or access software programs to design them electronically. Alternatively, you can download and print an assortment of graphic organizers for classroom use from the websites listed in Figure 3.10 (p. 67). Peruse these and other websites carefully to ensure you are selecting the appropriate types and ranges of organizers based on several factors: lesson goals and purpose, student task, complex text, grade, and learning style and readiness level of your students. Do not feel compelled to use only what is readily available. Customize your own organizer aligned to a specific task if it makes good sense.

Be mindful that some students might need more direction than others, and some will need partially completed organizers or a word bank. When using organizers to access complex text, depending on the complexity of the text and students' ability levels, consider presenting a small section of text at a time. Alternatively, begin by modeling for the whole class or a small group how to cull salient information from the text and chart the information onto a selected graphic organizer.

Concept Maps

Concept maps are an effective visual representation tool for organizing, synthesizing, summarizing, and identifying knowledge related to a problem, issue, or topic (Novak & Musonda, 1991). This type of graphic organizer, which is an excellent tool to elucidate complex text, shows connections between and among concepts and ideas, which allows students to visualize the relationships and show cohesion among information. Concept maps are predicated on a hierarchical structure (although sometimes procedures are embedded) with a key concept or idea typically at the top and subordinate and connected relationships extending below or out from there. A central element of concept maps is the use of linking words or phrases, which connect one cell to another—thus diagraming the various relationships to further enhance understanding. Some examples of linking terms are *includes, such as, for example, causes, requires, influences, produces, uses, determines, contains,* and *as a result of.* Another important aspect is that each concept, subconcept, or idea is entered once; however, arrows and linking words can indicate its function in multiple ways. See the concept map example (for photosynthesis) in Figure 6.4.

The following list features activity ideas related to concept maps that are designed to illuminate complex text.

- Before creating concept maps, expose students to surface knowledge relevant to the complex text as a stepping stone to key and subordinate concepts. Have them use this information to begin constructing a concept map and continue to add to and refine it as they reread the text and respond to text-dependent questions.
- To check for understanding, ask students to brainstorm a list of significant terms and phrases pertaining to the content. As a class, critique and revise this list as needed. Then ask students to use the terms and phrases to create their own concept maps.
- To differentiate, provide students with a partially completed map for those who need the support.
- As students create their concept maps, write statements that show the relationship between concepts (see Figure 6.4). Students will use this map and these statements to write a cohesive summary paragraph.
- Have students color code or use consistent shapes to indicate groupings of particular concepts. In fact, they can begin their concept maps with color-coded sticky notes so they can easily move concepts and linking words around as they recognize different connections and new additions.
- In addition to using concept maps to make sense of complex text, this strategy can also be used as a prewriting tool to brainstorm and organize ideas in preparation for researching and writing about a topic.

FIGURE 6.4

Photosynthesis Concept Map

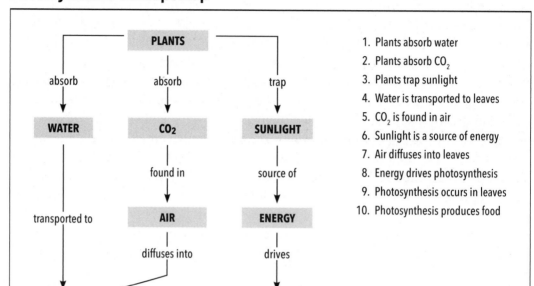

1. Plants absorb water
2. Plants absorb CO_2
3. Plants trap sunlight
4. Water is transported to leaves
5. CO_2 is found in air
6. Sunlight is a source of energy
7. Air diffuses into leaves
8. Energy drives photosynthesis
9. Photosynthesis occurs in leaves
10. Photosynthesis produces food

Source: From "Concept Mapping in Biology," by I. M. Kinchin, 2000, *Journal of Biological Education, 34*(2), p. 66. Copyright 2000 by Taylor & Francis. Reprinted with permission.

When assessing a concept map, look for several factors to gain insight into students' thinking so you can redirect, reinforce, or validate, as needed. The overall structure students use can uncover accurate or faulty impressions of the content that is the basis for the map. Additionally, review the concepts they use as an indicator of accuracy and completeness. Equally important is assessing how students connect the concepts and ideas. If the arrows and linking terms are not correct, this can lead to future misleading interpretations. After reviewing students' concept maps, immediate feedback is critical so they know what, if any, corrections need to be made to continue learning on the right path. In general, timely feedback for all formative assessments is a prudent practice that contributes greatly to student success.

4-Square

The 4-Square is a versatile graphic organizer with innumerable possibilities. In the series of examples shown in Figure 6.5, each quadrant has a different prompt that relates to a central stimulus. Use these examples to customize an organizer based on a particular learning focus for your class. For grouping, students can work in pairs or small groups, or you can conduct a Think-Pair-Share in which they complete the organizer individually, discuss with a partner, and then share with another pair or the whole class.

- In the first example, students place a stimulus in the center box. This version can be adapted to suit countless topics across content areas: historical or current event, war, Supreme Court case, scientific discovery, innovation, technological invention, natural phenomenon, progressive artistic movement, and so forth.
- The second example focuses on a specific perspective. A particular event or situation is placed in the center, and students respond to it through the eyes of various individuals or groups of people. Of course, any number of people can be included in the quadrants; individuals associated with the Civil War is just one example. Students can complete organizers for each topic they study and then compare the organizers throughout the year to determine similar themes. You can also adapt and use this organizer in other subject areas to compare and contrast different points of view.
- The third example is a variation—4-Square +1—that focuses on characterization. It can be used for literary characters, historical figures, scientists . . . almost any individual. After students complete the quadrants with information from the text, they use this information to assign a personality trait that is ultimately derived from text evidence.
- Finally, the fourth example asks students to determine the social, political, and economic impact of the central topic. This can include an event, idea, innovation, law, scientific or medical discovery, environmental condition, and so forth. In addition, students should consider how that topic connects to something from either the past or today. This version can also be used as an expansion of ideas first laid out in a basic 4-Square, such as the first example.

· · · · · ·

Manipulatives

Manipulatives are referred to as any item that students physically handle that supports hands-on learning. Math manipulatives—pattern blocks, counters, shapes, tiles, and so forth—are routinely used to practice and teach skills and concepts to increase understanding. You can also make manipulatives that address skills to support comprehension. For this activity example, sentence strip manipulatives are used to teach students how to identify and critique plot elements and sequence.

Figure 6.6 shows sentence strips for the plot of a version of *Cinderella*. A complete set is given to each small group of students in the class. Students lay out the strips and arrange them on the floor or a large table in sequential order. They then organize the

FIGURE 6.5
4-Square Examples

What is (or what caused): _____?	What happened because of : _____?
What do proponents or supporters say about: _____?	What do opponents say about: _____?

Union soldier	Confederate soldier
How do others react to . . .?	
Father of Union soldier	President Lincoln

What others say about _____, or what _____ says:	What _____ does:
Character or Individual:	
What _____ thinks or feels:	What _____ looks like:
Based on the organizer, what personality trait(s) does this character or person exhibit?	

What is the social impact?	What is the political impact?
What is the economic impact?	What are connections throughout time or today?

strips in an inverted check to mirror the sequence of a plot diagram (see Figure 6.3). When groups finish, ask and discuss these kinds of plot-related questions: "Which strip did you use for the central conflict? The story's climax? Why?" After modeling this activity with a familiar story such as *Cinderella*, replicate it by preparing cards or strips based on the complex text students are reading in class.

To use manipulatives in other ways, prepare cards with words, terms, phrases, or sentences from the text. Direct students to sequence, sort, or cluster the cards based on a prompt that aligns with your lesson goals. Students can also sort or sequence pictures, objects, instruments, sheet music, or other nonprint material that aligns to a subject area based on a particular purpose. Alternatively, ask students to use the cards to create a graphic organizer that makes sense to them. During discussion, encourage students to compare the graphic organizers they created, using evidence from the text to support their structures.

FIGURE 6.6
Cinderella Story Strips

Once upon a time, a girl named Cinderella lived happily with her father. Her mother had died so the two lived alone.
Her father remarries a mean woman with two evil daughters.
Cinderella's father dies, and the evil stepmother forces Cinderella to work all the time.
An invitation arrives inviting all the ladies of the kingdom to a palace ball.
The stepmother will not let Cinderella go to the ball.
The fairy godmother appears and makes it possible for Cinderella to go to the ball.
The fairy godmother tells Cinderella that she must leave the ball before the clock strikes midnight.
Cinderella goes to the ball, and the prince falls in love with her.
The clock strikes 12 and Cinderella must leave.
Cinderella drops her glass slipper.
There is a search to find the owner of the glass slipper.
The evil stepfamily refuses to let Cinderella try on the slipper, but the prince insists.
The slipper fits Cinderella.
Cinderella and the prince get married.
Cinderella lets her stepfamily live at the palace with her.
They all live happily ever after.

· · · · · ·

Diamanté Poem Adaptation

A diamanté poem is a poem whose lines are organized into a diamond-shaped frame. This format has been popular in language arts classrooms to focus on two opposing characters in a literary work for younger students (e.g., Cinderella and her stepmother). However, like many of these strategies, it is certainly adaptable across content areas and grades. It could easily be used to focus on protagonists and antagonists in high school texts (Beowulf and Grendel), words (*overt* and *covert*), ideas (dystopia and utopia), groups (Union and Confederate soldiers), individuals (Mother Theresa and Attila the Hun), scientific terms (protons and electrons), and so forth. Figure 6.7 includes two examples—one for vocabulary and the other for literary characters.

FIGURE 6.7
Diamanté Poem Examples

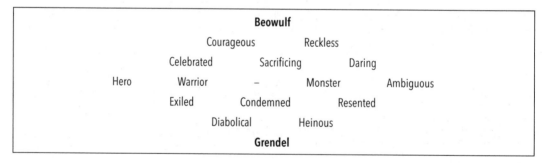

Directions for what words to enter on each line are shown below:

Line 1: Write one topic; skip to Line 7 and write the opposing topic.
Line 2: Write two adjectives that describe the topic in Line 1.
Line 3: Write three participles (i.e., verb forms ending with -*ed* or -*ing* that function as adjectives) that relate to Line 1.

Line 4: Write four nouns; the first two relate to Line 1, and the last two nouns relate to Line 7.

Line 5: Write three participles that relate to Line 7.

Line 6: Write two adjectives that describe the topic in Line 7.

Line 7: Write the topic that is in opposition to the one in Line 1.

If participles and participial phrases are included in your grade-level standards, then by all means capitalize on this opportunity to teach and include them for Lines 3 and 5. You can also have students replace them with verbs.

To model this strategy, use a text that is familiar to students. Think aloud to identify topics within the text that are potential candidates, and choose two that are most appropriate for Lines 1 and 7. Then articulate what you know about these topics and assign words to complete the other lines of the poem. If students know what they want to say but don't have the vocabulary to support it, then create an opportunity to teach new words (e.g., *heinous* and *diabolical* in the *Beowulf* example from Figure 6.7). Therefore, this activity can double as a content lesson to check for understanding and as a vocabulary acquisition lesson.

Students can create a diamanté individually or in pairs. Like any strategy, be creative! For example, small groups can create two versions: a finished diamanté and another one that is partially filled out. They pass their partially completed poem to another group to see how they would finish it and then compare their versions. Consider also that the task of brainstorming topics based on the text can itself be a fruitful cognitive activity, so don't be so quick to hand out a prepared list.

· · · · · ·

 Active Participation Strategies

The results of formal assessments—such as quiz answers, quick write or journal responses, presentations, graphic organizers, or homework assignments—are often used to ascertain how well students are grasping content. Likewise, informal formative assessments can also be an appropriate vehicle for obtaining information.

Similar to some electronic handheld devices, active participation strategies are a type of informal assessment that allow you to quickly gauge what your students know by asking them to use their fingers or thumbs to signify a response. Alternatively, students can write on a mini-whiteboard or hold up a prepared card.

By collecting information prior to launching into a unit or particular lesson, this strategy can be used as a preassessment. During a lesson, it becomes an ongoing or formative assessment to check for understanding. Since active participation feedback provides an informal way to check for understanding, you might also need to conduct formal assessments at strategic parts of the lesson to more fully determine how well students are grasping the content or text. These informal strategies are helpful, but they are not an effective instructional method for deep analysis and critique of complex text. For example, using active participation to ascertain students' ability to define similes, metaphors, or personification can be one facet of a lesson on figurative language. However, it's important also to engage students in discussions and tasks around text-dependent questions to have them examine the effects of figurative language on the complex text. Use the information you glean in all kinds of assessments, including active participation, to determine the next steps in your instruction.

As mentioned earlier, students can actively respond to a given prompt using their fingers, their thumbs, a card, or even a small whiteboard. In any of these examples, when you ask students to signal, give them the option of showing a closed fist if they are unsure or do not know the answer. In lieu of a fist, they can signal uncertainty by placing a card or the whiteboard flat on their desks; include a suitable option if students use a handheld electronic device. Being cognizant of your students' own lack of clarity is equally important information to the right or wrong response.

You can focus on foundational knowledge through discussion around text-dependent questions, as well as through these active participation suggestions. Sometimes a combination of both is worthwhile, given the goals of a lesson. Either way, when students determine the key details, they are positioned to grapple with the complexities and intricacies of concepts and content to arrive at a deeper meaning. Additionally, consider active participation strategies to reinforce general academic and domain-specific words.

Although this strategy can be adapted and used across the content areas in many ways, the focus of this book is on instruction around complex text. Therefore, the examples I've included here center on the text and its related content. Remember that these strategies provide a quick sense of what students know, so follow them up with other strategies if you feel you are not gleaning enough information. Students can make the prompts for the examples that follow, so allow them time to study the text, create their own active participation exercises, and try them out on classmates. Different versions of these active participation suggestions have been used for all grades; however, they may not work as well with high school students so, like everything you do, use your professional judgment when determining which strategy is most effective for your own students and, of course, the text they are studying.

Finger Signaling

Figure 6.8 features three examples from different content areas in which fingers are used to signal a response. Note the following:

- All prompts include a key at the top so students know how many fingers are associated with each correct response.
- Some prompts might be direct quotes because students are identifying methods of characterization, examples of a literary or rhetorical devices, text evidence in support of a topic, and so forth. In these instances, use direct quotes from the text

so there is direct applicability. This is the case with the first example in the figure that focuses on figurative language.

- The second example is a cursory check based on content from different units of study to cycle back to previous learning. This technique can also serve to preview new content to see what students might know.
- The third example (renewable and nonrenewable resources) can also be a thumbs up or thumbs down situation.

FIGURE 6.8
Finger Signals

What Type of Figurative Language?
1: Simile | 2: Personification | 3: Both | 4: None | Fist: I'm unsure.
a. "Miles guided the rowboat near a spot where lily pads lay like upturned palms on the surface." (p. 83) b. "Instead, he was gazing at the body on the ground, leaning forward slightly, his brows drawn down, his mouth a little open. It was as if he were entranced and–yes, envious–like a starving man looking through a window at a banquet." (p. 103) c. "An ancient green-plush sofa lolled alone in the center, like yet another mossy fallen log, facing a soot-streaked fireplace still deep in last winter's ashes." (p. 51) d. "Streaks of light swam and danced and wavered like a bright mirage, reflected through the windows from the sunlit surface of the pond." (p. 52) e. "The sky was a ragged blaze of red and pink and orange, and its double trembled on the surface of the pond like colors spilled from a paint box." (p. 60) (Quotes from *Tuck Everlasting* by Natalie Babbitt)

Who Made These Contributions?
1: Ancient Hebrews | 2: Ancient Greeks | 3: Ancient Chinese | Fist: I don't know.
a. First monotheistic religion based on the concept of one God who sets down moral laws for humanity b. Literature: *Iliad, Odyssey,* and *Aesop's Fables* c. Teachings of Confucius d. Mythology e. Silk Road (trade) f. Socratic method of teaching

Is This Resource Renewable or Nonrenewable?	
1: renewable | 2: nonrenewable | Fist: I'm unsure.	
a. fish	h. solar power
b. tides	i. leather
c. wind	j. wind power
d. oxygen	k. coal
e. water	l. diesel
f. forest	m. soil
g. hydropower	n. coffee

For another version, see Figure 6.9, which is an adaptation of the popular road trip or board game "three truths and a fib." Many teachers use this strategy as an icebreaker, but this example is for content. To conduct this exercise, read all four choices in succession (maybe even twice), allow some wait time, and then ask students to signal with their fingers which item is untrue. The first example in Figure 6.9 is related to text content; the second and third are for vocabulary acquisition.

FIGURE 6.9
Which Statement Is False?

Which statement is incorrect for the Bill of Rights?
1. The Second Amendment–the right to bear arms–is constantly debated. Some feel it is an archaic amendment written during a time when most people had guns in their homes to protect them from enemies. 2. The Third Amendment states that people are not forced to house–or quarter–soldiers during peacetime or war. 3. The Sixth Amendment states that in a criminal prosecution, the accused has the right to a speedy and public trial. 4. The Bill of Rights includes the first 15 amendments to the Constitution. They include natural or human rights.
Which statement uses the word *discriminate* incorrectly?
1. The musician was able to discriminate between the horn instruments used in the symphony. 2. The Jim Crow laws unfairly discriminated against African Americans. 3. She had discriminating taste in perfume and only wore products from the finest designers. 4. Those who discriminate treat everyone fairly and are unbiased.
Which statement uses the word *serenity* incorrectly?
1. *Serenity* and *tranquility* are synonyms. 2. A rock star, a carpenter, and a mechanic practice serenity each day in their jobs. 3. An example of a serene place is a tropical island marked by peacefulness. 4. One who values serenity might be someone who prefers being alone.

Thumbs Up / Thumbs Down

Create and issue prompts so students can respond to true/false or yes/no questions by signaling up or down with their thumbs. Such is the case with the first example about Islam in Figure 6.10. Another way to use this strategy is to include a combination of items around content knowledge and also personal impressions and habits. The second example around aerobic activity shows this approach. Prompts like these two examples can be issued more than one time—at the outset of a lesson or unit and again after covering some of the content to get a cursory take on what students have gleaned or if their mindsets or habits have changed. The last example includes rudimentary prompts about characters in a novel so teachers can determine if students understand key details before continuing to read.

FIGURE 6.10
Thumbs Up / Thumbs Down

Islam
Thumbs Up = True | Thumbs Down = False | Fist: I'm not sure.
1. Muslims believe that Muhammad was a prophet.
2. When Muslims pray, they face the holy city of Mecca.
3. Muhammad was a religious leader who brought the message of Hinduism.
4. Islam is a religion founded by Mohammed and follows the teachings of the Koran.
5. Those who follow the Islamic faith are called Buddhists.
6. The lives of nomads revolved around the seasons.
7. A pilgrimage is an example of God's words revealed through Mohammed.

Aerobic Activity
Thumbs Up = True | Thumbs Down = False | Fist: I'm not sure.
1. Examples of aerobic activity include biking, swimming, and walking.
2. Aerobic activity makes your heart beat faster, which is a benefit.
3. Aerobic activity eliminates all health risks.
4. Being physically active helps elevate people's moods.
5. When people exercise regularly and eat a healthy diet, they can lose weight and keep it off.
6. I engage in physical activity each day.
7. Physical activity is not a priority for me; I rarely do it.
8. If I don't eat breakfast and exercise in the morning, that is okay.
9. I would like to know more about different kinds of aerobic activity and how to make it part of my life.

To Kill a Mockingbird
Thumbs Up = True | Thumbs Down = False | Fist: I'm not sure.
1. Atticus is a lawyer in a southern town.
2. Scout Finch, a girl, is the protagonist of the story.
3. Jem Finch is Scout's older brother.
4. Atticus is Jem and Scout's uncle.
5. Boo Radley is the Finches' neighbor who loves to socialize and is seen frequently at neighborhood gatherings.
6. Dill Harris is the Finches' summer neighbor and friend.
7. Bob Ewell is an upstanding member of the community.

Two-Sided Cards

Read a prompt or quote related to the text, and have students show their responses by flashing one side of a prepared card or signaling if they are unsure of the answer by laying the card flat on the desk. Examples of what can be on each side of the card include *yes/no* (as an alternative to thumbs up/down), two characters (Romeo/Juliet), topics (angiosperm/gymnosperm), historical figures (Lincoln/Douglas), or governance (communism/capitalism). As mentioned earlier, it's important to follow up active participation with other assessments and activities that require more analysis and introspection.

Guidelines for Conducting Active Participation

For hand gestures, convey the following guidelines to students. (If students are using a handheld device, adjust these procedures accordingly.) Ask students to look straight ahead and signal at chest level so they are not influenced by one another's answers. Emphasize that signaling is a communication between each student and a teacher who needs to collect information and adjust teaching, as needed. Have students wait to signal until you give the proper indication. Wait time is important so students can think before responding with whatever first pops into their heads.

Explain to students that they should follow this sequence during an active participation exercise:

1. Review the directions. These should be at the top of the sheet to show whether students are expected to signal with a thumbs up or down or with a set number of fingers associated with specific answers. A fist always indicates uncertainty, unless they are using a card or whiteboard.
2. Emphasize that this is not a graded exercise, so students should respond as best as they can and feel comfortable showing a fist if they really are unsure of a response.
3. For activities that involve "Which statement is incorrect?" prompts, read all four statements in succession. For other versions, read one at a time or even frontload information prior to reading the prompts.
4. After reading the prompt(s), say, "Wait." Then allow several seconds of silence for students to process the prompt and think of a response.
5. Say, "Show" or "Signal," and scan the room to collect students' responses.
6. State the correct response, such as "Thumbs up is the correct answer." Specifically, be careful not to quantify the results, such as "Most of you got it right." This kind of statement only makes those who got the incorrect answer feel deficient. Then solicit input from volunteers to elaborate on responses and explain what made an answer correct using textual evidence, examples, or definitions of a particular word.

How many prompts are enough? When are there too many? There is not a set number of prompts that should be issued when using this strategy. However, I suggest that you have a sufficient number so you can gather enough information about what students know or do not know. The purpose of this informal strategy, like other assessments, is to inform instruction. It serves as a differentiation springboard since what you discover can help determine if you need to pull a small group and reteach or reread, move the class a little faster or slow it down, or enrich a handful of students. Therefore, you need to be the one to determine the right number of prompts that will give you an idea of how to proceed. Plus, you might also find that you need another more formal gauge of how students are doing if you are uncertain of the results, since these strategies are more cursory in nature.

Find Someone Who

This active participation strategy requires students to circulate around the room and find various classmates who will respond to teacher- or student-prepared prompts. Figure 6.11 features three versions. The vocabulary and literature examples are more suitable for self-directed students who can engage in a conversation without supplying proof of staying on task, since they are predicated on a discussion between different pairs of students. Alternatively, the nonfiction example shows an accountability measure whereby students have to engage in a discussion with various partners and then record their answers to different areas of the text under investigation. Select which type of involvement you expect of your students based on their work habits. Collect students' sheets for a more formal assessment.

FIGURE 6.11
Find Someone Who

Vocabulary

Directions: Find a different classmate who can respond to each of the six boxes. Once a task is completed to your satisfaction, ask for a signature on the provided line.

Find someone who . . .

Can provide an example of a character or individual who is **heinous** and what he or she does that supports this word.	Can draw a symbol for **serene**.	Can say an antonym for **gregarious**.
Can act out the word **saunter**.	Can tell you three examples for **reflection**.	Can use **pejorative** in a sentence that shows its meaning.

(continued)

FIGURE 6.11
Find Someone Who (*continued*)

Literature

Directions: Find a different classmate who can perform the action in each box. Once each person completes a task, verify that you think it is correct and then ask him or her to provide a signature on the line provided.

Find someone who . . .

Can find a place in the text where the author uses imagery and explain the underlying meaning of this passage. _____	Can make two inferences based on evidence from the text. _____
Can find two unknown words in the text and use context clues to define them. _____	Can find a part in the text that might be confusing to others and explain what it means. _____

Nonfiction

Directions: Find a different classmate who can perform the action in each box for separate sections of the text. Once each person completes the task, verify that you think it is correct and then ask him or her to provide a signature on the line provided.

Find someone who . . .

Can explain what a particular chart or table in a section of the text means. Write a one- or two-sentence explanation about the significance of this chart or table. Page or Figure #: _____ _____	Can find and explain a term used in the text selection. Write down two examples and nonexamples of this term. Term: _____ Examples: Nonexamples: _____
Can determine the main idea of a passage within the text selection. Write a one- or two-sentence summary of this passage below. Page # of passage: _____ _____	Can provide an analogy of a passage within the text selection. Write what this passage is like below. Page # of passage: _____ _____

Closing

Although many of the strategies mentioned in this chapter can certainly be used within a variety of instructional sequences (not necessarily related to complex text), take note of the advice that reading strategies should not be taught in isolation and disconnected from the text. Rather, these kinds of lessons should be in direct reference to the complex text that is the focus of instruction. This way, the reading strategies have a direct correlation and application to what students are studying.

Nevertheless, you undoubtedly are familiar with a broad range of instructional strategies and teaching methods. You knew many of these before reading this book; hopefully you now have several more to add to your inventory. What you as a teacher do completely matters to students. When you are deliberate and visible about your teaching it makes an impact. One expression of this is that you can redirect when students aren't learning and not continue to reuse the same strategies that have proven ineffective. In other words, you should implement alternative strategies for individual students or the whole class when the ones you've been using do not produce the desired results. As you consider these various strategies, the factors that guide you should be the learning goals of your unit, the text at hand, and—most importantly—your students' success or lack thereof.

> The only game in town is the impact of the choice of teaching method on all students learning. . . . Teachers need to be evaluators of the effect of the methods that they choose. When students do not learn via one method, it is more likely that it then needs to be retaught using a different method; it will not be enough merely to repeat the same method again and again. We, as teachers, need to change if the students do not change in their learning. (Hattie, 2012, pp. 95–96)

Remember to pay careful attention as you collect evidence in myriad ways for how students are progressing. Observe how they work in class, listen to how they interact and collaborate with others, heed their contributions during discussions, and review what they produce from various activities. Use all of this feedback and students' self-assessments to meet their needs so formative assessments truly become assessment *for* learning.

07
Writing About Text

Speaking or writing about a source text contributes to deeper comprehension than merely reading since both actions require intense scrutiny and examination. Reading and then engaging in a meaningful and fruitful discussion with others challenges us to extend our thinking, arrive at new insights, and consider different perspectives. Writing about what we read requires critical thinking and active engagement in order to compose a coherent piece for a particular purpose and audience. Therefore, learning experiences that include writing, speaking, and listening tasks foster further introspection and analysis of text.

Throughout this book are various writing, speaking, and listening ideas, such as annotation and peer conversations, questioning techniques, dialectical journals, graphic organizers, and reciprocal teaching sequences. What follows are additional writing opportunities, some of which include speaking and listening aspects, that extend students' understanding of the text. The emphasis on the link between reading and writing is rooted in sound research:

> The evidence is clear: writing can be a vehicle for improving reading. In particular, having students write about a text they are reading enhances how well they comprehend it. The same result occurs when students write about a text from different content areas, such as science and social studies. . . . Writing about a text should enhance comprehension because it provides students with a tool for visibly and permanently recording, connecting, analyzing, personalizing, and manipulating key ideas in text. (Graham & Hebert, 2010, pp. 6, 11)

Types of Writing Assessments

Writing assignments connected to complex text can run the gamut from short formative assessments to extensive summative ones. For example, suppose students are reading a novel or textbook unit that is divided into chapters or sections. For each chapter or section, student engage in a variety of activities and respond to text-dependent questions that help them examine the text in many ways. This helps them do justice to the author's work and meet learning goals (e.g., synthesize, infer, investigate word usage, cite evidence, etc.). All the while, they produce a variety of formative assessments that you review to inform subsequent instruction and that students themselves can use to gauge their learning progress. After several chapters or sections, students demonstrate an understanding of skills based on this particular chunk of learning, which is one kind of summative assessment. Eventually, the class will finish the novel or textbook unit and students will work on an all-encompassing summative or culminating assessment that reflects how well they have mastered the learning targets for the whole work. (For a succinct review of types of assessments, see Chapter 2.)

Writing Prompts

When crafting writing prompts or tasks, be clear about your unit and lesson goals and align to them. A combination of both formative and summative assessments is warranted to give you a comprehensive picture of students' level and pace of understanding. Consider if the purpose of the assignment is to check for understanding, hence more formative in nature, or whether it is a summative. You can issue formative writing prompts in which students write in their journals or on an exit card and then review their responses to inform instruction. Although you should provide students with a clear set of expectations for both formative and summative writing, use rubrics to score a summative.

Literacy Design Collaborative (LDC), a nonprofit agency funded by the Gates Foundation, has a rich repository of frameworks—called "template tasks"—that you can use to fashion writing prompts for summative and formative assessments. Each task incorporates literacy standards that align to almost any content area. The tasks are divided among the three writing types: argumentation, informational/explanatory, and narrative. Each template includes blanks for customizing the writing assignment for a particular subject area, specific writing genre, and the focus for the task. In responding to each prompt, students are required to read text, examine it carefully, and demonstrate an understanding through writing.

Figure 7.1 features three different templates and corresponding examples, which can qualify as summative assessments. To increase the challenge and depth of any prompt, you can add one of the eight provided Demands (D) to any template task. For instance, for the argumentation example, I added this D1: "Be sure to acknowledge competing views." Although this is part of the CCSS argumentation writing standard for ELA in grades 7–12, you might add it as a preview or enrichment in other grades where counterclaims are not yet an expectation. D6 is rather open-ended: "Use _____ (stylistic devices) to develop your work." Each of the narrative examples include this Demand. Although Figure 7.1 shows various Demands added to a summative task to evoke a more cognitively challenging response, each Demand can be used alone for a minitask or formative assessment.

As you peruse all of the template tasks (http://ldc.org/sites/default/files/LDC-Template-Task-Collection-2.0.A.pdf), pay attention to the variety of choices within each writing type since they are designed for flexibility. For example, argumentation templates might have prompts with an emphasis on analysis, definition, comparison, and more. Notice that each prompt is intended to be customized so students produce evidence of their understanding. Additionally, it's important to offer choice for differentiation purposes when it makes sense, such as the kinds of sources students use as references and the type of writing they will produce.

Be mindful of the broader definition of complex text as discussed in Chapter 1. Some subject-area teachers might replace reading literature or informational text with an alternative complex text required of their particular discipline. To illustrate, a culinary arts teachers might adapt a prompt to read, "After tasting and examining three different loaves of freshly baked bread, write a food review in which you compare the different loaves and argue for the one that is superior. Support your position with evidence from the food product using proper terminology to show your understanding of what contributes to quality."

The templates available from the Literacy Design Collaborative reflect a versatile and comprehensive resource for crafting your own prompts. However, you might have your own inventory of writing prompts from which to draw. No matter your source, be sure to use prompts that provide opportunities for students to demonstrate deep understanding of both the text content and targeted writing skills. Broaden assignments you already have used, if needed, so that students not only write about a topic (e.g., Write an information report about an entrepreneur) but also think deeply about concepts, interactions, implications, or relationships. Insert guiding questions into the prompt, and fashion the task in a way that calls upon students to focus on major insights they gleaned from the text so they can demonstrate deep understanding. Certainly ask that they pull evidence from the text to explain and support their ideas.

Checklists

Writing assessments should typically include not only the specific prompt (such as those discussed previously) but also a checklist and—especially for summative assessments—an accompanying rubric. When you are clear about the learning goals students are expected to meet and the complex text at the center of instruction, you can design assessments and criteria for success. Communicate the criteria to students so they are aware of the expectations for high-quality work and what the measure of success looks like. Prepare the checklist and rubric so that they both align to standards and reflect the skills you expect students to demonstrate. Make sure they are specific to the writing task and include clearly articulated expectations to support students in accomplishing their task. If you want students to participate in formulating the criteria, have them brainstorm items, then distribute your prepared checklist or rubric and compare the two versions. This exercise serves as a check for understanding of specific writing expectations and also allows students an opportunity to be invested in what they are about to write. Discuss any discrepancies between your criteria sheet and your students' and make prudent adjustments to your sheet based on valid student input.

FIGURE 7.1
Literacy Design Collaborative Template Task Examples

Task 2 (**Argumentation/Analysis**): *[Insert optional question]* After reading _____ *(literature or informational texts),* write _____ *(an essay or substitute)* in which you address the question and argue _____ *(content).* Support your position with evidence from the text(s). **Demand (D) 1:** Be sure to acknowledge competing views. **D2:** Give _____ *(#)* example/s from past or current _____ *(events; issues)* to illustrate and clarify your position.

SUBJECTS	PROMPTS
ELA	Would you recommend living forever? After reading *Tuck Everlasting*, write an essay in which you address the question and argue why immortality is a benefit or liability. Support your position with evidence from the text. **D1:** Be sure to acknowledge competing views.
ELA	Are characters' conflicts attributed to cultural influences or innate self-destructive tendencies? After reading Amy Tan's memoir *The Opposite of Fate* and watching the movie based on her novel *The Joy Luck Club*, write an argumentative essay that addresses the question. Support your position with evidence from both the book and movie. **D1:** Be sure to acknowledge competing views.
Social Studies	If Malcolm X were alive today, what message would he impart to social justice activists? Read "What Would Malcolm X Think?" by Malcolm X's daughter Ilyasah Shabazz and an excerpt from one of his final speeches. Then write a letter from Malcolm X's point of view to a social justice activist today in which you address the question and argue his perspective. Support your position with evidence from both texts.
Art	Do artists have an obligation to be conscientious about the work they produce, or should there be sanctions? After studying various forms of (socially or politically) controversial artwork and reading commentaries about both sides of this issue, write an argumentation that addresses the question and argues for a particular side. Support your position with evidence from the texts. **D1:** Be sure to acknowledge competing views. **D2:** Give one example from past or current events to illustrate and clarify your position.

(continued)

FIGURE 7.1

Literacy Design Collaborative Template Task Examples (*continued*)

Task 12 (Informational or Explanatory/Definition): *[Insert optional question]* After reading _____ *(literature or informational texts),* write _____ *(an essay, report, or substitute)* in which you define _____ *(term or concept)* and explain _____ *(content).* Support your discussion with evidence from the text(s).

SUBJECTS	PROMPTS
ELA	How does figurative language enhance a poet's message? After reading a collection of poetry from at least three different poets, write an essay that defines forms of figurative language and explains how poets use those forms to enhance their writing. Support your discussion with evidence from the poems.
Science	How are different species of arthropods living in our homes an example of biodiversity? Read "The Bugs in Our Homes" and at least two articles about arthropods posted online. Then write a report in which you define and explain the benefits of urban biodiversity in relation to arthropods.

Task 27 (Narrative/Description): *[Insert optional question]* After reading _____ *(literature or informational texts),* write _____ *(a narrative or substitute)* from the perspective of _____ *(content).* **D6:** Use _____ *(stylistic devices)* to develop your work.

SUBJECTS	PROMPTS
ELA	How do characters cope and survive emotionally and physically in the face of enormous strife and injustice? After reading *When the Emperor Was Divine* by Julie Otsuka, write a sequel to the novel from the perspective of one of the characters in response to this question. **D6:** Use imagery and mood to develop a narrative effect in your work that mirrors the author's.
Social Studies	What was it like to be an early explorer of the Americas? After reading accounts of a selected early explorer, write a series of journal entries from his or her perspective about life on an expedition, including details about tools, routes, obstacles, and discoveries. **D6:** Use sensory details to develop your journal entries so readers can visualize this explorer's experiences.

Source: Tasks from Literacy Design Collaborative (2013), *Template Task Collection 2.0.* Available at http://ldc.org/how-ldc-works/modules.

Student checklists have specific characteristics and ways they can be introduced and used. If they are used for a summative assessment, share them early in a unit so students are aware of what they are expected to work toward; this transparency contributes to student achievement. Here is a summary of the upcoming discussion, which elucidates each point for using a student checklist for a comprehensive summative assessment writing assignment. For formative assessments, some of these points might very well apply to some degree. Just remember that for any assessment, students need to have clear expectations so they can take care of their own learning and partner with you to make necessary progress.

- Students use the checklist as a guide while writing.
- Checklists are written from the first person point of view and with present-tense verbs.
- Checklists include brief statements that reflect skills they need to apply.
- Teachers conduct formal lessons around most of the items on the checklist.
- Teachers should lead a lesson around the checklist to foster ownership rather than distribute it without a proper introduction.
- Checklists should be customized for a particular writing assignment (e.g., argumentation, summary, literary critique).

Checklists can be brief and used repeatedly for various types of formative assessments (e.g., journal responses, weekly vocabulary paragraphs). They can be used as a guide while students are writing or working on a project. Therefore, they should be written from the first-person point of view and in the present tense. In this way, they serve a bit like a recipe. When baking, I do not get out all of my ingredients, tie an apron around my waist, bake the cake, take it out of the oven, and then review the recipe to check that I followed it completely. How sorry would I be if I omitted the baking soda and the cake didn't rise? Instead of reading the recipe afterward, I prop it up on the counter so I can consult it as I measure and stir in each ingredient. When composing the first and subsequent drafts of a major piece of writing, students use checklists to guide them while creating and revising their work. They do this to be aware of the expectations and double check that they are satisfying them in real time. In high school, students might use a rubric rather than a checklist to ensure they satisfy the expectations of a given assignment.

The line items on a checklist are brief and can represent formal lessons that you might conduct throughout the unit (e.g., I properly format my works cited document.). However, there may be some items that you don't. For example, older students may not need direct instruction to punctuate quotations correctly. Additionally, those who teach subjects other than language arts may not conduct lessons associated with conventions and grammar. Line items about these basic writing skills can be included on the checklist as a reminder, so students can access prior knowledge along with any pertinent resources. However, it is a good idea for colleagues to collaborate and divvy up teaching different skills if they share the same group of students. For example, the language arts teacher can focus on sentence structure, transitions, and well-constructed paragraphs while the science or social teacher addresses research skills including collecting evidence. For comprehensive assignments, it is helpful for students if teachers capitalize on one another's expertise to address standards collectively across content areas where it makes sense.

Another important recommendation is to conduct an exercise that reveals the checklist instead of merely passing it out to students. To do this, ask students to brainstorm a list in response to the question "What does a strong argumentation essay (or short story, informational essay, or other writing type) include?" After students generate a list—first in groups and then with the whole class—distribute a prepared checklist and have students compare the two. This exercise validates what they think will be included in this writing piece and reveals what else is expected. Conduct this exercise a week or so after beginning a unit of study. In doing so, this exercise has a dual purpose of introducing students to the checklist and checking for understanding (to assess their knowledge of the structure and characteristics of the specific writing type).

A detailed checklist can be customized to a particular task. For example, see Figure 7.2 for items aligned to a summative argument or summary writing assignment. Augment these genre-specific expectations with "Checklist Item Options" on the same figure. Finally, select subheadings to organize your tailored checklist. As mentioned earlier, providing students with criteria for success is worthwhile so they are aware of well-defined expectations not only for summative but also for formative assessments. Although this section focuses more on summative assessments, remember to consider creating a checklist for shorter assignments used for formative assessment, such as journal writes, annotations, or vocabulary practice that might be routine.

FIGURE 7.2
Checklist Item Options

Argument Writing Checklist

☐ I write an argument paper that focuses on one claim, and I stay on topic.
☐ I write an introduction that provides context for the reader and includes a thesis to establish my claim.
☐ Each of my body paragraphs begins with a topic sentence. Each topic sentence is a reason to support my major claim.
☐ I include sufficient and relevant supporting evidence (e.g., quotes, facts, data, examples, and other information) from the text(s). I integrate the evidence into my paper smoothly.
☐ I have proper attribution for textual evidence, as needed.
☐ I elaborate on the evidence I include to provide an explanation, interpretation, or analysis.
☐ I write concluding sentences for my body paragraphs.
☐ I organize my reasons and evidence logically. My strongest argument is in my final body paragraph.
☐ I acknowledge and address opposing viewpoints.
☐ I provide an effective conclusion to my paper that restates my major points and leaves an impression on readers.

Summary Checklist

☐ I include an appropriate title that is not the title of the text I am summarizing.
☐ I write an appropriate beginning that provides context, including the author and title.
☐ I write a thesis that states the main idea of the text I am summarizing.
☐ I include significant details about the text.
☐ I include quotes and paraphrase from the text where appropriate.
☐ My conclusion restates the thesis.

Checklist Item Options

Choose items from this list to accompany genre-specific expectations:

☐ I include an appropriate title.
☐ I show that I'm aware of my task, purpose, and audience.
☐ My paper shows that I understand the text well.
☐ I use appropriate transitional words and phrases to connect ideas and create cohesion.
☐ I use correct terms and precise language, and I avoid unnecessary repetition.
☐ I adhere to proper grammar and conventions.
☐ I maintain a consistent third person point of view.
☐ I maintain a consistent point of view. I do not include the second person pronoun *you*.
☐ I establish and maintain a formal writing style.
☐ My writing style is appropriate for the purpose and audience.
☐ My sentences begin in a variety of ways.
☐ I use a variety of sentence structures.
☐ I indent all paragraphs correctly.
☐ I use accurate and credible sources.
☐ My paper is properly formatted, and I use the correct heading.
☐ I include a works cited list and correctly format it.
☐ I have no run-on sentences or fragments.

Subheading Options

Organize the checklist in sections using these or other subheadings:

- Statement of Purpose/Focus/Content
- Written Expression
- Support/Evidence
- Organization
- Vocabulary or Word Choice
- Style
- Grammar/Usage and Conventions

Rubric Format and Scoring Examples

Rubrics should align to the checklist and be used as scoring guides to assess student work. There are many possible formats for rubrics and various scoring scales that you have undoubtedly seen and probably used. In this section, I focus on analytic rubrics, which entail more specificity than a holistic rubric and are used to score students in your classroom.

Design your checklist and then create an analytic rubric (or vice versa) that includes the same indicators of success so you are operating from the same set of expectations as your students. Figure 7.3 includes one particular format with sample items that may be a bit different than one you have used. In it, each specific skill has a dedicated row. This way, strengths and weaknesses in each particular area of focus can be easily ascertained so you and your students get a clear sense of performance. Any line item can be weighted. For example, some items might be worth 4 (on a 4-point scale), and others can be doubled. For a skill worth 8 points, you can score values anywhere from 0 or 1 to 8. Apply this same principle if you are using a 5- or 6-point rubric.

Determine instances where you will issue 0s or 1s for particular line items. The example in Figure 7.3 shows how a 0 could be assigned for the title, which is a pretty cut-and-dried situation because either there is a title or it is missing. However, the row for the introduction includes a 1 as the lowest possible score, indicating that a student attempted to write it but fell quite short. You can still score a 0 for papers where the introduction is entirely absent. For an on-demand writing assessment, this situation might happen, though this is a significant oversight in a comprehensive writing piece and is unlikely to occur if students progress through the writing process—including multiple drafts and feedback.

Some teachers present students with the rubric. Others use the rubric to score and just show students the checklist. Still other teachers use both for different purposes. You can feature just one section of the checklist or rubric at a time and conduct lessons around complementary items. Rely on your professional judgment and your student population to determine which criteria to share and embed in a lesson. Any scenario can work, as long as the tool to assess it is presented to students in advance of them working on the project. Clear expectations are vital.

FIGURE 7.3
Rubric Item Examples

Title *Include a unique title to support topic.*	**2**–Good **1**–Weak **0**–No title
Introduction *Create context for reading; establish claim through a thesis statement.*	**8**–Effective opening provides context for argument and entirely draws in readers; thesis establishes a claim clearly and is based on a debatable topic; sophisticated **6**–Opening somewhat provides context and draws in readers; thesis establishes a claim on a debatable topic **4**–Weak opening does not provide context or grab readers' attention; weakly stated thesis; topic not debatable **1**–No context or thesis provided; introduction clearly incomplete; claim unclear and not debatable
Sentence Variety *Vary sentence beginnings (e.g., subjects, adverbs, dependent clauses).*	**4**–Appropriate and consistent variety in sentence beginnings; sophisticated **3**–Uses some variety in sentence beginnings **2**–Most sentences begin the same way **1**–All sentences begin the same way

Other Assessments

Earlier in this chapter, you read about template tasks that can be used to design summative—and even formative—assessments that are quality-driven and develop literacy skills related to content across subject areas. The assessments that are in this section involve writing as well, but they are alternatives to traditional writing tasks. They can be used as formative assessments to collect information about students' progress or as summative assessments to gauge what students have learned. Create checklists, rubrics, or both, depending on the formality of the assignment so students are aware of the criteria for success and can work toward those goals.

Attribute Poem

In this writing assessment, students create a poem with multiple stanzas based on mostly any animate or inanimate topic (e.g., character, individual, concept, object). The key feature of the poem is that it reflects the personality traits of the topic along with supporting evidence from the text. You might ask them to create a stanza or two after each section of reading. Then, at the end of the book, unit, or larger segment of reading, students can collectively review all of the stanzas they generated and arrive at a global statement about the individual, character, or other topic. For example, an overarching takeaway can involve insights about a transformation, a pivotal event or decision, an obstacle that had to be overcome, lasting effects, and so forth. If the text includes several topics or subtopics, then each student can create a poem focusing on one topic and have classmates guess the identity based on the detailed description of the poem.

Figure 7.4 features three stanza examples from three different content areas and topics to reflect the versatility of this assignment. Notice that they all purposely begin with pronouns. In this way, students are using these poems in an activity designed to guess the identity of these subjects. Specifically, students create their poems and omit the title, and then classmates guess the subject of the poem along with pertinent personality traits. Otherwise, students should avoid redundant pronouns and be more creative.

To conduct an activity around this writing assessment, students read the complex text carefully so they are well versed in the topic and can demonstrate what they glean. Instruct them to follow these steps:

1. Select an individual, a character, or topic. An inanimate object or an idea is certainly fine.
2. Determine a personality trait. Remember that personality traits are expressed as adjectives. *(Teacher: It might be useful to conduct a brainstorming activity to generate a list of such words and then post the list for easy access.)*

3. Create stanzas for a poem using evidence from the text to support the personality trait you identify. You do not have to quote the text within the poem. However, you need to provide the resource(s) you used on a separate sheet so we have a reference if we need it.

4. Include verbs other than forms of the verb *to be* (e.g., *is, are, was*). Instead, use descriptive action verbs (e.g., *appreciates, craves, cringes, discriminates, exploits, imagines, justifies, proposes, realizes*).

5. *Optional:* Play a game to guess the identities of one another's poem topics.

FIGURE 7.4
Attribute Poem Examples

Vulnerable Cinderella	Adolf Hitler: A Demented and Maniacal Man	Football: An Intense Sport
She cringes at the sound of her step-mother's voice.	He instilled fear and hatred in many.	It is not suited for small-boned individuals.
She sheepishly responds to her step-sisters' demands.	He dreamed of a world free of non-Aryans: Jews, Gypsies, and homosexuals.	It creates a surge of physical and emotional energy in dedicated players.
She runs away at midnight to escape undesirable consequences.	He hungered for fame, attention, and domination.	It requires endurance and stamina.
She longs for happiness.		It sometimes turns mild-mannered male television views into aggressors.

Complex Instruction

Complex instruction is a cooperative learning strategy that is unique in that it is specifically orchestrated to highlight each student's strengths (Cohen, 1994). In this strategy, the assumption is that some students are reluctant to participate because they do not feel valued or have little to offer the group. As a consequence, they often feel ignored and achieve low academic status. Aim to equalize the stature of group members by offering many complex learning tasks so each student can select a task that capitalizes on his or her strengths. By completing a project that speaks to their talents, all students can feel successful by exhibiting competence among their peers. Visibly pay attention to students' products, particularly those who might otherwise be overlooked, and tactfully point them out so that others notice their achievement.

Figure 7.5 features three examples of complex text assignment sheets—one for character (or individual) transformation, another for early exploration in social studies, and a third for a performing dance class. There are six tasks on each example; however, there are typically four students in each group. Offering six tasks gives students the opportunity to choose among several options. Since the goal is for students to appreciate one another's intellectual strengths, offering a variety of products can help ensure that students select one that helps them shine. Although the tasks represent creative ways to show understanding, all of them include a writing component. Students work on their individual tasks, but group work is a feature of this strategy. Select and present these collaboration options to students, or suggest other ways groups can work together:

- Read and review all of the tasks, and decide which one each group member will complete.
- Discuss responses to the guiding questions to be clear about the content before beginning a project.
- Solicit and receive feedback from group members while working on projects.
- Prepare for a group presentation to the class that shows cohesion among the tasks and makes it clear you rehearsed.
- Present together to the class.

FIGURE 7.5
Complex Instruction Task Examples

How do characters change over time?

Task Card #1	Task Card #2	Task Card #3
Create a timeline with words and pictures that show how a character has changed from the beginning to the end of the story.	Design a poster with pictures and captions that focuses on what others say about a character that indicate a change.	Develop a graphic organizer that shows the causes and effects of a character's actions that lead to change.
Task Card #4	Task Card #5	Task Card #6
Draw two detailed pictures of a character: one that depicts this character at the beginning of the story and another at the end. Write captions using imagery to reflect change.	Write and conduct an interview with a character that includes a rationale for a change in his or her perspective. Use costumes and props.	Create a PowerPoint presentation focusing on how a character changes by using at least two methods of characterization.

European Exploration

Directions: Choose one task and complete it. Within your project, make sure to respond to these two guiding questions using evidence from your text: *Why did Europeans choose to explore the Americas? How did European explorers get to their destinations?*

Task Card #1	Task Card #2	Task Card #3
Write a <u>letter</u> from a crew member's point of view to a friend or family relation back in Europe. In your letter,	Chanteys were <u>work songs</u> that sailors created and sang to lighten certain backbreaking tasks and for	Create a properly formatted <u>PowerPoint</u> presentation (large font, noncluttered pages, visuals, consistent

(*continued*)

FIGURE 7.5

Complex Instruction Task Examples (*continued*)

Task Card #1	Task Card #2	Task Card #3
describe your trip so far and your hopes for when you reach your destination. Address the guiding questions within the body of your letter and write in a style reflective of the time period.	entertainment when they were not working. The words and music were a reflection of their daily lives. Although the term wasn't used until the mid-19th century, crews involved in a European exploration might have created songs. Create one they might have sung that describes their experiences on the voyage and answers the guiding questions. Lead the entire class in your song.	design) that addresses the guiding questions. Present your project without reading off of each slide. Add commentary to your slides to demonstrate your understanding.
Task Card #4	Task Card #5	Task Card #6
On a map of the world, draw and label the routes of several explorers. Create a key of map features and include an explanation of the goals of each explorer. Respond to the guiding questions in a paragraph or a list of bulleted sentences.	Create a script for a skit based on the guiding questions. Invite your group members to perform the skit with you. Include props and costumes.	Create a timeline highlighting the major events of exploration. In your map, include dates, events, and drawings. Address the guiding questions in your timeline.

How do dances vary historically, culturally, and socially?

Directions: Choose and complete one task in response to this guiding question: *How do dances vary historically, culturally, or socially with respect to different attributes?* Use evidence from your resources, such as videos, photographs, or text, to create your project. Examples include social dances (e.g., wedding celebrations, high school prom), ceremonial dances (e.g., harvest, rites of passage), or dances for entertainment or competition (e.g., ballet, street dance).

Attributes:

- Attire
- Props
- Setting
- Rhythmic pattern of music
- Purpose of dance
- Roles dancers portray

- Number and characteristics of dancers (e.g., men, women, children)
- Shape or pattern of movement (e.g., angular, curved, twisted)
- Choreographic form (e.g., call and response, rondo, canon)

Task Card #1	Task Card #2	Task Card #3
Create and perform a dance to share with the class. Write a brief explanation of how the dance responds to the guiding question.	Write a comparison/contrast essay that addresses the guiding question.	Create a poster with images and words in response to the guiding question.

Task Card #4	Task Card #5	Task Card #6
Create a video montage along with an annotation that responds to the guiding question. Share the montage with the class.	Write a script and conduct an interview (live or pre-taped) that includes responses to the guiding question. Assign various people to assume roles. Use costumes and props to depict these different people.	Prepare a PowerPoint that addresses the guiding question. Adhere to format (e.g., large font, non-cluttered pages, visuals, consistent design). Present your project by adding commentary instead of reading off of each slide.

Source: Portions adapted from *Dance: Kindergarten to Grade 7: Curriculum 2010* by the British Columbia Ministry of Education, 2010. Copyright 2010 by the Ministry of Education, Province of British Columbia.

RAFT

RAFT is an acronym whose letters stand for *role, audience, format, topic* (Santa et al., 1988). In this strategy, students assume a *role* (not necessarily themselves) and address an *audience* (who doesn't have to be the teacher) on a *topic* (linked to the text or curriculum) in a particular *format* (that aligns to the role, audience, and topic). It might sound complicated, but it's a very simple structure that yields a host of possibilities for demonstrating understanding of a text. In creating a product under this structure, students use critical thinking skills, analyze a text deeply, and consider different perspectives.

It is a highly motivating exercise because it offers students choice in the role they assume, the audience they address, their topic of focus, and the format of the product they create. All four aspects can vary and are highly versatile. Figure 7.6 provides an explanation and a partial list of possible examples.

RAFT topics are based on the content so students can demonstrate understanding of the complex text and subject matter. You might create a RAFT chart as a formative assessment geared to a text section. When doing so, provide at least four choices so each student can select one that is personally motivating. To differentiate by readiness, create three or four different charts based on readiness levels.

Figure 7.7 features examples of RAFT tasks that can be used across various content areas. To illustrate how to "read" these tasks, follow this example for the first line: Write a complaint letter from the point of view of a Los Angeles citizen to a Chinese official that addresses this guiding question: How do the pollution issues in China affect Los Angeles citizens? Encourage students to create their own RAFTs and pass them to classmates to complete. The cognitive energy it takes not only to complete but also to create RAFTs is a telling exercise of how well students know the content.

FIGURE 7.6
RAFT

Definitions	Examples (Partial List)
Role What role and point of view will the student assume?	**Will the student assume the role and point of view of…?** • **Fiction:** character in a story, animated character, animal • **Individual (type or actual person):** student, reporter, eyewitness, banker, poet, businessperson, historical figure, scientist, inventor, Robert E. Lee, Albert Einstein, Julia Child • **Inanimate Object:** raindrop, number, literary device, punctuation mark, electron, graph, shape, type of rock, planet, Mt. Rushmore, Nile River • **Concept:** diversity, energy, evolution, immigration, pattern, productivity, rhythm, social justice, symmetry • See "Audience" examples
Audience Who will see, read, watch, or use the product students create?	**Who is the student's audience based on the role and point of view?** • Other students, teacher, community members, school board, parents, newspaper editor, local Congressperson, self, online blog audience • See "Role" examples
Format What will be the format of the product students create?	**What type of product will the student create?** • **Writing:** essay, report, letter of advice, letter to the editor, poem, eulogy, thank-you note, news article, travel guide, complaint letter, summary, petition, campaign speech, children's book, recipe, journal • **Visual or Performing Arts:** three-dimensional model, sculpture, illustration, poster, craft, mobile, skit, musical, pantomime • **Technology:** PowerPoint or Keynote presentation, iMovie, webpage, blog, WebQuest, multimedia project, Excel spreadsheet • **Other:** lab experiment, terrarium, weather map, blueprint, portfolio, artifact, bulletin board, chart, infographic
Topic What is the basis for the product? What is the focus?	**What is the focus or point of the product?** • Guiding question or the focus based on complex text and learning goals • Topic examples: social inequality, immigration reform, gravitation force, symbolism, allusion, jazz versus classical, effects of peer pressure, women's suffrage then and now • Possible beginning phrases or frames: Identify attributes of . . ., Describe the effects of . . ., Explain why . . ., Analyze the relationship between . . ., Convince _____ to _____, If _____ could . . .

Closing

Writing about text has been proven to increase comprehension across content areas and therefore should be a mainstay within lesson design to promote understanding of what students read. The cognitive activities of reading and writing are intimately interrelated. Students must first deeply comprehend an author's work by employing various reading strategies to make inferences, analyze, synthesize, and examine it carefully. Then they must grasp the writing task and its expectations and determine the best way to demonstrate the required understanding in writing. To do so means not only writing in an organized fashion according to a particular text structure but also pulling salient evidence, providing elaboration, and developing the topic coherently and effectively.

There are many opportunities for students to write in response to complex text along a continuum of formative to summative assessments. For example, they can write annotations, notes, journal entries, graphic organizers, or poetry to more formal writing such as newspaper articles, summaries, and arguments based on information and evidence from the core text. The options are endless, so convey the purpose for reading and writing in response to it and craft a meaningful and clear prompt or task so students can show what they learned. Remember to be transparent about your expectations through a checklist, rubric, or both—as appropriate—so students are primed for success.

· · · · · ·

A Final Thought

Reading for understanding, as described by Adler and Van Doren (1972), is the kind of reading that occurs when an author's work exceeds the capabilities of the reader. As such, the reader must work hard to master the art of reading in order to fully attain an increased understanding. While reading, it becomes clear that we do not understand the text perfectly. In fact, we understand enough to know that it might be somewhat over our heads—or downright incomprehensible. To grasp the author's work, we have to really exert ourselves. However, as adults, we realize that the book has something to teach us, and our goal is to master the particular skills and talents to increase our understanding. Such is the situation when encountering complex text.

When reading frustrates us, we are cognizant that it is difficult. In such situations, we instinctively call upon our reserve of strategies to forge ahead and seek clarity and answers to what confuses us. We know that we don't know—we're cognitively aware of our reading shortcomings, but we're equipped to overcome these reading obstacles.

As educators, we have an obligation to supply students with those tools, strategies, and skills necessary to read deeply for understanding. We must work hard to endow our students with the gift of self-agency so they can discover how reading can lead them along unexplored future paths. I hope this book has provided you with additional support to boost your professionalism and add to your reservoir of knowledge and tools. Forge ahead and continue to bring students to new heights. You make a difference each and every day.

FIGURE 7.7
RAFT Examples

Role	Audience	Format	Topic
Science			
Los Angeles citizen	Chinese official	Observations	How do the pollution issues in China affect Los Angeles citizens?
High school student	3rd grade student	Illustrated children's book	How does the process of meiosis produce different types of children?
Social Studies			
American government official	Japanese American individual	Letter of justification	Identify the reasons for the federal mandate to intern those of Japanese origin
Japanese American individual	American government official	Editorial in a newspaper	Counter the reasons for interning those of Japanese origin
Native American leader	President Polk	Formal plea	Urging the government to forbid the killing of buffalo and reasons why this is critical
Language Arts			
Protagonist	Antagonist	Advice column	Why you need to change your attitude and some suggestions for doing so
Thesis statement	Topic sentence	List examples	Explain the relationship between a thesis and topic sentences
Historical fiction	Fantasy	Comparison/ contrast graphic organizer	Describe the similarities and differences between these two narrative genres
Miscellaneous			
Engine	Mechanic	Procedure manual	How to tune me
Airplane passenger	Design engineer	Revised design of airplane interior with description for changes	Suggestions to improve poor layout and design of the interior of passenger jets

Resource A

Measuring Text Complexity

Three-Part Model for Measuring Text Complexity

Sections of Appendix A of the Common Core State Standards (CCSS) (CCSSI, 2010b) and the addendum that presents further research on text complexity (CCSSI, 2013) provide a three-part model educators can use to determine if a text is the appropriate challenge level for specific students. This model helps to pinpoint where a text falls on a continuum from easy to difficult. An abbreviated version of each part is explained below. Besides Appendix A and the addendum, other resources are widely available. An excellent one is Fisher, Frey, and Lapp's *Text Complexity: Raising Rigor in Reading* (2012).

Much of what is referenced in this section is from the website Achieve the Core (www.achievethecore.org). Besides offering a rich bank of tools for measuring text complexity, the site includes a pervasive amount of math and literacy resources for those who address college and career readiness standards. (I've also referenced this website at points throughout this book.) Although it is designed for supporting CCSS implementation, anyone interested in teaching to standards similar to the CCSS will still find this website most helpful.

Quantitative measures. The first part of the three-part model focuses on assigning a text to a grade-level band according to quantitative features. Specifically, this means determining word length or frequency, sentence length, text cohesion, and other calculable properties of a text. Such aspects are difficult, or perhaps impossible, for human readers to evaluate efficiently; therefore, computer software is used. Figure A.1 shows a number of these quantitative tools that are available to help determine an appropriate grade-level span for a particular text with regard to these quantitative features. This reference chart of metrics from six different tools (e.g., Lexile, Flesch-Kincaid) includes conversions for CCSS grade bands for each of these multiple measures. "While there is variance between and among the measures about where they

FIGURE A.1

Updated Text Complexity Grade Bands and Associated Ranges from Multiple Measures

Common Core Band	ATOS	Degrees of Reading Power	Flesch-Kincaid	The Lexile Framework	Reading Maturity	SourceRater
2nd–3rd	2.75–5.14	42–54	1.98–5.34	420–820	3.53–6.13	0.05–2.48
4th–5th	4.97–7.03	52–60	4.51–7.73	740–1010	5.42–7.92	0.84–5.75
6th–8th	7.00–9.98	57–67	6.51–10.34	925–1185	7.04–9.57	4.11–10.66
9th–10th	9.67–12.01	62–72	8.32–12.12	1050–1335	8.41–10.81	9.02–13.93
11th–CCR	11.20–14.10	67–74	10.34–14.2	1185–1385	9.57–12.00	12.30–14.50

Source: "Finding Common Core Grade Levels for Texts: Quick Reference Chart" at: http://achievethecore.org/dashboard/300/search/1/1/0/1/2/3/4/5/6/7/8/9/10/11/12/page/642/text-complexity-collection-list-pg

place any single text, they all climb reliably—though differently—up the text complexity ladder to college and career readiness. Choosing any one of the text-analyzer tools from second grade through high school will provide a scale by which to rate text complexity over a student's career, culminating in levels that match college and career readiness" (CCSSI, 2013, p. 4). To determine how to use each quantitative analysis tool, access the links and instructions from the document "Finding Common Core Grade Levels for Texts: Guide to Online Tools," which is available here: www.achievethecore.org/text-complexity.

Using any one of the three parts of the model as the sole measure of complexity is incomplete and can mislead teachers about the appropriate challenge level of a particular text. In fact, sometimes quantitative measures can often underestimate complex narrative fiction. For example, John Steinbeck's *The Grapes of Wrath* measures in a Grade 2–3 band because of relatively basic grammar and syntax, yet the content is clearly too mature for students in these grades. Therefore, it is wise to consider the qualitative aspect of each text as well as specific reading and task considerations.

Qualitative measures. This part of the model refers to attributes that attentive readers can identify to determine if a text is appropriate for students: complexity of the text's structure (e.g., organization, use of graphics, text features), language features and clarity (e.g., literal or figurative language, contemporary or archaic vocabulary, general academic and domain-specific language, sentence structure), level of meaning (literary) or purpose (informational), and knowledge demands (e.g., cultural or literary references, life experiences, and discipline knowledge for informational). The Achieve the Core website has rubrics you can use to evaluate the complexity level of each of these qualitative features for both literary and informational text which appear in Figures A.2 and A.3.

FIGURE A.2
Text Complexity: Qualitative Measures Rubric for Literature

Text Title: _____   Text Author: _____

	Exceedingly Complex	**Very Complex**	**Moderately Complex**	**Slightly Complex**
TEXT STRUCTURE	**Organization:** Is intricate with regard to such elements as point of view, time shifts, multiple characters, storylines, and detail **Use of Graphics:** If used, illustrations or graphics are essential for understanding the meaning of the text	**Organization:** May include subplots, time shifts, and more complex characters **Use of Graphics:** If used, illustrations or graphics support or extend the meaning of the text	**Organization:** May have two or more storylines and occasionally be difficult to predict **Use of Graphics:** If used, a range of illustrations or graphics support selected parts of the text	**Organization:** Is clear, chronological or easy to predict **Use of Graphics:** If used, either illustrations directly support and assist in interpreting the text or are not necessary to understanding the meaning of the text
LANGUAGE FEATURES	**Conventionality:** Dense and complex; contains abstract, ironic, and/or figurative language **Vocabulary:** Complex, generally unfamiliar, archaic, subject-specific, or overly academic language; may be ambiguous or purposefully misleading **Sentence Structure:** Mainly complex sentences with several subordinate clauses or phrases; sentences often contain multiple concepts	**Conventionality:** Fairly complex; contains some abstract, ironic, and/or figurative language **Vocabulary:** Fairly complex language that is sometimes unfamiliar, archaic, subject-specific, or overly academic **Sentence Structure:** Many complex sentences with several subordinate phrases or clauses and transition words	**Conventionality:** Largely explicit and easy to understand with some occasions for more complex meaning **Vocabulary:** Mostly contemporary, familiar, conversational; rarely unfamiliar or overly academic **Sentence Structure:** Primarily simple and compound sentences, with some complex constructions	**Conventionality:** Explicit, literal, straightforward, easy to understand **Vocabulary:** Contemporary, familiar, conversational language **Sentence Structure:** Mainly simple sentences
MEANING	**Meaning:** Multiple competing levels of meaning that are difficult to identify, separate, and interpret; theme is implicit or subtle, often ambiguous, and revealed over the entirety of the text	**Meaning:** Multiple levels of meaning that may be difficult to identify or separate; theme is implicit or subtle and may be revealed over the entirety of the text	**Meaning:** Multiple levels of meaning clearly distinguished from each other; theme is clear but may be conveyed with some subtlety	**Meaning:** One level of meaning; theme is obvious and revealed early in the text

(continued)

FIGURE A.2

Text Complexity: Qualitative Measures Rubric for Literature (*continued*)

Text Title: _____ Text Author: _____

	Exceedingly Complex	Very Complex	Moderately Complex	Slightly Complex
KNOWLEDGE DEMANDS	**Life Experiences:** Explores complex, sophisticated, or abstract themes; experiences portrayed are distinctly different from the common reader	**Life Experiences:** Explores themes of varying levels of complexity or abstraction; experiences portrayed are uncommon to most readers	**Life Experiences:** Explores several themes; experiences portrayed are common to many readers	**Life Experiences:** Explores a single theme; experiences portrayed are everyday and common to most readers
	Intertextuality and Cultural Knowledge: Many references or allusions to other texts or cultural elements	**Intertextuality and Cultural Knowledge:** Some references or allusions to other texts or cultural elements	**Intertextuality and Cultural Knowledge:** Few references or allusions to other texts or cultural elements	**Intertextuality and Cultural Knowledge:** No references or allusions to other texts or cultural elements

Source: Adapted from Appendix A: Research Supporting Key Elements of the Standards, *Common Core State Standards for English Language Arts and Literacy in History/Social Studies and Science and Technical Subjects.* Copyright 2010 by National Governors Association Center for Best Practices, Council of Chief State School Officers. Retrieved from http://achievethecore.org/content/upload/SCASS_Text_Complexity_Qualitative_Measures_Lit_Rubric_2.8.pdf

Alternatively, you can use a worksheet to gauge the complexity level. With this tool, you can determine where a text falls among a scale that indicates if the text is appropriate for the beginning of a given grade-level span, near the end, or unsuitable for the span altogether in each category similar to those featured in the rubrics. Blank worksheets for each grade-level span and a completed sample of one are located under the tab "Finding CCSS Grade Levels for Texts: Qualitative Scales" in the same link referenced earlier (www.achievethecore.org/text-complexity). When using this worksheet, consider this: "Few (if any) authentic texts will be at the low or high ends on all of these measures, and some elements of the dimensions are better suited to literary or to informational texts" (CCSSI, 2013, p. 4). Peruse both assessment tools—the rubric and worksheet—to help determine which one is most appropriate for your specific situation.

Reading and task considerations. This part of the model deals with the variables specific to particular readers and the task students are asked to perform. As a teacher, you are expected to use your professional judgment, experience, and knowledge of students and the particular subject when issuing assessments. Pay attention to readers' cognitive capabilities (i.e., attention, memory, analytical thinking), motivation, knowledge (i.e., vocabulary, topic, linguistic, comprehension strategies), and experiences. In addition, consider the assigned task, which includes the purpose for reading, complexity level, and questions posed.

FIGURE A.3
Text Complexity: Qualitative Measures Rubric for Informational Texts

Text Title: _____ Text Author: _____

	Exceedingly Complex	**Very Complex**	**Moderately Complex**	**Slightly Complex**
TEXT STRUCTURE	**Organization:** Connections between an extensive range of ideas, processes or events are deep, intricate and often ambiguous; organization is intricate or discipline-specific	**Organization:** Connections between an expanded range of ideas, processes or events are often implicit or subtle; organization may contain multiple pathways or exhibit some discipline-specific traits	**Organization:** Connections between some ideas or events are implicit or subtle; organization is evident and generally sequential or chronological	**Organization:** Connections between ideas, processes or events are explicit and clear; organization of text is chronological, sequential, or easy to predict
	Text Features: If used, are essential in understanding content	**Text Features**: If used, directly enhance the reader's understanding of content	**Text Features**: If used, enhance the reader's understanding of content	**Text Features**: If used, help the reader navigate and understand content but are not essential to understanding content.
	Use of Graphics: If used, intricate, extensive graphics, tables, charts, etc., are extensive or are integral to making meaning of the text; may provide information not otherwise conveyed in the text	**Use of Graphics:** If used, graphics, tables, charts, etc., support or are integral to understanding the text	**Use of Graphics:** If used, graphic, pictures, tables, and charts, etc., are mostly supplementary to understanding the text	**Use of Graphics:** If used, graphic, pictures, tables, and charts, etc., are simple and unnecessary to understanding the text but they may support and assist readers in understanding the written text
LANGUAGE FEATURES	**Conventionality**: Dense and complex; contains considerable abstract, ironic, and/or figurative language	**Conventionality**: Fairly complex; contains some abstract, ironic, and/or figurative language	**Conventionality**: Largely explicit and easy to understand with some occasions for more complex meaning	**Conventionality**: Explicit, literal, straightforward, easy to understand
	Vocabulary: Complex, generally unfamiliar, archaic, subject-specific, or overly academic language; may be ambiguous or purposefully misleading	**Vocabulary:** Fairly complex language that is sometimes unfamiliar, archaic, subject-specific, or overly academic	**Vocabulary:** Mostly contemporary, familiar, conversational; rarely overly academic	**Vocabulary:** Contemporary, familiar, conversational language
	Sentence Structure: Mainly complex sentences with several subordinate clauses or phrases and transition words; sentences often contain multiple concepts	**Sentence Structure:** Many complex sentences with several subordinate phrases or clauses and transition words	**Sentence Structure:** Primarily simple and compound sentences, with some complex constructions	**Sentence Structure:** Mainly simple sentences

(continued)

FIGURE A.3

Text Complexity: Qualitative Measures Rubric for Informational Texts (*continued*)

Text Title: _____ Text Author: _____

PURPOSE	**Purpose:** Subtle and intricate, difficult to determine; includes many theoretical or abstract elements	**Purpose:** Implicit or subtle but fairly easy to infer; more theoretical or abstract than concrete	**Purpose:** Implied but easy to identify based upon context or source	**Purpose:** Explicitly stated, clear, concrete, narrowly focused
KNOWLEDGE DEMANDS	**Subject Matter Knowledge:** Relies on extensive levels of discipline-specific or theoretical knowledge; includes a range of challenging abstract concepts	**Subject Matter Knowledge:** Relies on moderate levels of discipline-specific or theoretical knowledge; includes a mix of recognizable ideas and challenging abstract concepts	**Subject Matter Knowledge:** Relies on common practical knowledge and some discipline-specific content knowledge; includes a mix of simple and more complicated, abstract ideas	**Subject Matter Knowledge:** Relies on everyday, practical knowledge; includes simple, concrete ideas
	Intertextuality: Many references or allusions to other texts or outside ideas, theories, etc.	**Intertextuality:** Some references or allusions to other texts or outside ideas, theories, etc.	**Intertextuality:** Few references or allusions to other texts or outside ideas, theories, etc.	**Intertextuality:** No references or allusions to other texts, or outside ideas, theories, etc.

Source: Retrieved from http://achievethecore.org/content/upload/SCASS_Info_Text_Complexity_Qualitative_Measures_Info_Rubric_2.8.pdf

Recap about measures. The three-part measures are intertwined, and each represents important considerations when ascertaining the complexity level of text, which is sometimes tricky to determine. Using these multiple measures will help ensure reliability for specific grade-level bands (e.g., grades 4–5, 6–8, etc.). Once the band is determined—based on these quantitative measures—focus on qualitative features to consider a specific text for a certain grade.

Even though the model is generally effective, there are always situations where it is not quite foolproof. As discussed earlier, texts such as *The Grapes of Wrath* are deceivingly simplistic, so using a quantitative measure alone would be incomplete. In fact, in this case, the qualitative measure would supersede the quantitative: "sometimes quantitative considerations will trump quantitative measures in identifying the grade band of a text, particularly with narrative nonfiction in later grades. Research showed more disagreement among the quantitative measures when applied to narrative fiction in higher complexity bands than with informational text or texts in lower grades. Given this, preference should sometimes be given to qualitative measures when evaluating narrative fiction intended for students in grade 6 and above" (CCSSI, 2013, p. 8). Another exception occurs for certain kinds of text—such as poetry, drama, and K–1 texts—where the quantitative measures are not as valid or even applicable. For these texts, rely more heavily on qualitative and reader and task considerations.

For a more detailed explanation of this three-part model and associated research, read "Supplemental Information for Appendix A of the Common Core State Standards for English Language Arts and Literacy: New Research on Text Complexity" available here: www.achievethecore.org/text-complexity (under the abbreviated title "Supplement to Appendix A").

For suggestions on how to find texts and compile a fiction and nonfiction list of titles, see Resource B of this book.

Resource B

Text Selection for Fiction and Nonfiction Literature

School or District Project: Fiction and Nonfiction Text Selection

There are many factors to consider when creating a list of appropriate texts that is intended for use at various grade levels throughout a school or across a district. Careful planning, awareness of what constitutes complex text, and familiarity with available resources are contributing factors that help ensure a well-balanced and sound instructional program. With that in mind, this Resource can serve as a guide for teachers, administrators, or other designated educators to embark on a selection process to compile a comprehensive core text list for classrooms either within a school or across a district that aligns with the existing curriculum. What follows is a recommended distribution of text types across grade levels, suggested steps in a selection process including roles of various individuals, and resources for choosing titles to help you with this project. You know your school and district best, so take what you read here and customize, as needed.

Recommended Distribution of Text Types Across Grade Levels

Before beginning the selection of appropriate texts, familiarize yourself with the recommended balance of distribution across grade spans. Regardless of whether your school is in a state that has adopted the CCSS, it would still behoove you to be aware of the prescribed literary and informational percentage distribution that the National Assessment of Educational Progress (NAEP) requires (see Figure B.1). Since informational text is a priority as students advance through the grades, the CCSS emphasizes literacy across the content areas. Therefore, all teachers contribute to the goals reflected in this distribution and should consider a cross-curricular focus when assigning texts—while still being cognizant of the primary responsibilities of language arts teachers. "Because the ELA classroom must focus on literature (stories, drama, and poetry) as well as literary nonfiction, a great deal of informational reading in grades 6–12 must take place in other classes if the NAEP assessment framework is to be matched instructionally" (CCSSI, 2010a, p. 5).

FIGURE B.1

Distribution of Literary and Informational Passages

Grade	Literary	Informational
4	50%	50%
8	45%	55%
12	30%	70%

Source: Reading framework for the 2009 National Assessment of Educational Progress, by National Assessment Governing Board, 2008, Washington, DC.

Suggested Steps and Individual Roles in the Selection Process

The following are suggested steps for the process of text selection. Figure B.2 shows an abbreviated version of what is detailed in this section. Consider these suggestions and personalize them to relate to your own school and district. Collecting input from numerous stakeholders will help ensure a smooth process, so a cross section of educators is embedded within the process. The culture of your school will help determine the specific role that parents should play as it can span a continuum of involvement. Include them in the process where you deem their input to be necessary. For example, you might solicit their feedback by making them active participants in the process by assigning parents to the committee, alerting them that the project is taking place and asking for input, and/or distributing a list of books after the selection process to inform them of the final product.

Step 1: Appoint a committee facilitator *(Ownership: district-level administrator)*: Before commencing a project to select appropriate texts, find an able and experienced committee facilitator to lead this project. This person does not need to have read every book across all grade levels, which would be a tall order to say the least, but he or she should be familiar with a wide array of titles. More importantly, this person needs to know where to access and recommend resources for text titles. (I've provided these later in this Resource.) In addition, the facilitator should be well acquainted with the tools required to determine text complexity.

FIGURE B.2
Steps in the Text Selection Process

Ownership	Steps in Process
District-level administrator	1. Appoint a committee facilitator.
Facilitator	2. Select committee members. 3. Launch the text-selection process.
Committee members	4. Explain the selection process to colleagues. 5. Gather grade-level text suggestions. 6. Vet and recommend suggested books.
Facilitator	7. Collect book recommendations and prepare for sharing the information.
Facilitator and committee members	8. Present recommendations and compile a list. 9. Distribute a Fiction and Nonfiction Text List (and survey).
Teachers	10. Design a unit of study and submit feedback.

He or she will be expected not only to lead meetings but also to spend time researching, planning, and executing tasks—including reading or familiarizing himself or herself with recommended texts that are eventually identified as serious contenders. In addition, this person should possess strong facilitation skills and a knack for diplomacy, especially consensus building. It is likely that situations will arise in which teachers demand that certain texts be kept in a particular grade level despite the fact that they might be inappropriate (because they are too complex, are not complex enough, have sophisticated subject matter, and so forth). Therefore, it will be necessary to tactfully pry some teachers away from using "time-honored" books that are no longer in alignment with the expectations of current standards. In order to suggest a reassignment of titles, a facilitator needs to be cognizant of available resources to identify texts and ascertain text complexity and of content-area standards so he or she can suggest appropriate texts that align to them.

Work in collaboration with the facilitator to discuss specific issues related to the scope of the project, implementation, selection of committee members, communication about meetings, decisions around contentious situations, and so forth. Determine compensation for facilitators and committee members.

Step 2: Select committee members (*Ownership: facilitator*): Depending on the size of the district, search for and select one or two grade-level representatives to serve on the core committee. In large districts, more than two might be needed. Besides grade-level teachers, encourage other relevant staff—such as librarians and literacy coaches—to serve on the committee. Determine how educators will be selected. Will teachers apply for a spot on the committee or merely volunteer? What is the application process? Are there qualifications, such as years of service or subject-area expertise? Should people solicit recommendations from peers? What is the timeline for committee selection?

Step 3: Launch the text-selection process *(Ownership: facilitator)*: Once committee members are chosen, plan for and send out invitations to an introductory meeting to launch the process. To prepare for this initial meeting with committee members, read Resource A on text complexity and this Resource to familiarize yourself with what the entire process of text selection entails. From this information, your own professional expertise, and input from committee members, you can begin to develop a plan for the committee's goals and how it can be accomplished.

For the initial meeting, consider the following agenda draft:

- Conduct a brief icebreaker if the grade-level representatives on the committee have never met.
- Share the goals of the meeting with committee members. Allow time for reading and discussion of any materials in this Resource or Resource A that you think committee members should read. Perhaps even lead a Jigsaw activity designed for this purpose.
- Share and discuss the proposed steps of the text-selection process (Figure B.2), timeline of the entire process, possible dates and locations of meetings, and expectations for committee members. Distribute or direct members to appropriate resources they will need during the process.
- Introduce the quantitative tool(s) that you will use (e.g., Lexile, ATOS, DRP) and which form(s) reviewers will use for qualitative measurements (see Resource A and aligned figures). There needs to be consistency throughout the school or district, so make this decision early in the process.
- Plan agenda items for the next committee meeting. Identify agenda items that committee members should discuss with their grade-level colleagues.

Step 4: Explain the selection process *(Ownership: committee members)*: Committee members should meet with their grade-level colleagues to explain the selection process in general and each step in particular (see Figure B.2). There will ultimately be several texts selected at each grade level, so teachers should have the flexibility to choose and teach from a list. From a logistical standpoint, this is helpful in schools where there are not enough copies for all students to read the same book simultaneously. Teachers can also choose titles that they feel are appropriately engaging for their students and that they are passionate about teaching.

I realize that not having a list of mandated titles might be controversial for some people, but I feel that it's important for teachers to have a choice in their instruction—provided that the texts have been appropriately vetted for complexity and that they relate to subject-specific standards and content. Like students, teachers need to feel motivated and engaged by a text; otherwise, they will not feel as passionate about the unit of instruction surrounding the text.

Step 5: Gather grade-level text suggestions *(Ownership: committee members)*: Core committee members should begin by soliciting text suggestions from their grade-level colleagues. Invite teachers from all content areas to make recommendations. For example, a history teacher might advocate for a particular work of historical fiction or a journal or memoir tied to the curriculum (e.g., *I Have Lived a Thousand Years* by Livia Bitton-Jackson, *Warriors Don't Cry* by Melba Pattillo Beals). Likewise, a science teacher might recommend a book focusing on a scientific idea or a scientist's biography/autobiography (e.g., *Venom* by Marilyn Singer, books about Marie Curie, Isaac Newton, Charles Darwin, Gregor Mendel).

Committee members should brief grade-level colleagues on the process for determining text complexity. Explain that recommended texts that have been vetted will be cross referenced with other grade levels. Some titles might be eliminated or exchanged because of redundancy or to better align with different grade-level selections. This explanation is important so teachers understand why a recommended book may not appear on the final list.

Share the resources for text titles found in Figure B.3 to assist with researching and compiling titles to recommend and review. This figure is a good launching pad for finding longer works; certainly there are other resources available so welcome suggestions from colleagues as mentioned in this step. Those who review and suggest books for the committee's consideration should complete the appropriate forms. See the next step about vetting books for a fuller description of what that entails.

Step 6: Vet and recommend suggested books *(Ownership: committee members)*: Examining texts carefully requires an investment, so consider providing ample time—such as during a long school break—for committee members to properly vet books. Before spending time reviewing titles, committee members might create an interactive document (e.g., Google doc) that lists what each person is reviewing. This will insure that two or more committee members are not focusing on the same text. Divide up the task of reviewing books that are strong candidates for recommendation to the whole committee. For each text under consideration, complete and submit to the facilitator Figure B.4, which is essentially a cover sheet that provides a synopsis of the key features of each recommended book. For measuring text complexity, reviewers should read about the three-part model in Resource A to understand what is involved in identifying appropriately complex text for all students. Below is a recap of tools from Resource A to use in completing Figure B.4:

- **Quantitative Measures:** Access the agreed-upon quantitative measurement tool online and determine a grade band (see Figure A.1). Remember that a consistent measure needs to be used (e.g., Lexile, Flesch-Kincaid).

FIGURE B.3
Resources for Text Titles

The following online options provide a good starting point for researching potential titles for longer works. Solicit suggestions from other school districts, colleagues, bookstore owners, and local librarians for their input and recommendations. In addition, search the Internet for titles of award-winning and high-quality books. Be sure to use the three-part complexity model (see Resource A) to determine complexity levels of suggested titles.

• The California Department of Education has a recommended literature list on its website that includes a compilation of PreK–12 titles across content areas. The search tool is customized so users can compile a list or find a particular book based on certain criteria. For example, users can search for classifications (e.g., alphabet books, concept books, graphic novels, picture books, photo essays, wordless books), awards (e.g., Caldecott, California Young Reader Medal Program, Golden Kite Author and Illustrator Aware, National Book Award, Nobel Prize), content standards alignment, cultural designations (e.g., African, Filipino, Korean, Middle Eastern, Native American), language, genres (e.g., drama, fantasy, humor, tall tale, nonfiction, speech), and more. Link: http://www.cde.ca.gov/ci/cr/rl

• Appendix B of the CCSS (2010c) includes a list of complex text suggestions (certainly not mandates) for grade-level bands (e.g. 4–5, 6–8, 9–10). Within each grade span are various titles across content areas that are categorized by text type. Some entries are titles only; others might be passages–not necessarily whole works–so if a potential entry is intriguing, access the entire text and review it before making a recommendation. When using these titles in the classroom, educators should refer and expose students to the original text sources (rather than excerpts) whenever possible. In addition to the list of titles, sample performance tasks are featured to illustrate the kinds of assessments educators might issue. Link: www.corestandards.org/assets/Appendix_B.pdf

• National Council of Teachers of English (NCTE): Below are two awards NCTE grants each year; check the link cited below for other awards for outstanding books at all levels and content areas.
   - Orbis Pictus Award promotes and recognizes excellence in the writing of nonfiction for children across content areas. One title is awarded each year; however, up to five Honor Books are also recognized and eight additional recommended books can be named. This is the homepage link for awards: http://www.ncte.org/awards
   - The NCTE Charlotte Huck Award for Outstanding Fiction for Children promotes and recognizes excellence in the writing of fiction for children. The criteria focus on titles that have the potential to transform children's lives by inviting compassion, imagination, and wonder. This is the homepage link for awards: http://www.ncte.org/awards

• The International Literacy Association's (ILA–formerly IRA) Choices Reading Lists compile a rich resource of literary titles with annotated lists. Link: http://www.reading.org/Resources/Booklists.aspx
   - Children's Choices (K–6): This list consists of 100 favorite book titles chosen by approximately 10,000 children. Anyone who wishes to encourage young people to read for pleasure will be interested in this list. Therefore, it is not solely compiled for teachers, librarians, and bookstore owners; it is also geared to parents, grandparents, guardians, and caregivers. This list is a project of a joint committee supported by ILA and The Children's Book Council.
   - Teachers' Choices (K–8): The approximately 30 books on this list have been identified as outstanding trade books that teams of teachers, librarians, and reading specialists find exceptional for curriculum use and that readers ages 5–15 will enjoy reading.
   - Young Adults' Choices (Grades 7–12): This project has a threefold purpose: encourage young adults to read; make teens, teachers, librarians, and parents aware of new literature for this population; and provide young adults with an opportunity to voice their opinions about books targeted to them. The list includes about 30 titles that approximately 4,500 teenage reviewers read and select.

- **Qualitative Measures:** Access and complete either the informational or literature rubric (Figures A.2 and A.3) or the worksheets from www.achievethecore.org that were all referenced in Resource A.
- **Reader-Task Considerations:** Are students who will read this text highly knowledgeable in the content? Are they skilled readers? Is their motivation and interest high or low? What prior experiences might they have concerning the text? What task might they be asked to complete? Identify any of these particular factors with regard to students' characteristics that need consideration in relation to this text.

FIGURE B.4
Fiction and Nonfiction Text List Recommendation

Title:			Author:		
Recommended Grade-Level Placement	Genre (e.g., biography, historical fiction, informational text)	Format (e.g., chapter book, graphic novel, speech)	Listed in CCSS Appendix B?	Qualitative Measure (See Resource A)	Quantitative Measure (Input grade band and # that indicates grade band; see Resource A)
			Yes No	attach	

Reader-Task Considerations:
Does the text tie in with another content area? If so, which content area(s) and in what way?
Other comments:

Step 7: Collect book recommendations and prepare for sharing the information *(Ownership: facilitator)*: Before the selection committee reconvenes as an entire group, collect the recommendations from each member (i.e., completed Figure B.4). Compile a master list, perhaps on a spreadsheet, so their collective information can be viewed easily. Look for a clear articulation of complexity growth from grade to grade using the quantitative and qualitative measures. Also pay attention to a variety of genres and formats, and instances of redundancies. Highlight these areas on the spreadsheet to bring to the committee for discussion, as needed.

Plan for how committee members will present recommendations to each other and how you will facilitate the meeting. These questions can help guide you as you plan an agenda for the committee meeting; they can also be a springboard for you to consider other items:

- What is the order for presenting (e.g., chronologically by grade level, by subject matter)?
- Will each committee member be given a time limit for sharing recommendations?
- What should each committee member bring and share during the presentations (e.g., copies of his or her qualitative measurement [Figure A.2, A.3 or spreadsheet], copy of the actual text)?
- Is there a process for giving feedback, such as after each person shares or at the end of hearing from a cluster of grade level or subject matter representatives?
- Will recommendations be shared in small grade level or subject matter groups or with all committee members?
- If the recommendation presentations are conducted in small groups, how will all committee members learn of the discussions?
- What if there are not enough recommendations given for a particular grade or even subject?
- What if there is not an appropriate distribution of literary and informational text (see Figure B.1)?
- If there are discrepancies, what will help eradicate them? Suggestions: have objective criteria available that addresses sticky points like the quantitative or qualitative measures, or Figure B.1 that shows a distribution of text types.
- What is the agenda for a follow-up meeting?

Step 8: Present recommendations and compile a list *(Ownership: facilitator and committee members)*: The facilitator shares the prepared agenda using the considerations in the previous step, and distributes the master list of compiled input. Each committee member presents his or her recommendations. The overall aim is to arrive at a whole-group consensus and compile a final list of text recommendations that adheres to the qualifications of text complexity and provides articulation from grade to grade. As groups present, they can approve a text title, table it for further discussion, or reject it for concrete reasons that members should discuss. The facilitator takes copious notes from which a final text list will be created that can include any of the items detailed below. Before the meeting adjourns, the facilitator should discuss any next steps in the process (e.g., further discussion, school or districtwide communication about list).

- title and author
- description
- recommended grade level
- content tie-in
- quantitative and qualitative measures
- text and reader considerations
- genre, format, and page count
- key standards

Step 9: Distribute a fiction and nonfiction text list (and survey) *(Ownership: facilitator)*: Distribute final recommended titles to pertinent district personnel and other stakeholders. It might be helpful to create a survey to collect information on students' and teachers' impressions of each title after they have had an opportunity to study or teach it. It can include specific feedback about students' interest in the text, content tie-in, activities and assessments teachers conducted and how students performed, teacher and student resources aligned to the text, and so forth.

Step 10: Design a unit of study and submit feedback *(Ownership: teachers)*: Teachers need to read each text and have a solid curriculum in place to teach it. They need sufficient time and resources to develop, pilot, and refine a unit of instruction around each text. If, however, teachers feel the text is not an optimal selection for a number of valid reasons, there needs to be a venue (provide feedback to the facilitator or district administrator) for them to discuss these issues and determine if the text should stay on the list or be replaced.

References

ACT. (2006). *Reading between the lines: What the ACT reveals about college readiness in reading.* Iowa City, IA: Author. Retrieved from https://www.act.org/research/policymakers/pdf/reading_report.pdf

Adams, G. L., & Engelmann, S. (1996). *Research on direct instruction: 20 years beyond DISTAR.* Seattle, WA: Educational Achievement Systems.

Adler, M. J., & Van Doren, C. (1972). *How to read a book: The classic guide to intelligent reading.* New York: Simon & Schuster.

Babbitt, N. (1975). *Tuck everlasting.* New York: Farrar, Straus and Giroux.

Bacon, F. (2012). *The essays.* Available: www.goodreads.com/quotes/28623-read-not-to-contradict-and-confute-nor-to-believe-and

Beck, I. L., McKeown, M. G., & Kucan, L. (2002). *Bringing words to life: Robust vocabulary instruction.* New York: Guilford Press.

Beck, I. L., McKeown, M. G., & Kucan, L. (2013). *Bringing words to life: Robust vocabulary instruction,* (2nd ed.). New York: Guilford Press.

Beck, I. L., McKeown, M. G., & Omanson, R. C. (1987). The effects and uses of diverse vocabulary instructional techniques. In M. G. McDeown & M. E. Curtis (Eds.), *The nature of vocabulary acquisition* (pp. 147–163). Hillsdale, NJ: Erlbaum.

Bradbury, R. (1951, Aug. 7). "The Pedestrian." *The Reporter.*

Brantley, S. R. (1997). *Volcanoes of the United States.* USGS. Retrieved from http://pubs.usgs.gov/gip/volcus/titlepage.html

British Columbia Ministry of Education. (2010). *Dance: Kindergarten to grade 7: Curriculum 2010.* Retrieved from http://www.bced.gov.bc.ca/irp/pdfs/arts_education/2010dancek7.pdf

Carnegie, A. (1889). "Gospel of Wealth." *North American Review, No. CCCXCI.* Retrieved from www.swarthmore.edu/SocSci/rbannis1/AIH19th/Carnegie.html

Cisneros, S. (1991). Eleven. In *Woman hollering creek and other stories.* New York: Random House.

Cohen, E. (1994). *Designing groupwork: Strategies for the heterogeneous classroom* (2nd ed.). New York: Teachers College Press.

Coleman, D. (2012). Middle school ELA curriculum video: Close reading of a text: MLK "Letter from Birmingham Jail" Retrieved from http://www.engageny.org/resource/middle-school-ela-curriculum-video-close-reading-of-a-text-mlk-letter-from-birmingham-jail

Coleman, D., & Pimentel, S. (2012). *Revised publishers' criteria for the Common Core Standards in English Language Arts and Literacy, Grades 3–12.* Retrieved from www.corestandards.org/assets/ Publishers_Criteria_for_3–12.pdf

Common Core State Standards Initiative (CCSSI). (2010a). *Common Core State Standards for English language arts and literacy in history/social studies, science, and technical subjects.* Washington, DC: CCSSO & National Governors Associations. Retrieved from http://www.corestandards.org/assets/CCSSI_ELA%20Standards.pdf

Common Core State Standards Initiative. (2010b). *Common Core State Standards for English language arts and literacy in history/social studies, science, and technical subjects: Appendix A: Research supporting key elements of the standards.* Washington, DC: CCSSO & National Governors Associations. Retrieved from http://www.corestandards.org/assets/ Appendix_A.pdf

Common Core State Standards Initiative. (2010c). *Common Core State Standards for English language arts and literacy in history/social studies, science, and technical subjects: Appendix B: Text exemplars and sample performance tasks.* Washington, DC: CCSSO & National Governors Associations. Retrieved from http://www.corestandards.org/assets/Appendix_B.pdf

Common Core State Standards Initiative. (2010d). *Key shifts in English language arts.* Washington, DC: CCSSO & National Governors Associations. Retrieved from http://www.corestandards.org/other-resources/key-shifts-in-english-language-arts/

Dale, E., O'Rourke, J., & Barbe, W. B. (1986). *Vocabulary building: Process, principles and application.* Columbus, OH: Zaner-Bloser.

Erickson, H. L. (2002). *Concept-based curriculum and instruction: Teaching beyond the facts.* Thousand Oaks, CA: Corwin.

Erickson, H. L., & Lanning, L. A. (2014). *Transitioning to concept-based curriculum and instruction: How to bring content and process together.* Thousand Oaks, CA: Corwin.

Fisher, D., & Frey, N. (2014). *Better learning through structured teaching: A framework for the gradual release of responsibility.* Alexandria, VA: ASCD.

Fisher, D., Frey, N., & Lapp, D. (2012). *Text complexity: Raising rigor in reading.* Newark, DE: International Reading Association.

Fountas, I. C., & Pinnell, G. S. (2012). *Genre study: Teaching with fiction and nonfiction books.* Portsmouth, NY: Heinemann.

Glass, K. T. (2012). *Mapping comprehensive units to the ELA common core, K–5.* Thousand Oaks, CA: Corwin.

Glass, K. T. (2013). *Mapping comprehensive units to the ELA common core, 6–12.* Thousand Oaks, CA: Corwin.

Goerss, B. L., Beck, I. L., & McKeown, M. G. (1999). Increasing remedial students' ability to derive word meaning from context. *Reading Psychology, 20*(2), 151–175.

Graham, S., & Hebert, M. (2010). *Writing to read: Evidence for how writing can improve reading: A report from the Carnegie Corporation of New York.* Retrieved from http://carnegie.org/fileadmin/Media/Publications/WritingToRead_01.pdf

Hattie, J. (2009). *Visible learning: A synthesis of over 800 meta-analyses relating to achievement.* New York: Routledge.

Hattie, J. (2012). *Visible learning for teachers: Maximizing impact on learning.* New York: Routledge.

Kinchin, I. M. (2000). Concept mapping in biology. *Journal of Biological Education, 34*(2), 61–68.

Levitt, S., & Dubner, S. (2005). *Freakonomics: A rogue economist explores the hidden side of everything.* New York: HarperCollins.

Literacy Design Collaborative. (2013). LDC Template Task Collection 2.0. Retrieved from http://ldc.org/sites/default/files/LDC-Template-Task-Collection-2.0.A.pdf

London, J. (1982). *To build a fire.* New York: Bantam Dell.

Lyman, F. T. (1981). The responsive classroom discussion: The inclusion of all students. In A. Anderson (Ed.), *Mainstreaming digest* (pp. 109–113). College Park, MD: University of Maryland Press.

Marzano, R. J. (2004). *Building background knowledge for academic achievement: Research on what works in schools.* Alexandria, VA: ASCD.

Marzano, R. J., & Pickering, D. J. (2005). *Building academic vocabulary: Teacher's manual.* Alexandria, VA: ASCD.

Marzano, R. J., & Simms, J.A. (2013). *Vocabulary for the common core.* Bloomington, IN: Marzano Research Laboratory.

McKeown M. G., Beck, I. L, Omanson, R. C., & Pople, M. T. (1985). Some effects of the nature and frequency of vocabulary instruction on the knowledge and use of words. *Reading Research Quarterly, 20*(5), 522–535.

McKinstry, C. M. (2013). *While the word watching: A Birmingham bombing survivor comes of age during the civil rights movement.* Carol Stream, IL: Tyndale House.

Meyer, B. J. F., & Ray, M. N. (2011). Structure strategy interventions: Increasing reading comprehension of expository texts. *International Electronic Journal of Elementary Education, 4*(1), 127–152.

National Governors Association (NGA) Center for Best Practices, & the Council of Chief State School Officers (CCSSO). (2013) *Supplemental Information for Appendix A of the Common Core State Standards for English Language Arts and Literacy: New research on text complexity.* Washington, DC: NGA Center and CCSSO.

National Reading Panel. (2000). *Teaching children to read: An evidence-based assessment of scientific research literature on reading and its implications for reading instruction.* Bethesda, MD: National Institutes of Health. Retrieved from http://www.nichd.nih.gov/publications/pubs/nrp/Documents/ch4-I.pdf

Novak, J. D., & Musonda, D. (1991). A twelve-year longitudinal study of science concept learning. *American Educational Research Journal, 28,* 117–153.

Ontario Ministry of Eduation. (2006). *The Ontario curriculum: Grades 1–8: Language.* Retrieved from http://www.edu.gov.on.ca/eng/curriculum/elementary/language18currb.pdf

Palincsar, A. S., & Brown, A. L. (1984). Reciprocal teaching of comprehension-fostering and comprehension-monitoring activities. *Cognition and Instruction, 1,* 117–175.

Partnership for Assessment Readiness for College and Careers (PARCC). (2011). Structure of the model content frameworks for ELA/literacy. Retrieved from www.parcconline.org/mcf/english-language-artsliteracy/structure-model-content-frameworks-elaliteracy

Pearson, P. D., & Gallagher, M. (1983a). The gradual release of responsibility model of instruction. *Contemporary Educational Psychology, 8*, 112–123.

Pearson, P. D., & Gallagher, M. C. (1983b). The instruction of reading comprehension. Center for the Study of Reading, Technical Report No. 297, University of Illinois at Urbana-Champaign. Retrieved from https://www.ideals.illinois.edu/bitstream/handle/2142/17939/ctrstreadtechrepv01983i00297_opt.pdf?sequence=1

Rothstein, D., & Santana, L. (2011). Teaching students to ask their own questions. *Harvard Education Letter, 27*(5). Retrieved from http://hepg.org/hel/article/507

Santa, C. M., Havens, L., Nelson, M., Danner, M., Scalf, L., & Scalf, J. (1988). *Content reading including study systems: Reading, writing, and studying across the curriculum.* Dubuque, IA: Kendall/Hunt.

Shanahan, T. (2012, June 18). Shanahan on literacy: What is close reading? Retrieved from http://www.shanahanonliteracy.com/2012/06/what-is-close-reading.html

Snow, C. E. (2013). Cold versus warm close reading: Building students' stamina for struggling with text. *Reading Today, 30*(6), 19.

Speare, E. G. (1986). *The witch of blackbird pond.* New York: Houghton Mifflin Harcourt.

Swift, J. (1729). *A modest proposal.* Retrieved from http://www.online-literature.com/swift/947/

Texas Education Agency. (2010). *Texas Essential Knowledge and Skills.* Figure 19 TAC §110.10(b). Retrieved from http://ritter.tea.state.tx.us/rules/tac/chapter110/ch110a.html#110.10

Texas Reading Initiative. (2002). Promoting vocabulary development: Components of effective vocabulary instruction. Austin, TX: Texas Education Agency.

Tomlinson, C. A., & McTighe, J. (2006). *Integrating differentiated instruction and understanding by design.* Alexandria, VA: ASCD.

Tomlinson, C. A., & Moon, T. R. (2013). *Assessment and student success in a differentiated classroom.* Alexandria, VA: ASCD.

Virginia Department of Education. (2010). Standards of learning documents for English. Retrieved from http://www.doe.virginia.gov/testing/sol/standards_docs/english/2010/stds_all_english.pdf

Wolf, M., & Barzillai, M. (2009). The importance of deep reading. *Educational Leadership, 66*(6), 32–37.

Index

The letter *f* following a page number denotes a figure.

About the Author

Kathy T. Glass consults nationally with schools and districts, presents at conferences, and teaches seminars for university and county programs delivering customized professional development. A former master teacher, she has been in education for more than 25 years and works with administrators and teachers in groups of varying sizes from kindergarten through high school. Her expertise revolves around areas of curriculum and instruction, such as implementation of the ELA Common Core State Standards or other standards-based curricula; backward design; differentiated tools, strategies, and assessments; pre-, formative, self-, and summative assessments; writing instruction and assessment; unit and yearlong curriculum maps; text-dependent questions; and engaging instructional strategies that facilitate close reading. By providing educators with practical application of research-based methods, she works to strengthen their teaching or coaching and extend their professional capacities to help improve student achievement.

In addition to this book, she has written *Mapping Comprehensive Units to the ELA Common Core Standards, 6–12* (Corwin, 2013) and *K–5* (Corwin, 2012); *Lesson Design for Differentiated Instruction, Grades 4–9* (Corwin, 2009); *Curriculum Mapping: A Step-by- Step Guide to Creating Curriculum Year Overviews* (Corwin, 2007); and *Curriculum Design for Writing Instruction: Creating Standards-Based Lesson Plans and Rubrics* (Corwin, 2005). With Cindy Strickland, she has coauthored the *Staff Development Guide for the Parallel Curriculum* (Corwin, 2009). In addition, Kathy served as a differentiation consultant for Pearson Learning's social studies textbook series for K–5 (2013).

Originally from Indianapolis, Kathy resides in the San Francisco Bay Area. She can be reached at kathy@kathyglassconsulting.com. Her website is www.kathyglass-consulting.com.

Related ASCD Resources

At the time of publication, the following ASCD resources were available (ASCD stock numbers appear in parentheses). For up-to-date information about ASCD resources, go to www.ascd.org. You can search the complete archives of *Educational Leadership* at http://www.ascd.org/el.

ASCD Edge™

Exchange ideas and connect with other educators on the social networking site ASCD Edge at http://ascdedge.ascd.org/

Print Products

A Close Look at Close Reading: Teaching Students to Analyze Complex Texts, Grades K-5 by Diane Lapp, Barbara Moss, Maria Grant, and Kelly Johnson (#114008)

A Close Look at Close Reading: Teaching Students to Analyze Complex Texts, Grades 6-12 by Barbara Moss, Diane Lapp, Maria Grant, and Kelly Johnson (#115002)

Building Student Literacy Through Sustained Silent Reading by Steve Gardiner (#105027)

Creating Literacy-Rich Schools for Adolescents by Gay Ivey and Douglas Fisher (#105142)

Encouragement in the Classroom: How do I help students stay positive and focused? By Joan Young (#SF114049)

Reading for Meaning: How to Build Students' Comprehension, Reasoning, and Problem-Solving by Harvey F. Silver, Susan C. Morris, and Victor Klein (#110128)

Real-World Projects: How do I design relevant and engaging learning experiences? By Suzie Boss (#SF115043)

Teaching Reading in the Content Areas: If Not Me, Then Who? 3rd Ed. by Vicki Urquhart and Dana Frazee (#112024)

Vocab Rehab: How do I teach vocabulary effectively with limited time? By Marilee Sprenger (#SF114047)

The Whole Child Initiative helps schools and communities create learning environments that allow students to be healthy, safe, engaged, supported, and challenged. To learn more about other books and resources that relate to the whole child, visit www.wholechildeducation.org.

For more information: send e-mail to member@ascd.org; call 1-800-933-2723 or 703-578-9600, press 2; send a fax to 703-575-5400; or write to Information Services, ASCD, 1703 N. Beauregard St., Alexandria, VA 22311-1714 USA.